Dreams and Nightmares

CRITICAL EXPLORATIONS IN SCIENCE FICTION AND FANTASY
(a series edited by Donald E. Palumbo and C.W. Sullivan III)

1. *Worlds Apart? Dualism and Transgression in Contemporary Female Dystopias* (Dunja M. Mohr, 2005)

2. *Tolkien and Shakespeare: Essays on Shared Themes and Language* (edited by Janet Brennan Croft, 2007)

3. *Culture, Identities and Technology in the* Star Wars *Films: Essays on the Two Trilogies* (edited by Carl Silvio and Tony M. Vinci, 2007)

4. *The Influence of* Star Trek *on Television, Film and Culture* (edited by Lincoln Geraghty, 2007)

5. *Hugo Gernsback and the Century of Science Fiction* (Gary Westfahl, 2007)

6. *One Earth, One People: The Mythopoeic Fantasy Series of Ursula K. Le Guin, Lloyd Alexander, Madeleine L'Engle and Orson Scott Card* (Marek Oziewicz, 2008)

7. *The Evolution of Tolkien's Mythology: A Study of the History of Middle-earth* (Elizabeth A. Whittingham, 2008)

8. *H. Beam Piper: A Biography* (John F. Carr, 2008)

9. *Dreams and Nightmares: Science and Technology in Myth and Fiction* (Mordecai Roshwald, 2008)

10. Lilith *in a New Light: Essays on the George MacDonald Fantasy Novel* (edited by Lucas H. Harriman, 2008)

11. *Feminist Narrative and the Supernatural: The Function of Fantastic Devices in Seven Recent Novels* (Katherine J. Weese, 2008)

Dreams and Nightmares

Science and Technology in Myth and Fiction

MORDECAI ROSHWALD

CRITICAL EXPLORATIONS IN
SCIENCE FICTION AND FANTASY, 9
Donald E. Palumbo *and* C.W. Sullivan III, *series editors*

McFarland & Company, Inc., Publishers
Jefferson, North Carolina, and London

LIBRARY OF CONGRESS CATALOGUING-IN-PUBLICATION DATA

Roshwald, Mordecai, 1921–
　　Dreams and nightmares : science and technology in myth and fiction / Mordecai Roshwald.
　　　　p.　　cm. — (Critical explorations in science fiction and fantasy ; 9)
　　Includes bibliographical references and index.

　　ISBN 978-0-7864-3694-1
　　softcover : 50# alkaline paper

　　1. Science in literature.　　2. Technology in literature.　　I. Title.
PN55.R67　　2008
809'.93356—dc22　　　　　　　　　　　　　　　　　　　　2008013475

British Library cataloguing data are available

©2008 Mordecai Roshwald. All rights reserved

No part of this book may be reproduced or transmitted in any form or by any means, electronic or mechanical, including photocopying or recording, or by any information storage and retrieval system, without permission in writing from the publisher.

Cover images ©2008 Shutterstock

Manufactured in the United States of America

McFarland & Company, Inc., Publishers
　Box 611, Jefferson, North Carolina 28640
　　www.mcfarlandpub.com

Table of Contents

Introduction	1
1 • The Bible	5
2 • Greek Mythology	20
3 • The Middle Ages	35
4 • Age of Reason	45
5 • Science and Human Nature	57
6 • The Machine Prophet	73
7 • Evolution: Natural and Designed	93
8 • Mind Control	112
9 • The Menace of the Machine	139
10 • The Threat of Paradise	161
11 • The Suicide of Civilization	187
Conclusion	209
Chapter Notes	211
Bibliography	217
Index	219

Introduction

On the face of it, science and technology belong to a realm of human endeavor which is far removed from the domain of myth and fiction. Science, and its application to human needs and desires, is founded on reason, logic, careful observation, experimentation. Scientists, inventors, and engineers pursue their paths of inquiry and invention guided and confined by strict rules, which must not be ignored or transgressed. Any laxity in this regard may well lead to errors in scientific conclusions and to mishaps and calamities in technological inventions. The world of fantasy and imagination, in which myths and fiction deliberately indulge, is not subject to such strict rules, and their creators, whether anonymous or known, enjoy the freedom of going beyond the known facts, of introducing surreal elements, of mixing physical reality with emotion, of reality with dreams. Both domains are clearly human, but they each belong to a different department of the human mind, and express a different propensity of humanity. Unless they are kept apart, we face the menace of confusion and calamity. No sane person would cross a bridge constructed by a hallucinating engineer, or, for that matter, hardly anyone would read the mathematical calculations of an engineer for literary entertainment.

What is the point, then, of inquiring into the manner in which myth and fiction deal with science and technology? We might as well pursue the attitude of shoemakers to philosophy, or the stance of mathematicians toward drama. Even if such an inquiry could produce valid conclusions, these would be of little general interest. In other words, they would be trivial.

Yet this analysis is less than correct. For humanity is not clearly divided into systematic thinkers and dreamers, into scientists and fantasists, into practical people and wishful thinkers. In most people, perhaps in every human being, the opposite elements — reason and yearning, realism and dreaming, logic and fantasy — coexist. The one or the other may be developed to a greater or lesser degree, but both play a role in human consciousness. Moreover, these

Introduction

opposite elements do not exist in hermetically separated departments of our mind, but they come into contact with each other and influence one another. This does not mean that they are confused with each other: if they are, the person concerned is in trouble, and if he is allowed to apply his confusion to practical concerns, the society may face an even greater trouble. Nobody wants to trust dreaming drivers or fantasizing engineers.

Yet if the two domains must not be *confused* with one another, they can come in *contact* with each other, and such a contact can be mutually beneficial. Imagination can profit from science and technology can reap benefits from fantasy. For example, unless fancy becomes quite outlandish, it takes into consideration current knowledge and applied science. The myth of Sisyphus accepts the laws of physics which make a stone roll down a slope. On the other hand, perhaps the airplane would not have been invented had there not been the Greek myth of Daedalus and the Arabian stories of the flying carpet. Thus, the contact and the mutual relationship between the domain of science and technology and the sphere of myth and fiction become a valid and interesting field of inquiry. We shall pursue this relationship as it is manifest in diverse myths and stories.

Such myths and stories often reflect human striving for a better life, which knowledge and technology hold out. The imaginative garb appeals to us, to a certain propensity in us, and thus lends wings to the substance of the quest. For the hidden or ostensible aim of the stories is to improve life by giving more control over environment, by creating ingenious machines and systems, by adapting reality to human needs and aspirations.

The notion of harmony between the human quest for scientific and technological progress and human wellbeing, which is assumed in some stories and legends, as well as in design and planning of scientific applications, cannot be taken for granted. Indeed, it has not been accepted in myth and fiction as an unquestionable truth. As experience has shown, humanity has not limited its quest for knowledge and technical progress to the exclusive pursuit of human wellbeing. Science, and particularly technology, have also been pursued for the sake of increasing human power, human control over nature, and the dominance of one human society over another. Thus, imperceptibly, we enter into the domain of human relations — not all amicable — and the use of techniques to control, vanquish, subdue. These aspects have also found a prominent expression in the fictional treatment of science and technology.

Then there is another, and in some way the most puzzling aspect of technology, namely that an invention, designed as a means, becomes an active

Introduction

agent and leads to unintended and unforeseen consequences. As is said "Science can be a wonderful servant, but a terrifying master." While such unintended consequences can and often have been explored in a purely rational and scientific manner, they have occasionally been brought to public attention with more vigor and persuasive power by mythical and fictional description. The freer rein of imagination has thus contributed to a wider, and perhaps more intense concern about this kind of danger inherent in measures and techniques ostensibly designed to make humans proud.

The treatment of science and technology in myth and fiction deals both with their actual and potential role, with what they have achieved or with what they may achieve. Myth and fiction deal with both real and imaginary benefits of science and technology, and with their actual or feared dangers. They see them as they are, but also in the gargantuan dimensions they may assume. They look at them as obedient servants, as well as sinister masters. They explore all the possibilities, even reaching to spheres which may be considered beyond the possible — only to convince us that nothing can be excluded from the potential reach of science and technology.

They make us giddy with expectation and they make us tremble in fear.

In the following exploration of various and diverse myths and stories, attention will be paid to these cardinal consequences and implications of science and technology, as well as to the peculiarities of each fictional treatment of them. The cases explored are no more than examples, but they are restricted to important and instructive samples of the broad issue.

The cases are culled from antiquity to our own times, presented in chronological sequence, complemented by or mixed with thematic classification. The selection out of a great wealth of texts, is necessarily personal. While I've tried to avoid repetition, overlapping of similar approaches and parallel themes cannot be avoided. Despite such similarities, each of the selected works is sufficiently distinctive to deserve attention and require interpretation.

1

The Bible

The Bible remains largely reticent about the role of technology in human life. To be sure, it mentions the "fathers" of a few basic skills: Abel was "a keeper of sheep," Cain "a tiller of the ground" (Genesis 4:2), Jabal the father of tent dwellers and cattle raisers (Genesis 4:20), Jubal the father of musicians (4:21), and Tubal-cain a metal worker (4:22). But in none of these cases is there any special stress on the significance of the technological skill, on the role it fulfills in human life. There is no reflective or philosophical comment about these skills, no wonder or admiration expressed for these achievements.

We find very detailed instructions, on the other hand, for the construction of the tabernacle and its various implements (Exodus, 35–39), and the men entrusted with the job are praised as "wise hearted ... in whom the Lord put wisdom and understanding to know how to work all manner of work for the service of the sanctuary" (Exodus 36:1). Significantly, it is the construction of God's mobile abode, as it were, accompanying the wandering Israelites in the wilderness of Sinai, that these passages are concerned with, not the building of human dwellings. Solomon's construction of the "house of the Lord," again recounted in detail, falls into the same category, though the opportunity is used to provide some information about the palaces of the king and his pharaonic wife (1 Kings, 6–7).

The detached, almost indifferent, attitude to human-related technology that seems to characterize biblical text, may be due to the virtually single-minded preoccupation of the Bible with religious and moral issues, to the exclusion of other problems. Thus, it is the moral failure of Cain, the fratricide, rather than his and Abel's occupations and skills, which are the focus of the story of the two brothers. Technology, being morally neutral, does not figure as an important issue of biblical philosophy or reflection. Yet there are some notable exceptions to this.

The Flood and the Rescue

The story of the flood and the rescue of Noah and his company is recounted in Genesis 6:5–9:17. The tale gives prominence to the ark Noah built in order to save himself and his family, as well as some other specimens of living creatures, and thus assure the continuation of life. The tale grips us — and not only because it appears in first book of the Bible. There is an intrinsic quality to it of horror and fascination. The horror is in the description of the eradication of mankind by an act of God; the fascination is in the rescue of Noah and the other inhabitants of the ark through an ingenious device. The contrast between catastrophe and salvation offers a dramatic tension and a cathartic relief. In our own age, when scenarios of global catastrophe and mankind's demise have transcended the realm of fantasy and poetic imagination, the story of biblical deluge may appear particularly relevant, and thus likely to appeal to modern sophisticated public. Such a public may find new meaning in the simple tale, and even see it as a parable for our own era.

The familiar biblical story is not entirely unique and original, as is well established today. Stories of deluge can be found in various cultures, including those of ancient Greece, India and China, though they vary considerably in scope and detail.

The oldest tales originated in Mesopotamia, as testified by a Sumerian text from the end of the third millennium B.C., and a subsequent Accadian text, known as the eleventh tablet of the Gilgamesh Epic. The biblical story has a considerable resemblance to the Mesopotamian text, which is therefore assumed to have been its prototype, or evidence that both originated from a common, even earlier source. Still, there remains a distinctive feature of the biblical tale. Unlike the others, it is linked to the belief in one universal God, a just God who punishes the wicked and saves the righteous and shows compassion for them.[1] The stamp of ethical monotheism is imprinted on the story and lends it meaning in the context of, and consistent with, the cardinal teaching of the Bible.

The biblical tale of the flood is quite familiar. It opens with God's realization of the corruption of mankind. "And God saw that great was the wickedness of man in the land, and all the forming of the thoughts of his heart was only evil all day long" (Genesis 6:5). So God repented having created man and decided: "I will wipe off man whom I have created from the surface of the earth, both man and beast and crawling creatures and the fowl of heaven" (6:7).

But "Noah was a just and perfect man" (6:9). So God told Noah to build an ark, for himself and his family and specimens of all the living creatures to hide in, and to equip it with food, while God was going to flood and destroy all he had created. And, indeed, God poured down rain for forty days, as well as opened the fountains of the depths and the earth was flooded, while the ark was lifted up on the water. All the living creatures on the land, died, and only Noah and his company in the ark survived. Eventually, as the flood stopped the waters started to recede, till Noah and all the living creatures in the ark could finally leave it. Then God made a covenant with Noah and his seed after him and with every living creature that "never shall all flesh be cut off by the waters of the flood" (9:11). As a token of the covenant God set his bow in the cloud. Seeing it, he will recollect the covenant and refrain from turning the water into a devastating flood (9:12–17).

This famous story can be characterized as a tale of crime, punishment and redemption, or as a parable of divine justice, meting out punishment to the wicked and taking care of the just, or as a lesson and stern warning to humanity to adhere to moral conduct. The story also weaves in a charming mythical explanation of the rainbow, which creates a linkage between God the creator and God the supervisor, judge and redeemer of mankind. Yet, besides these salient characteristics of the tale, there are here elements which express or are linked to the realm of science and technology, and thus are of special interest for the present study.

For one thing, it should be noted that the divine punishment inflicted on humankind is of a naturalistic kind. A deluge of torrential rains and even overflowing of ground waters is only a quantitative increase of an observed and experienced natural phenomenon. Though it is ascribed to God it may accord with actual observation and thus be regarded as conforming with a scientifically feasible scenario. Or, looked at from a religious perspective, it reveals a perception of God enacting his will through natural means.

Then it is possible to look at the story as a remarkable instance of human sagacity in view of a natural calamity. Noah, who has an advance notice of a catastrophic flood, does the sensible thing: he builds an ark which would float on water and thus save him and whomever he includes in the rescue plan. The ark should and does serve as a floating shelter. That in the story he does it all on the instructions of God does not diminish the fundamental sense of the story, or at least one of its lessons, that an impending natural menace has to be met with technological resourcefulness. Thus, nature is confronted here with civilization, even if the latter is guided by divine counsel.

Significantly, the story goes into some technical details, which make sense and testify to the realization of the importance of the right technological means. God presents Noah with exact specifications as to how to construct the ark. "Make thee an ark of gopher wood; thou shalt make it [divided into] cells; and have it pitched on the inside and on the outside" (6:14). The material of construction is indicated, though we do not know what kind of wood "gopher" is (as referred to in the original Hebrew). The pitching is clearly aimed at preventing water penetration. The division into cells is apparently intended for securing separate accommodation for the various species, for storage and the like. Then we have the dimensions of the ark. "The length of the ark shall be three hundred cubits, the breadth of it fifty cubits, and the height of it thirty cubits" (6:15). The ratio of 30 to 5 to 3 makes sense to the lay person. An ark of such dimensions seems fairly stable and not likely to topple, especially as it is not designed as a navigable ship, but as an essentially stationary floating shelter.

Then there are additional structural details. The ark is to be equipped with a skylight—which seems a better translation of *tsohar* than window (6:16) and an opening or a door in the side of it, for the obvious need of entry and exit. The ark is designed to contain three levels, or stories (6:16). Then there is an indication of a peculiar technical arrangement. Literally translated it reads: "and thou shalt finish it to the cubit from above"[2] (6:16). Though the intent is clearly a technical detail, its exact meaning remains somewhat elusive. One plausible explanation is that the cover of the ark ought to be sloping on its two sides along the entire structure, so that at its highest point it will be a cubit above the height of the walls, in order that the raining water would flow down the roof.[3] To be sure, all this does not amount to a detailed architectural and engineering blueprint. Yet the intent to convey a sensible design and a technologically feasible construction is evident.

Interestingly, the scientific orientation of the story is not confined to the design and construction of the ark. As already mentioned, God takes care that specimens of living species are included in the refuge—a clear biological concern for the continuation of life. Noah, too, resorts to rational observation of animal behavior in order to find out the outside situation. He first sends a raven, "which kept going forth and back until the waters were dried up from off the earth" (8:7); that is to say, its conduct led to no conclusion till the situation became quite clear anyway, or perhaps it was judged by Noah as erratic. Yet, in what could be regarded as an indication of an experimental approach, Noah sent another bird, a dove, to find out "if the waters were abated from off the surface of the earth" (8:8). The dove — as is well known, a long-distance flyer — found no rest and returned to the ark, which indicated to Noah that the earth was still covered with water. Seven days later he repeated the experiment, "And the dove came in to him in the evening, and in her mouth was an olive leaf plucked off: so Noah knew that the waters were abated from off the earth" (8:11). Yet, he repeated the same experiment seven days later, and this time the dove did not return anymore, which was a proof that the earth was dry and the ark could be opened and its occupants leave their refuge.

The ingenious approach of Noah to find out the condition of the earth and whether it was safe to leave the ark is an interesting revelation of a thoughtful, rational, experimental approach to the solution of a pressing problem. It is this spirit which is at least partly responsible for scientific inquiry and for technological invention, and it is noteworthy to encounter it in an ancient text, whose focal concern is outside the realm of science and technology.

Significantly, following the story of the flood, the Bible tells us that "Noah, a man of the land, began and planted a vineyard" (9:20).[4] This suggests, in an extremely terse manner, that Noah started cultivating the land, or returned to the cultivation of the land — after Cain, the first tiller of the land, had murdered Abel and was cursed from the earth (Genesis 4:11). At least Noah appears the first to cultivate grapes. Thus, a significant techno-scientific skill is attributed to him.

It is noteworthy that in the rabbinical literature there is an emphasis on the constructive technological skills and achievements of Noah. This point is made in a commentary on a biblical verse concerning the birth of Noah and the meaning of his name: "And he [Lamech, Noah's father] called his name Noah, saying, This one shall console (and relieve) us from our work and from the toil of our hands, due to the earth which the Lord hath cursed" (5:29).[5] While the etymological connection between *Noah* and *nahem* (console) is dubious, it is made in the biblical text, and built upon in the following midrashic commentary.

> Before Noah was born, when they sowed they would not reap, but they would sow wheat and barley and reap thorns and thistles. As Noah was born, the world returned to its settled condition: they reaped what they sowed — they sow wheat and they reap wheat, they sow barley and they reap barley. Moreover, until Noah was born, they labored with their hands, wherefore it is written "and from the toil of our hands." As Noah was born, he made them ploughs and sickles and hoes and all the tools.[6]

Thus Noah is presented here as the founder of the material civilization of humankind, which is linked to the founding of agriculture and the use of implements, that is to say, technology.

Not least important in the story of the flood and the rescue of Noah is the overall linkage between righteousness and resourcefulness, between ethics and technology, between morality and knowledge. Whether the source of knowledge is God, who is also righteous, or whether the just Noah participates in providing rescue for himself and his party, the linkage between the realm of morality and the domain of applied knowledge persists. In the rabbinical commentary this connection is even enhanced, as Noah, the righteous survivor and the originator of the new humanity, is also something of a Prometheus, taking care of his human progeny. Implicit in this reading of the story is the idea — indeed, the ideal — of the combination of morality and knowledge as the foundation of human civilization.

Such an ideal remains as relevant today as its realization continues to be elusive.

The Tower of Babel

If we should single out one biblical story which touches on the problem of technology with a measure of direct concern, it is the story of the tower of Babel, as told in Genesis 11:1–9. Though the story is quite familiar, its brevity allows us to reproduce it here in *toto*, in two parts, for the convenience of the reader.

> And the whole earth was of one language, and of one speech. And it came to pass, as they journeyed from the east, that they found a plain in the land of Shinar; and they dwelt there. And they said one to another, Go to, let us make brick, and burn them thoroughly. And they had brick for stone, and slime had they for mortar. And they said, Go to, let us build us a city and a tower, whose top may reach unto heaven [literally, "and its top in heaven"[7]] and let us make us a name [perhaps, "a landmark"]; lest we be scattered abroad upon the face of the whole earth [Genesis 11:1–4].

Interestingly, and characteristically for the biblical myths, the story is told in a factual manner and related to concrete geographical locations. *Shinar* is the name occasionally used for Babylonia. The geographical connection is further reinforced by reference to burned bricks as the building material, which was typical of ancient Mesopotamia. In other words, there is an attempt to plant the myth in reality, or to lend the myth the air of an actual historical event.

Then there is the technological element — this, too, rooted in actual experience, though soaring beyond it. The burned brick, recognized as a reliable and efficient building material, is attributed to the inventiveness of early humanity, as is the use of slime for joining the bricks. Out of the simple building blocks, great structures could be erected. The actual and the symbolical capacity of technology is clearly and vividly presented.

But then a new element makes its appearance: the attempt of humans to use skill and practical ingenuity for a purpose beyond the pedestrian need. We witness the marriage between known technique and daring ambition, between reality and aspiration. Humanity suddenly reveals the tendency to reach beyond daily needs, into the realm of fancy. Humans try to surpass themselves, as it were, and to reach for the sky. They want not merely a city, but a tower, "whose top may reach unto heaven." To be sure, this ambition is justified by a practical concern: the erection of a landmark which will serve as a focus for a growing and expanding humanity, and thus assure its cohesion and unity. Still, even such a concrete objective testifies to vision and foresight. It is evidence to the power of human intelligence and to the range of human spirit.

However, as the story continues, this daring of humankind and its application to concrete endeavors sounds alarm bells in heaven. God himself is looking askance at the monumental achievement of humanity, which may well be a portent of things to come. The sequel of the text conveys the divine concern and consequent action, and its impact on humanity.

> And the Lord came down to see the city and the tower, which the children of Adam[8] builded. And the Lord said, Behold, the people is one, and they have all one language and this being their beginning deed, there will be nothing of all they plan to do that will be impossible.[9] Go to, let us go down, and there confound their language, that they may not understand one another's speech. So the Lord scattered them abroad from thence upon the surface of the entire earth[10]: and they left off to build the city. Therefore is the name of it called Babel; because the Lord did there confound the[11] language of the entire earth: and from thence did the Lord scatter them abroad upon the surface of the entire earth (Genesis 11:5–9).

The divine reaction to humans' grand design strikes one as atypical, almost alien, in the biblical text, for God appears here as being envious of human achievement, rather than as the concerned and benevolent father of mankind and Israel, as he usually does in the Bible. The notion of divine envy of man is a familiar motif in the Greek legend, where it is much more easily acceptable, as the Greek gods are described in the image of men and women, with their known frailties. An idea of this kind could have found its way from some alien — not necessarily Greek — sources into the Hebrew Bible. Still, the idea of divine envy appears strange even in the context of a pre-monotheistic belief, and could be regarded as a manifestation of human megalomania: for why should the powerful and the immortal envy the weak and the transient? One could turn the tables and explain the attribution of envy to gods, or to God, as due to a psychological twist: humans try to justify their own failings by putting the blame on superior beings.

Why don't humans achieve whatever they plan? Given bricks, which can be put on top of one another, and given social unity, the tower of civilization might have reached "unto heaven." So why did humans fail? Because of divine envy! The blame for human failure is conveniently put on God. Significantly, it is not technology which is the Achilles' heel in human endeavor; the culprit is social cohesion. It is the linguistic confusion and the following dispersal that are the cause of the failure. Even if the blame is put on divinity, the indication of the nature of the human flaw remains transparent. The symbolical tale conveys a perennial moral.

It is possible to interpret the story of the tower of Babel in a different manner, more consonant with the religious, moral tone of the Bible. The intent of the story could be to point to the sinfulness of a colossal technological design. The combining of social forces, facilitated by a common language, for a great technological project encroaches in intent on the omnipotence of God; it is the expression of sinful hubris. Humans should walk humbly with God and not try to overreach themselves. Technology, the art of using bricks, may well be useful, but should not be applied to grand designs. Humans must restrain their impulse to use science for projects beyond their limited needs. Build yourself a hut, but do not try to construct a tower.

If this sounds like a pietistic, self-effacing message, it may be suggested that it contains a moral even if the religious element is set aside. The story could be read as a warning to a self-confident humanity which relies on its technological know-how in its quest for limitless power. Technology, the human means to power, should be used with caution and moderation. It is but a means and should be proportioned to people's true needs, and not serve megalomaniac ambitions. Otherwise, it becomes a dangerous force which will lead people to moral failure and actual disaster. This may well sound more relevant to the modern scene than to earlier ages of human civilization.

As is well known, biblical texts have been the subject of commentaries and interpretations for many centuries, and they have offered an opportunity for the creation of homilies, less strictly confined to the intent of the biblical wording than a rigorous scholarly interpretation would allow. Thus, in a way, myths have been woven around the biblical stories. Some instances of commentaries and homilies related to the story of the tower of Babel may be adduced to shed additional light on the issues contained in the myth and the diverse perceptions of it.

Ibn Ezra (1092–1167), a medieval Jewish commentator on the Bible, distinguished by his scholarly-rationalistic approach, virtually debunks the supernatural and mythological nature of the story. The notion that the builders of the tower wanted to reach heaven is, in Ibn Ezra's opinion, absurd. "They were not so foolish as to think to climb to heaven." He substantiates this point by a simple linguistic analysis. "And be not surprised at the wording 'and its top in heaven' (Genesis 11:4), for in this manner Moses spoke, 'cities great and fortified in heaven' (Deuteronomy 9:1)."[12] In other words, "in heaven" is merely a figure of speech, indicating great height, used in other passages in the Bible. So there is no intent in the present text to suggest that people wanted to reach heaven, or the divine abode.

Indeed, argues Ibn Ezra, the biblical text reveals the desire and intention of the people "to build a big city to settle in and to construct a high tower to serve them as a landmark and renown and glory, and to recognize the location of the city for those like shepherds going out of it. Also their name will remain after them as long as the tower lasts, and that is what the scripture said, 'to make us a name.'" Thus, the tower is reduced to being a geographical or a topographical convenience, as well as an expression of the human penchant for collective glory and for historical remembrance. Technology and human organization are, rather sensibly, put in the service of human practical needs, as well as some higher human aspirations. Yet, there is hardly anything in this to provoke or justify divine displeasure.

Still, this positive interpretation cannot explain the sequel of the story, why God interfered with the plan. Since Ibn Ezra cannot ignore this aspect of the tale, he simply asserts that the Lord "did not thus plan." In other words, the innocent endeavor of humankind did not accord with the divine designs, about the nature of which the commentator seems to remain silent; or does he? For in commentary on Genesis 11:7 he indicates that the Lord's dispersal of humanity was good for them and in accordance with his earlier design, expressed in the blessing of Noah and his sons; "and fill the earth" (Genesis 9:11). For how could they multiply and fill the earth, if all resided in one place? The common-sense observation of Ibn Ezra all but nullifies the meaning of the story of the tower of Babel. The great technological achievement and collective effort become, in the long run, of minor importance.

Other commentaries focus on the confrontation of human endeavor and divine will, but rather than see God as jealously guarding his elevated position against human encroachment — a view contradicting the basic biblical notion of a just and compassionate God — put the blame on humans, thereby saving God's ethical image.

Thus, Ramban (Rabbi Moshe ben Nahman, or Nahmanides, 1194–c.1270) argues that the people "thought of an evil design." Rashi (Rabbi Shlomo Yitzhaqi, 1040–1105) suggests that "they ungratefully revolted against Him who lavished goodness on them and saved them from the flood."[13] (For they were the descendants of Noah.) Thus the technological enterprise was the expression of human waywardness and was justly obstructed by God.

One homiletic comment goes even further in putting the blame on mankind and thus justifying the divine interference in the bold human enterprise. It was human hubris and outright challenge to God's elevated status and his rule that constituted people's grand endeavor in building the tower. "They said: 'Not everything is in His hands, to choose for Himself the upper regions and give us the lower ones. So come and let us make a tower and establish an idol at its top and give a sword in its hand, so that it may be seen as if it waged a war on Him.'"[14] The idol and the sword in its hand, and the underpinning tower, symbolize the rebellion against God the just and merciful and the glorification of power and violence, which the builders of the tower wanted to embrace. This clearly required divine interference, so that humans would know their place and human civilization be averted from developing in a sinister way.

Having explored the story of the tower of Babel and its various interpretations, one can perhaps single out its salient message — at least as seen from modern perspective. In a sense, the tale expresses the conflict between humans' technological capacity, which appears virtually boundless (even the sky is not the limit), and humanity's social failing. Human ingenuity can assure man felicity and power; technology could offer an even greater bliss. However, the collapse of understanding among people, the failure of communication in the literal and wider sense, leads to calamities. Technology and social cohesion are two factors indispensable for human progress, but the advancement of the former without the cooperation of the latter leads to confusion and potential misery. If this reading of the myth sounds far-fetched, it may well be taken as another Midrash, or a latter-day homily, a testimony to the fecundity of the biblical tale.

The Plagues

The story of the oppression of the children of Israel in Egypt and their delivery and exodus from the land of their enslavement, told in the first fifteen chapters of Exodus, is associated with divine interference and with a series of miracles which made such an unusual achievement possible. This has been the traditional perception of the tale, and the biblical text fully justifies such a reading of the story. Ostensibly, miracles are the opposite of science and technology, for the latter depend on reason and know-how, while the former defy human capability and understanding.

Yet, reading the story, permeated with miraculous occurrences though it is, from the vantage point of the present, one can discern in it "technological" or "pseudo-technological" elements. For we face here not one great miracle, a single extraordinary event which cannot be attributed to natural forces, let alone to human ingenuity. We witness a series of unnatural phenomena, which God causes to occur, or rather which are enacted by humans — Moses, and occasionally Aaron — on divine instructions and with God's support. Thus, miracles become the embodiment of a system, a system of controlling and affecting events in accordance with the needs of some people or a certain society of people. Moses becomes a performer of miracles, a kind of a magician. He is not an autonomous magician, as each act of magic he performs is initiated by God and depends on God's determination. Still, to Pharaoh and his entourage, as well as to the children of Israel, he appears as a man with extraordinary powers, capable of deeds which defy human experience and reach beyond the normal human capacity.

In what way can this magic be related to technology? It can be said that what science fiction is to science, magic is to technology. Magic is a kind of technology fiction. It is a powerful, irresistible technique which can achieve outstanding results. Just as we speak of the miraculous achievements of modern technology, so we can imagine the yearning for, or even expectation of, desired objectives behind mysterious magical acts. The quest for an easy means to gain an important, or even vital, end is common to rational humans and to the credulous. Indeed, such a quest of the naive, who may hope to attain the objective through magic, may be the precursor of technological endeavor and a catalyst for scientific invention. Thus a bridge — perhaps only a narrow footbridge — is established between magic and technology.

The use of magic is first addressed to the establishment of Moses's credibility as God's messenger to the people of Israel and to Pharaoh. He has to show that he is the "engineer," entrusted to perform the great task. Thus, he is instructed by the Lord to convert the rod in his hand into a serpent, and then turn the serpent into the rod again (Exodus 4:3–4). Another technique, taught by God, is to strike Moses's hand with leprosy, and then make it look healthy again (4:6–7). A third feat is the conversion of water into blood (4:8). Armed with these extraordinary skills, Moses would be trusted by Israel, and eventually try to establish his stature as a man of miraculous capacity vis-à-vis Pharaoh (4:21).

Then the use of magic or pseudo-technology is applied to convince Pharaoh to let the Israelites leave for a feast in the desert — a prelude to a design to leave Egypt altogether, as the story reveals, and as Pharaoh gradually comes to understand it. The means resorted to are the famous ten plagues, starting with the conversion of all the waters of Egypt into blood, and then progressing through the plague of frogs, lice and so on, to the tenth and ultimate sanction of the death of the firstborn of all the Egyptians. The various means employed to make Pharaoh accept the demand made by the leader of Israel — whether supernatural as presented in the biblical text, or explainable rationally as attempted by various commentators, in respect of some plagues at least — are deliberately chosen "to soften the heart of Pharaoh," that is to say, to force him to comply with the demand. The series of the plagues and the responses of Pharaoh — starting with an absolute "no," and ending with a loud and clear "go"— are a drama of political negotiations between two hostile entities: the powerful master-people and the seemingly defenseless subdued nation. Yet the latter are empowered by mysterious techniques which eventually force the masters to submit to the demands of the enslaved, or demands made on their behalf.

Significantly, the drama is not presented as a single miraculous event, which one might have expected if the confrontation was between Pharaoh and God. Instead, there is give and take and use of techniques in a gradational way. No overkill here.

The magic, addressed at the ecological and environmental conditions of the Egyptian kingdom, is measured — perhaps out of concern for the host country of the Israelites. Thus, it is not all at once, an all-out attack, but, to use a modern concept, a limited warfare. As Pharaoh refuses to budge, however, the measures escalate till the crucial tenth plague forces him to give in.

As already indicated, the biblical story presents the dramatic sequence of events as planned and guided by God, but the element of human magic, or pseudo-science, is present as well. This is clear not only through the role given Moses (and Aaron) in performing the miracles and enacting the plagues, but also by referring to the prowess of the Egyptian magicians in this respect. When Aaron casts down his rod before Pharaoh and it turns into a snake, the Egyptian monarch calls the magicians and they perform the same deed (7:10–12). Similarly, the Egyptian magicians repeat the act of converting water to blood (7:22). The plague of the frogs was performed by the Egyptian experts, as well (8:7). Thus, the story appears to be a contest of two opponents, each with similar or comparable "technology." Yet, despite the similarity, there is no equality. The technique of Moses and Aaron is superior to that of the Egyptian magicians. This is shown gradually and sporadically, as if the advantages of the weapons of two enemies were pointed out. Thus, when the Egyptian magicians produce snakes out of rods, the rod-snake of Aaron "swallowed up their rods" (7:12). More significantly, when Aaron made the dust into lice, the attempts of the magicians to do the same failed (8:16–18). "Then the magicians said unto Pharaoh, This is the finger of God" (8:19). In the battle of technicians, one party is outwitted and beaten and admits its defeat. Moreover, it transfers the contest from the level of humanity to the domain of divinity. This is, of course, in line with biblical theology, though it puts a limitation on our "technological" interpretation.

The divine-mosaic technique's superiority and efficacy in achieving its goals is exemplified by further incidents. When the plague of "boils" (whatever the nature of the skin affliction *shehin* may have been) hits the Egyptians, "the [Egyptian] magicians could not stand before Moses," because they were afflicted together with their compatriots (9:11). When the plague of hail hit Egypt and devastated the entire country, there was a notable exclusion: "Only in the land of Goshen, where the children of Israel were, was there no hail" (9:26). Then, in the most horrific plague, which concluded the confrontation and made Pharaoh submit to the demands of Moses, when all the firstborn in Egypt were smitten, the children of Israel were passed over (12:12–13). Thus, the initial contest in the magical or pseudo-technological skills gives way to the clear and acknowledged superiority of the Israelite over the Egyptian knowledge, a superiority attributed to the divine will behind the techniques of Moses and Aaron.

The final act, testifying to the superiority of Israel, and assuring their success in escaping from the bondage of Egypt, while inflicting a calamity on the Egyptian army, occurs at the crossing of the Sea of Reeds, or the Red Sea, as described in Genesis 14. The Israelites are out of Egypt, but Pharaoh regrets having let them go and pursues them with a strong contingent of forces, including horsemen and chariots. When the Israelites see the pursuing Egyptians, they panic and openly regret having embarked on the entire scheme of escaping the servitude. Yet, at this crucial moment, again a technique is employed, which reverses the impending calamity into salvation, and makes the weak triumph over the powerful.

As the Egyptians are closing on the Israelites, Moses is instructed by God to lift his rod and stretch his hand over the sea and divide it, thus allowing the Israelites to cross it on dry ground, while the waters formed a wall on their right and left. When the Egyptians followed in hot pursuit, Moses repeated his act and the waters came back and flooded the Egyptians, whose chariots had sunk in the soft ground even before. In a trice the powerful army was destroyed and the threatened children of Israel saved.

History records many cases of attempts by the oppressed to gain freedom from their oppressors. This usually took the form of an armed rebellion — whether by the Helots against Sparta on various occasions, by the slaves led by Spartacus against Rome in 73–71 B.C., by various revolts of serfs in Europe, as well as ethnic or national entities against the rule of imperial powers, like Rome, Britain, and Russia. Whether a subdued class, or a conquered nation, the exploited and oppressed have attempted to gain freedom. The results of such rebellions varied, though, broadly speaking, they all too often tended to end with failure and calamity for the oppressed, and even when successful, involved heavy casualties.

It is the uneven situation, the poor chances of the enslaved or subdued to get their freedom from their oppressors, that may be seen as one of the salient features underlying the peculiar story of the exodus. For it is such a situation that breeds the dream of some miraculous "technology," of some unprecedented but effective means, which would be put at the command of the oppressed and enable them to force the oppressors to release them from bondage — and that without the heavy penalty of suffering. To have a "bag of tricks," a reliable choice of techniques — comparable to a variety of weapons but much more startling and effective, would offer a perfect solution. Such a magic, pseudo-technology, or mythical technology, is suggested by the biblical story. It certainly would awaken resonant emotions among other oppressed people.

To be sure, it is all related to divine will. It is God who commands and controls and guarantees the effectiveness of these extraordinary means. In a monotheistic ardent religion it could not be otherwise. It is noteworthy, however, that the simple religious faith is complemented here by the ingenious collection of techniques. Under the cover of religious belief, one can detect a quest for practical measures to achieve the vital aim of freedom. This quest produces and animates the myths of power, of pseudo-scientific means, capable of achieving the aim. While such wishful dreaming can be dismissed as a mere psychological phenomenon, it must not be forgotten that out of dreams and yearnings concrete technologies have occasionally been born.

2

Greek Mythology

The tales of the Greek mythology differ from the stories of the Bible. They differ both in substance and form. The substantive difference lies in the Greek myths being woven in the context of polytheistic beliefs which, by their very nature, are fairly vague and allow the creation of fables and stories without submission to the rigors of a dogmatic religious belief. Episodes about the doings of Zeus, or Athene, or Apollo could be woven without much attention being paid to their inner consistency or their compatibility with other stories. Mount Olympus was a rather chaotic place in this sense. What was true of gods applied also to various demigods and to humans in close contact with the gods and occasionally turning into immortal beings. The strict discipline of the Israelite monotheism would not endure such vagueness and diversity, any more than a Euclidean geometrician would tolerate the pronouncement of faulty or unfounded theorems. And if certain apparent inconsistencies could be discerned in the biblical text — whether due to the compilation of various older sources, or the pre-biblical origin of the story — the commentators assailed such contradictions with an ardor of monotheistic belief combined with the vigor of sharp minds in an endeavor to explain, or explain away, any such inconsistencies. The theological cohesion and consistency of the holy book was accepted as a tenet of faith and a principle of creed.

This substantive difference between the biblical stories and the Greek myths was complemented by the textual form. Whereas the ancient Israelite tales are formulated in one sacred text, the Bible, for all to read and comprehend or comment upon, the Greek myths about gods and men and their countless deeds and conflicts have no authoritative source. They had grown out of an oral tradition, or traditions, which have no recorded beginning and which were eventually used by various writers — either faithfully to record what they had heard, or as a theme for a literary composition. Whether a straightforward account or a highly literary creation, the tales did not entail a concern for strict adherence to truth. Indeed, in contrast to the perception of biblical stories, they may have been often viewed as myths in the first place, and so not subject to the criterion of truth and veracity. Where different versions of myths are extant, as often is the case, there is no issue of deciding which is the true one: they are all true and false. They are true, having been accepted in one tradition or another; they are false, being mere tales, with only some elements of them actually possible.

This laxity of the Greek myths, in substance and in the diversity of textual sources, allows a greater freedom in choosing the material for the present study and in describing and analyzing their messages. Conceivably, one could present a somewhat different image of the tale by making a different selection of sources. Our choice will be guided by an attempt to reach early written records — even though the dating of such material may be controversial. Another consideration will be the completeness of the source, for dealing with fragments would complicate the presentation and the analysis. Where a literary presentation of a myth, or its use in a broader composition, is extant, the attraction to such a source could hardly be resisted. A composition such as a dramatic masterpiece might be close to the original myth in time and in spirit. Moreover, a literary presentation would attempt to convey a clear, consistent, plausible and meaningful image of a hero and his actions, making the text comprehensible, enjoyable and even inspirational, as in the case of the biblical stories.

Our search, will be restricted to the theme of science and technology in Greek mythology. In the variety and diversity of myths and heroes, that characterize the Greek mythology, it is not surprising to find more than an occasional allusion or reference to science and technology, but a veritable preoccupation with these facets of human endeavor.

Daedalus

One figure that looms large in connection with our theme is that of Daedalus. While he was the protagonist of Sophocles' tragedy *Daedalus*, the work is lost, with only a few fragments extant. Consequently, the myth of Daedalus will be recounted and explored here following the account of Apollodorus (or Apollodoros) in his work *Bibliotheke*, translated as *The Library*, and the *Epitome* of this work, compounded from some additional or parallel manuscripts. Besides the Greek work of Apollodorus, the references to

Dreams and Nightmares

Daedalus in Ovid's *Metamorphoses* will be used. While the Latin work may well be somewhat removed from the original Greek sources used by Ovid, it is still relatively close to the Greek traditions. Moreover, unlike Apollodorus, Ovid weaves his tale into the fabric of a poetic composition and even suggests an interpretation of the story of Daedalus, which has a stimulating impact on our own interest and involvement.

While the identity of the Roman poet Ovidius Naso, his time (43 B.C.–18 A.D.) and his authorship of *Metamorphoses* are well established and not subject to any dispute, this is not the case of Apollodorus and *The Library*. The assumption that the work is the product of Apollodorus, an eminent Athenian grammarian of the second century B.C., has been discarded by modern scholars.

Instead, the work is thought to have been written in the first or second century A.D.— whether by a man called Apollodorus or someone else later confused with the earlier grammarian.[1] *The Library* is a straightforward account of Greek mythology, evidently based on a variety of earlier written sources. Scholars regard the book as an uncritical reproduction of various myths, but this limitation has the advantage of being an accurate and documentary account of the popular Greek beliefs.[2] Let us reproduce the essentials of the story of Daedalus, as conveyed in *The Library*.

Daedalus, an Athenian, was "an excellent architect and the first inventor of images"—*agalmatoi*, which may mean "glorious and delightful things" and thus suggest a wider range of creation. He threw down from the Acropolis his pupil Talos (or Calos) who happened to be his nephew, fearing that the latter might surpass him. Condemned by the Areopagos, he fled to Minos, king of Crete.[3] There Minos's wife, Pasiphae, having fallen in love with a bull, solicited Daedalus's help. He constructed a wooden cow, hollow inside, and put Pasiphae into it. The bull, mistaking it for a real cow, copulated with it, and Pasiphae gave birth to a monster, named Minotaur, with a bull's face and human body. Minos shut Minotaur up in the Labyrinth, a construction of Daedalus, a maze from which it was virtually impossible to find a way out.[4] The Minotaur was fed seven Athenian youths and seven maidens each year. When Theseus, the Athenian hero, voluntarily joined the sacrificial party, Ariadne, the daughter of Minos, having fallen in love with him, decided to save him. She turned to Daedalus to tell her how to get out of the Labyrinth. He suggested a clue, namely, to take a ball of thread and fasten one end to the lintel of the door on entering the maze, hold on to the unwinding ball, thus marking the way of return. Theseus followed the instructions and, having slain Minotaur, made his way out and returned to Athens.[5] Informed of the escape of Theseus and his party, and aware of the help provided byDaedalus, Minos imprisoned the architect and his son Icarus in the Labyrinth. Yet Daedalus constructed wings for himself and his son in order to escape Minos by air.

He instructed Icarus not to fly too high, lest the glue melt in the sun and the wings fall off, nor to fly too close to the sea, lest the pinions be detached by dampness. However, the heedless Icarus, disregarding the injunctions, soared ever higher and, the glue having melted, fell into the sea and perished. Daedalus, however, made his way to Camicus in Sicily, where he was concealed by its ruler Cocalus.

Minos, in pursuit of Daedalus, promised a great reward to whomever would pass a thread through a spiral shell of his, thus hoping to find Daedalus. And, indeed, when he proffered the shell to Cocalus, the latter gave it to Daedalus, who found a solution. He fastened the thread to an ant, and, having bored a hole in the shell, let the ant pass through the spiral. When Minos saw the solution of the task, he realized that Daedalus was behind Cocalus, and demanded his surrender. However, the daughters of Cocalus killed Minos.[6]

Ovid, in his dealing with the myth of Daedalus, expands on its most dramatic episode, namely the escape by air with Icarus, and the misadventure linked with it. Clearly this is a theme most amenable to poetic and literary imagination. It also happens to be the most ambitious of human yearnings for technological achievement.

The determination of Daedalus to escape from Crete is attributed to his hatred of the island and the long exile there — a perfectly understandable human reaction. The solution of the problem reveals another human characteristic, namely logical thinking. While Minos controls the sea and the land, thus precluding an escape by the available routes, Daedalus argues with himself, the sky remains open. "*Omnia possideat, non possidet aera Minos.*" Though Minos owns all, he does not own the air.[7] While the thinking is clear and strikes a responsive chord in the reader's mind, the speculation of Daedalus reaches beyond the imagination of an average man.

For though the logical argument is quite human, Daedalus's creative thinking is extraordinary. Daedalus does not say, "Minos controls the land and the sea around it, and so there is no way of escape for me." Instead he sees the sphere out of the mighty king's control — the air. The daring thoughts of an inventor see a possibility of escape, where ordinary men see nothing.

Significantly, one can discern here, in the presentation of Ovid, a note of defiance of the man of genius, of the great scientist and inventor, toward the great potentate. We face here a contest between Power and Mind, a contest in which Mind is destined to win.

The capacity of Mind, at least the ingenious mind of Daedalus, is not merely to challenge the power of the king in principle or in theory, which would have been a futile endeavor, but to do so in practice. This is achieved by an inventive technological device which should enable Daedalus, and his son Icarus, to escape through air by flying. In the words of Ovid, "Having said so [one might say, 'no sooner said than done'], he sets his mind to unknown arts, and changes [or 'renovates'] nature."[8] Here the dream of human inventiveness, of the capacity to interfere with what is perceived as natural order, is daringly expressed. The way in which nature can be renewed, reformed, changed, is not elaborated in general terms. The idea that natural laws cannot be changed, but can be used to achieve marvelous things, is not conveyed, or even suggested. Yet, to achieve the capacity of locomotion not given to humans by nature, is perceived as overcoming the natural order of things.

That this is done by imitating natural phenomenon, the flight of birds, is neither surprising nor detracts from the meta-natural achievement. One could say that it is only natural for man to take advantage of the natural phenomena and imitate them, if possible, to achieve his goals. Daedalus, in Ovid's description, takes great pains to construct his wings from birds' feathers. He is not only a man of great ideas, but a careful and exact engineer. This in contrast to Icarus, who excitedly tried to help, only hindering his father's work. Clearly, Ovid tries to emphasize the need for high competence and expertise in an engineering enterprise. Excitement is not enough, and indeed may interfere with the rational-systematic approach. The comment on the fumbling Icarus also serves as an indication of the impending tragical failing of the willing, but incompetent, disciple—a precursor, in a way, of Dukas's The Sorcerer's Apprentice.

Once airborne, the flying duo awakens the admiration of people on land, fishermen, shepherds, and plowmen. Stupefied, "they believe them to be gods, that they could fly through air."[9] The tableau vividly presents the simple folk wondering at the marvel of technology and taking it for a supernatural phenomenon.

By the same token, Ovid may have wished to indicate that such an achievement—merely a myth in his time—would elevate man to the level of the powerful dwellers of Olympus.

Yet, whatever the splendor of such an achievement, it remains firmly embedded in science and technology, in knowledge and technical competency. This is tragically conveyed by the accident which occurred to Icarus. His careless flight, too close to the sun, ended with a fall into the sea and death. The father's efforts to teach his son to fly and to follow his instructions failed, because of the son's inaptitude or carelessness — a lesson indicating that technology must follow strict rules if it is to prove successful.

Ovid stresses the personal tragedy of Daedalus and the irony that the father's ingenious invention became the cause of the son's untimely death. When Daedalus sees the wings of Icarus in the water, "he cursed his science [or skills] (*artes*)."[10] The technological success is linked here with a personal tragedy, a point which did not escape the sharp eye of a man of literary imagination.

Nor does Ovid miss another point, a matter of a clear moral nature. For as Daedalus is burying his son, a partridge utters a joyful song. The bird, in Ovid's tale, was the incarnation of Daedalus's sister, whose son had been murdered by the envious Daedalus. Her vindictive joy at the suffering of Daedalus reminds the reader of the just punishment meted out on a self-centered and unscrupulous inventor. It also conveys a cautionary reminder that a great man of science, an engineer of genius, can be morally flawed.

Let us highlight the salient features of the myth of Daedalus, looked at from our perspective. Significantly, Daedalus is not merely presented as an architect and a great inventor, but even his name has a meaning which points to his remarkable qualities. *Daidalos*, as an adjective, means "cunningly or curiously wrought." Hence the proper noun means "the cunning worker, the artist."[11] Thus, it could be said that Daedalus serves as an *allegory* of cunning, resourcefulness and inventiveness. At the same time, the story of Daedalus is presented as a *personal* adventure and drama. In a sense, Daedalus combines symbolism with real humanity, while both the allegory and the reality entail deeds and achievements plausible and fantastic, significant and trivial, monumental and bizarre.

The diversity of Daedalus's exploits is rather baffling. On the one hand, he is merely a clever man, as his advice to Theseus how to find his way out of the Labyrinth exemplifies. On the other hand, he is presented as a man of outstanding ingenuity who constructs the Labyrinth, and a man of genius who contrives a way of flying. Yet, it is not beyond him to engage in the petty problem of pulling a thread through a spiral shell. He is a sculptor and an architect, a riddle solver and a great inventor. He is endowed with a creative mind, as well as with good common sense. There is, however, a common root to this diversity of talent and achievement. It all springs from the man's intelligence. Intelligence is the power which underlies the good advice and the great invention.

Daedalus is the epitome of *Homo sapiens* with a fully developed mind, which is eagerly applied to any practical problem or objective of humanity — from the simplest to the most exalted, from the present to the future, from the earthbound maze to airborne travel.

A less obvious feature of the myth can perhaps be detected in the stories related to the maze. Daedalus constructs the perplexing Labyrinth — a structure with open doors in which humans get lost. Though this may be a far-fetched interpretation, such a construction may symbolize human inventions which turn into a trap for humanity. A foremost example of such a situation is offered in our times by nuclear weapons. Yet Daedalus finds a way for securing a way out of the trap — a search which has been emulated in connection with recent inventions of more complex nature. Even the bizarre way of passing a thread through a spiral shell may be seen as a symbol of man's capacity to overcome the complexities of nature — and not only those of his own creation.

In a sense, of course, almost any technological invention, however beneficial in general, may prove a trap in some cases.

The accidents in various modes of transportation, from the chariot to the airplane, are a clear testimony to this phenomenon. And, indeed, this risk of a trap, of a mishap, is clearly conveyed in the story of Icarus. Whatever the splendor of human invention, there is an element of fragility to it. As this fragility may affect the wellbeing of humans, it carries within itself an element of tragedy. Thus, the melting wings cause Icarus's death and Daedalus's deep sorrow. The inventor must beware. Technology is not given unequivocal, enthusiastic praise. It is admired, but this admiration is accompanied by a note of caution and anxiety.

Switching from the inventions to the inventor, what is the image of the great resourceful man of science and technology? His professional and mental qualities are clearly admired, but what about his moral traits as a human being? Here clearly his image is anything but bright. He seems to have no compunctions in creating the cow for Pasiphae, despite the abnormal and sinister purpose involved. He facilitates the imprisonment of Minotaur in the Labyrinth, conceivably a desirable deed; yet he does not foresee, and perhaps disregards, the human sacrifices to the monster. Nonetheless, he offers a solution to Theseus how to find his way out of the Labyrinth. In short, he appears to be a genius for hire — with little regard as to the desirability or undesirability of the objective he serves. He is a morally neutral engineer — not unlike some in our own times.

Yet the moral imperfections of Daedalus go deeper. His ambition to be the foremost inventor or artist is so important to him, that he commits a murder. He kills his own pupil and nephew, fearing that the latter may outshine him. Such an egocentric preoccupation with one's standing, such a ruthless commitment to one's career, far from glorifying one's profession, blemishes one's humanity. Thus in summation one can quote Sir J.G. Frazer's characterization of Daedalus: "Through the clouds of fable which gathered round his life and adventures we may discern the figure of a vagabond artist as versatile as Leonardo da Vinci and as unscrupulous as Benvenute Cellini."[12] With all the misgivings about technology and the doubts cast on the moral character of Daedalus the inventor and the artist, the myth, or the cluster of myths, seems to point to some kind of a happy ending. Daedalus succeeds in escaping the pursuing Minos. The clever and resourceful scientist-artist proves the winner in the confrontation with the powerful despot. The engineer escapes the wrath of his employer. In the contest of power and wit, wit proves the winner. There is here an expression of sympathy for the clever underdog, on the run from the ruthless man of power. Whether the happy ending is typical of such a situation is another matter.

Yet, one can discern another element in the conclusive story.

The trick which Minos uses to find Daedalus, namely a puzzle which can be solved only by an ingenious mind, testifies to the cleverness and resourcefulness of Minos himself. He realizes that Daedalus, the ardent inventor, will not resist the temptation of taking on a demanding task. He recognizes the Achilles' heel of the inventor, his dedication to, his obsession with, the solution of problems, and he uses this knowledge to set a trap for Daedalus, and proves successful. That this success is reversed is not due to the "logic" of the situation, but rather the result of extraneous and incidental factors.

Thus, the myth points to the weakness of the great inventor whose professional zeal is greater than his overall judgment of the situation. Daedalus seems to forget his lot and fortune when he faces a fascinating problem which challenges his genius. If he is ready to forget his own concerns when encountering a puzzling task, it may not be surprising that he shows little concern for morality when challenged by various difficult tasks, whether linked to Pasiphae's unnatural passion, or some tasks set by Minos. In a way, one could say that because Daedalus is more than human, he is occasionally less than human. This may be true of some of his successors.

The most prominent achievement of Daedalus, as far as science and technology are concerned, is his conquest of the air. It clearly conveys and symbolizes human aspirations to fly. It is noteworthy that this yearning is manifest in another myth, namely that of Bellerophon.

Bellerophon is not described as an inventor or an artist. He is merely a charming young man, encountering bad luck and persecution on false charges. His upright conduct in rejecting the amorous advances of the wife of Proetus, king of Tiryns, resulted in a false accusation of the spurned woman (reminiscent of the biblical story of Joseph), and consequent banishment to her royal father's court with a secret demand to kill the alleged seducer.

King Iobates, reluctant to kill his charming guest, asks him instead to kill Chimera, expecting that Bellerophon will perish in the fight. For Chimera was a terrible monster, "more than a match for many, let alone one." It was a three-headed creature, belching fire, and devastating the land around.[13] Bellerophon faces this challenge with the help of a winged horse, Pegasus. With divine assistance he mounts the horse, and, flying above the range of Chimera, shoots the monster and kills it. Some other exploits against powerful human enemies follow, all crowned with success. These, too, are attributed in some tales to the cooperation of Bellerophon and Pegasus. Having proved invincible, Bellerophon finally gains the favor of the king, who gives him his daughter for a wife and makes him the heir to the kingdom.

The link between the myths of Daedalus and Bellerophon, as indicated above, is the feature of air travel. Yet there are differences between the ways in which the two tales handle this aspiration. Whereas Bellerophon gets the cooperation of the flying horse through divine favor and while Pegasus himself is a semidivine creature, Daedalus invents the flying contraption. The myth of Bellerophon merely expresses the yearning for flying; the tale of Daedalus conveys the aspiration to fly and the ambition to achieve it by human ingenuity and art. The gap between the hope for a miracle and the quest for human achievement is clear and its importance must not be ignored.

A difference of another kind is that Daedalus's flight is used for a peaceful purpose: it is a dream for a new mode of transportation. The myth of Bellerophon and Pegasus clearly links the capacity to fly to a military objective, to gaining an advantage in a confrontation with an otherwise superior force. In the annals of military history enemies have always looked for a technological advantage which would facilitate a victory, and indeed such an advantage, especially when taking the other side by surprise, has often proved crucial in the fortunes of war. In the tale of Bellerophon the airborne fighter proves no match for his seemingly mightier enemies.

A tale of a warrior fighting from the air was nothing but a wishful dream till fairly recent times. Yet it embodied a yearning which came to fruition on a colossal scale in the past century.

To be sure, the ancient myth differs from the present reality in two cardinal respects. Bellerophon is essentially the virtuous fighter — at least in the case of Chimera, a dangerous and vicious monster. Thus, the big guns are on the side of the righteous.

The myth seems to ignore a situation in which the technological advantage is on the side of the wicked, threatening the righteous — as, alas, has often happened in human history.

Then the tale entrusts the new weapon to one side, and ignores the possibility of the other side being equipped with a similar technological advantage. What if Chimera had its own Pegasus? Probably there would have been another myth which would give one side — hopefully the good — another crucial advantage.

Prometheus

The mythical figure of Prometheus is particularly relevant to our study. For though Prometheus is a heroic figure, who combines rebellious self-assertion vis-à-vis the most powerful deity, Zeus, with compassion for weak humanity, and as such belongs in the realm of the dramatic conflict between crude power and charity, he deals with knowledge and technology in the course of his heroic action. It is this aspect that concerns us, but it must be explained in the context of the wider tale.

As is to be expected, there is no authoritative source extant for the myths about Prometheus. He is mentioned by Hesiodus, Apollodorus, and others. Yet, the most coherent and comprehensive picture is presented in the drama of Aeschylus, *Prometheus Bound*, which will be the main source for our analysis. (Aeschylus wrote two more dramas about Prometheus which are not extant.) The drama deals not only with Prometheus's role in science and technology, but also with the use of such skills by other *dramatis personae* — a point of interest in the context of this study.

The name Prometheus means "forethought," and it stands in contrast with Prometheus's mythological brother Epimetheus, who represents "afterthought." The clear intention of this juxtaposition is to indicate that thinking ahead is the manner of the wise and resourceful, while thinking after the event is the lot of the failing and stupid. Naturally, it is Prometheus who is associated with wisdom and skill, the means of forethought in the service of humanity.

Prometheus, in Greek mythology preceding the drama of Aeschylus, is a Titan, a divine being, which in the framework of Greek mythology does not deprive him of recognized human characteristics. Thus, in a way, he represents a human endowed with almost superhuman qualities of mind and character. According to the myth, Prometheus stole fire from heaven and gave it to humans, contrary to the will of Zeus. As a punishment for transgressing his orders, Zeus had Prometheus nailed to Mount Caucasus. There an eagle would swoop down and eat his liver, which regrew overnight to allow the continuous repetition of the torment. Eventually, Prometheus was released by Hercules.[14]

The myth, as used in Aeschylus's drama, is drawn in monumental proportions, and the plight of humanity plays a more elaborate and prominent role in it. The conflict between Zeus and Prometheus revolves around the issue of the human condition. Or, to put it in a more dramatic way, as Aeschylus does, the issue is the survival of humanity. Zeus plans the perdition of man; Prometheus is resolved to save the human kind. In the words of Aeschylus, put into the mouth of Prometheus:

> Of wretched humans he [Zeus] took no account, resolved
> To annihilate them and create another race.
> This purpose there was no one to oppose but I:
> I dared. I saved the human race from being ground
> To dust, from total death.[15]

Besides the obvious juxtaposition of the merciless Zeus and the compassionate Prometheus, it can be argued that the conflict expresses the philosophical puzzlement about the paradox in the human condition, namely that humans are biologically feeble and yet achieve success through knowledge and the use of artifacts. Humans by nature (symbolized by Zeus) destined for perdition, are saved by intelligence (symbolized by Prometheus), as further elaborated.

The transgression of Prometheus, in the myth and in the drama, consisted of stealing fire and bringing it as a gift — a saving gift — to mankind:

> ... For I am he
> Who hunted out the source of fire, and stole it, packed
> In pith of a dry fennel-stalk.
> And fire has proved
> For man a teacher in every art, their grand resource.[16]

Fire is conceived as the foundation of all technology and perhaps also as the symbol of all applied knowledge.

Indeed, the role of Prometheus, as described by Aeschylus, is not confined to the single act of stealing fire for humanity: he becomes the encyclopedic teacher of mankind, the founder of human civilization in the widest sense of the word. This is well elaborated in a monologue of Prometheus:

> ... What I did
> For mortals in their misery, hear now. At first
> Mindless, I gave them mind and reason...
> In those days they had eyes, but sight was meaningless;
> Heard sounds, but could not listen; all their length of life
> They passed like shapes in dreams, confused and purposeless.
> Of brick-built, sun-warmed houses, or of carpentry,
> They had no notion; lived in holes, like swarms of ants,
> Or deep in sunless caverns; knew no certain way
> To mark off winter, or flowery spring, or fruitful summer;
> Their every act was without knowledge, till I came.
> I taught them to determine when stars rise or set —
> A difficult art. Number, the primary science, I
> Invented for them, and how to set down words in writing —
> The all-remembering skill, mother of many arts.
> I was the first to harness beasts under a yoke
> With trace or saddle as man's slave, to take man's place
> Under the heaviest burdens; put the horse to chariot,
> Made him obey the rein, and be an ornament
> To wealth and greatness. No one before me discovered
> The sailor's waggon — flax-winged craft that roam the seas...
>   I showed them how to mix mild healing herbs
> And so protect themselves against all maladies...
>   ... Next the treasures of the earth,
> The bronze, iron, silver, gold hidden deep down — who else
> But I can claim to have found them first?[17] ...

Building, writing, arithmetic, transportation on land and water, medicine, mining, the saving arts of mankind are all gifts of Prometheus. It is through civilization — comprising knowledge and technology — that humans are elevated from a miserable biological condition to a decent level of existence.

Significantly, the philosophy conveyed here regards knowledge and its application to human needs — and not faith in God, as in Christianity — as the salvation of mankind. The mythical savior Prometheus does not atone for humans' original sin, but teaches humans in order to lift them from original ignorance. Though motivated by compassion for humanity, Prometheus does not preach and moralize, but instructs and enlightens. Salvation lies in knowledge and its application, and the savior is a scientist and a technologist.

As noted, the name Prometheus expresses the idea of foresight, of thinking ahead of events, or contingency. Thus, Prometheus comes to emphasize the significance and value of knowledge when applied to future situations and not to past events. Indeed, the ideal of the knowledge of the future is formulated by Prometheus himself:

> ... I know exactly every thing
> That is to be; no torment will come unforeseen.[18]

While this falls short of controlling and mastering future events — and there is in the last quotation an element of resignation to necessity — perhaps it is not too bold to conclude that the intent to control the future is implicitly assumed in *Prometheus Bound*. For if Prometheus can foresee the future and at the same time masters the arts and applies knowledge to human needs, it is plausible to expect that he will apply his skills to the foreseen situations, or at least to those which can be mastered.

The predictive capacity of Prometheus seems to veer from the visionary to the practical, from prophesy to prognosis. And, of course, prognosis invites human action to counter the feared situation, even if such action cannot be always assured of success. To be sure, prophecy — at least in the Israelite tradition — also invites human action, such as repentance and contrition and mending one's ways, in order to avert divine wrath. The book of Jonah is a prominent example of this. However, the response to prophecy is on the moral plane and is expected to affect God's decisions, whereas prognosis is essentially concerned with natural phenomena and is made to pave the way for the beneficial interference of human action. Prometheus brings foresight and knowledge, pre-science and science, down to earth and puts them at humans' command, thus elevating humans to a new level of comfort and power. In brief, the promise of Prometheus is the assurance of maximal wellbeing to humanity through knowledge, science and technology.

And yet, despite this praise and glorification of knowledge and technical skill, *Prometheus Bound* does not remain an unqualified hymn of glory to applied science. A subtle hint is introduced by Aeschylus which points to a danger looming in technology precisely where its advantage lies — namely, in the power it wields. In the opening passages of the play the following exchange takes place between Strength, allegorically representing ruthless power, and Hephaestus, the divine smith, who is commanded by Zeus to fetter Prometheus to a rock for the latter's transgression.

> HEPHAESTUS: I hate my craft, I hate the skill of my own hands.
> STRENGTH: Why do you hate it? Take the simple view:
> > Your craft
> > Is not to blame for what must be inflicted now.
> HEPHAESTUS: True — yet I wish some other had been given my skill.[19]

Unlike Strength, Hephaestus finds it hard to accept the moral neutrality of technology. Even though the command to inflict the cruel punishment is issued by Zeus, Hephaestus is employing his skill to execute that command, and Aeschylus seems to indicate that such an execution may well burden the conscience of the executioner. Or to put it in other words, had the technological skill not been there, this kind of cruel action would not have taken place. The technological know-how becomes, be it reluctantly, an ingredient in the cruel act, and the technologist a partner, be it an unwilling one, in the evil deed. In our own era, when the destructive power of technology seems limitless, this foresight, or Promethean insight, of Aeschylus is of particular relevance.

While Hephaestus finds it hard to dissociate himself from moral responsibility for the use of his technology, Strength fulfills his role in binding Prometheus without compunction, consoling himself with the philosophy that he, like others, is not free to act as he wishes:

> All tasks are burdensome — except to rule the gods.
> No one is free but Zeus.[20]

Though Aeschylus may well wish to convey here the truth about the actual limitations on a free, and possibly moral, action taken by anyone subject to a tyrannical ruler, it would be erroneous to conclude that this expresses his compliance with such a state of affairs. For the myth of Prometheus, as expounded in the play, can be understood as a passionate protest against the dissociation of conscience from power, of charity from knowledge, of compassion from technology. Indeed, it is the combination of these two elements in the symbolical figure of Prometheus that saves mankind, just as the combination of skill and cruelty results in iniquity and suffering. An additional, ironical twist lies in the fact that the charitable technologist may well become the victim of the cruelly used technology, that Prometheus is visited with punishment for his noble art. In his own words,

> I pitied mortal men; but being myself not thought
> To merit pity, am thus cruelly disciplined....[21]

To sum up the philosophy about the place of technology in human life, as conveyed in Aeschylus's *Prometheus Bound*, the following points can be made. Firstly, the overall attitude to technology is one of approval and admiration. It is the application of reason to human needs that produces the conditions of a tolerable life, as well as establishes human civilization. Science and technology are the salvation of mankind, they are the factors which convert wretched brutes into civilized human beings.

Still, the boon is not unqualified, for the danger always looms that knowledge and skill, applied science and technology, will be used by an evil and cruel mind for a sinister purpose.

The power inherent in technology is great, but only by combining it with charity will it serve a good purpose. Unfortunately, there is no inherent guarantee that this power will be used for a noble purpose. Thus the great boon of technology also casts a long shadow. The wellbeing resulting from the use of science is mixed with forebodings. Despite the dominance of the trust in technology in the dramatic presentation of the myth, a dissonant note is discernible, a degree of ambivalence is expressed.

3

The Middle Ages

To include the following two examples of tales or stories under the label "Middle Ages" is somewhat inaccurate. For though in both cases the myths associated with the texts explored may have originated in the Middle Ages, if not even earlier, the texts themselves are closer to modern times. Indeed, the old myths were creatively developed well into the modern era in one form or another, and thus defy chronological delimitation. Despite these reservations, it can be suggested that they belong in a genre of tales which we tend to associate with the Middle Ages — if not, strictly speaking, chronologically, then typologically, for they are characterized by the belief in magic. The achievement of an objective — one which is virtually unattainable by current scientific or technological means — is made feasible by an incantation, a mysterious contact with supernatural powers, an arcane manner of affecting or manipulating nature, or powers controlling nature. Such trust in magic, a power restricted to some individuals, may have been more typical of the Middle Ages than either the enlightened antiquity or the informed modernity, even if one must admit the practice of magic in ancient times and the sporadic belief in it in the modern era.

Still, it is the Middle Ages which are linked in our consciousness to such attempts as conversion of baser metals into gold by means of alchemy. Astrology, divining human destiny from the stars, though originating in antiquity and claiming followers to date, may again be typical of the Middle Ages. The tricks abounding in the stories of *Thousand and One Nights* are a clear example of the quest for magical power characteristic of the Middle Ages, even if the Arabic text was translated into French, and subsequently into other European languages, not before the early eighteenth century.[1] The original texts reach back to the Middle Ages, as do the folk stories which served as the source material.

Indeed, these stories heavily rely on magical means. It is not simply *deus ex machina* that provides the resolution of an intricate conflict, or the salvation of a deserving hero or heroine. It is the knowledge of an incantation, or the control over a magical implement or object, that offers a lucky man the means to attain his objective. Significantly, it is not an outstanding individual, such as Heracles or Theseus or Achilles in the Greek mythology, who occasionally gets the supernatural assistance of the gods when facing a difficult task; it is the ordinary fellow, an Aladdin or an Ali Baba who, by obtaining the know-how, the magical means, can attain his desire. Thus, magic replaces miracle, know-how substitutes heroism. Magic becomes a precursor of technology, the latter to be magic available to all.

The spoken formula "Open, Sesame" opens mysterious doors. A mechanical horse allows its rider to fly to his place of choice. Rubbing a ring produces a jinni, working instant miracles at the command of its owner. A lamp provides Aladdin with the services of another jinni. In short, whatever one wants, one gets — provided one has access to the magical contrivance or formula.

The world of our own modern age, with its means of locomotion, automatic doors and more intricate devices, is adumbrated in these tales, though the *means* to attain objectives are mysterious, irrational, magical, and not scientific and technological. Needless to say, the difference is crucial. Yet, the common human dream and quest underlie both magic and technology.

It is keeping in mind the magical perspective that the Golem legend and the Doctor Faustus Story will be explored.

The Golem

The legend of the Golem has been shaped through generations of Jewish mysticism and folktales. "Golem," a Hebrew word, is associated with unformed matter, but it came to mean a creature human-made. The two meanings are linked, because of the assumption that the creature is made of earth or clay — that is to say, shapeless but moldable matter — and also (as we shall see later) because the finished synthetic creature retains some of the earthly, and thus less than perfect, quality. The story of the Golem has been woven over centuries: some of its elements can be traced in the Talmud, to the first half of the first millennium, while some final touches have been added to it in the Jewish folklore of early nineteenth century. Moreover, the legend has been used as material for various literary and artistic compositions, by Jews and non–Jews alike, from early nineteenth century through our times.

Poems, stories, novels, dramas, musical compositions, even a film or two, are included among these modern uses of the old tale.[2]

One of the basic and oldest elements in the legend is the idea that humans can create a living creature, even another human being. Thus, a Talmudic statement attributes to the righteous the capacity to create a world, and one sage is reported to have made a man and sent him to another scholar. (Significantly, however, the factitious human did not have the capacity to respond when spoken to.)

The creation of such a being is achieved by the knowledge of the right formula for using the holy letters of which the name of God, as well as the books of his laws and teaching, consist. These letters, in the right combination, are believed to have the creative force. They are said to have been used by God in the creation of the world and are thought to be usable by the devout scholar who knows the mysterious formula.[3]

The idea of a magical creation of a living being becomes at a later date (about the sixteenth century) linked with stories and speculations focusing not on the process of creation and the personality of the creator, but on the nature of the creature — the Golem. The Golem in these stories is usually seen as a being fulfilling a certain useful function, such as being a servant to his pious rabbinical maker.[4] This aspect of the legend seems to originate in medieval stories about the creation of an automatic human[5] — one could say, a kind of a living robot. An additional element is added to the Golem fable among Polish Jews in the seventeenth century — namely, the danger inherent in the creature. The Golem is described as continuously growing in size and strength and thus causing fear among people and in his rabbinical maker. Then the latter, who had put life into his body, removes it, and the creature falls apart. In the moment of disintegration, however, the Golem, or the weight of his mass, injures, or even kills his creator.[6]

The legend of the Golem from the seventeenth century on has taken a variety of forms and been linked to several rabbis. The most famous version of the legend dates from early nineteenth century and attributes the creation of the Golem to a prominent scholar of the sixteenth century, Rabbi Loew of Prague.

According to this story, Rabbi Loew created a Golem who served him through the week. On the eve of the Sabbath, the universal day of rest, the rabbi would remove the name of God from the Golem, who would turn back into the clay of which he was made. When the rest day was over, the Golem was revived by the reinsertion of the sacred name. On one occasion, however, the rabbi forgot to remove the name on Sabbath eve and the Golem started to get wild, to shake the houses and to threaten general destruction, which he was able to cause due to his enormous strength. The Rabbi was summoned from the synagogue, succeeded in tearing out the sacred name and thus turned the Golem into earth. The rabbi did not revive the Golem anymore, and his remains were put into the attic of the Alt-Neu synagogue of Prague, still in existence.[7]

Looking at the legend as a whole, not only at this particular version, and bearing in mind the various elements which have been incorporated in it over the ages, there are certain salient features of special relevance to our subject matter. One is the human intent to create life. In a way, this constitutes the highest, most ambitious, dream, the peak of hubris, for in creating life humans achieve the creative capacity of God. Indeed, the making of the Golem is conceived in some medieval traditions as repeating the divine creation of Adam.[8] Such an aspiration transcends the most audacious technological designs of any time. But even in the later, post–Renaissance versions of the Golem legend, when the creature becomes more robot-like, a semi-mechanical and only partially living being, the human creator still retains the ambitious profile of a superman; the rabbinical miracle worker remains a Faustian figure.[9]

It is noteworthy and typical of the spirit of the Judaism which informs these legends that the attempt to imitate God or to aspire to deeds beyond the normal human capacity is not done against God or in defiance of his commandments. As aptly noted, Rabbi Loew, the Jewish Faust in the legend, is not, like his prototype, in alliance with the devil.[10] Typically, in one medieval text an argument is raised that the fabrication of a human will make people believe that the human creator is divine and that God does not exist. The fear of such a consequence makes the human creator destroy the work, concluding that the study of the techniques of creation should be undertaken only in order to understand the power of God, but not with the intent to apply the know-how to practice.[11]

Thus the human dream remains curtailed by self-control, by moral discipline. The sense of religious awe dominates the human aspiration to become godlike. To be sure, humankind does use magic to achieve miraculous objectives, but it is magic relying on the sacred name of God, and imitating the works of God, and not the magic of the fallen man.[12] Significantly, the creation of the Golem is, as a rule, ascribed to a righteous, saintly, scholar or rabbi, that is to say, to someone steeped in the ways of the Lord, and consequently fully aware of the right ways of conduct and of human responsibility to God and to people.

Another aspect of the legend is the emphasis on the limitations of the Golem, which clearly implies the supremacy of humanity over the most miraculous artifact. As already noted, even in the earliest versions of the tale the fabricated creature does not know to answer when spoken to — an obvious allusion to its mental limitations.

The point was elaborated upon by medieval commentators who stress in a variety of ways, that the Golem, while possessing a certain kind of vitality, does not have reason, spirit, soul.[13] The stature of the Golem is further diminished by various anecdotes about him from more recent centuries. One tells of the Golem instructed to grease the Rabbi's wagon and applying the grease to the entire vehicle. Another story has the Golem set fire to a house, when told to light a candle.[14] Stories like these both introduce an element of humor into the legend, which in itself belittles the achievement of making a Golem, and point to the limitations of the creature. The Golem may be powerful, much stronger than ordinary human beings, but he is inferior to them, for his intelligence, if it may be called so, is mechanical, and thus limited to the execution of orders at best. However ingenious the creature may be, humankind, endowed with mind and spirit, stands much higher — indeed, can claim a qualitative superiority.

Yet, this belittling of the Golem and the relative aggrandizement of humans do not preclude the misgivings and forebodings about the possible danger inherent in the Golem. The danger may be due to the excessive power of the creature, or perhaps the result of its mental limitations, or because of the combination of power with the absence of reason. Or, to convey the same idea in theological terms, the danger may originate in the telluric, earthly, element, which without the divine control becomes chaotic and destructive.[15] The danger may ultimately lie in the very attempt of someone, even a righteous and pious person, to attempt such a colossal thing as the creation of a semihuman being.[16]

The legend of the Golem is a blend of a naive folk tale and mystical speculation. It could be described as being to religious belief and Judaism what science fiction is to science. As a scientist will not accept science fiction at its face value, so a devout person will not view the Golem story as literally true. Yet, as a scientist may detect instructive insights in some science fiction, so a religious person — and perhaps even an agnostic — may discern some wisdom and a pertinent moral in the story of the Golem.

How will such conclusions affect the perception of the place of technology in human affairs? Underlying the legend of the Golem, and therefore informing any conclusions derived from it, is a basic religious-philosophical outlook. It is committed to a belief in an ordered universe in which God is the supreme authority and thus superior to humans, while the latter must ascertain their own superiority over any device they may be able to invent or create. To ensure this harmonious order, any daring attempt of people to master the elements and to use them to their advantage must be entrusted to responsible, moral, wise ones—people who combine knowledge with conscience and are imbued with a sense of religious awe. Yet, even such an arrangement is not foolproof, and an invention of great daring may turn against humankind, even if it essentially remains subhuman and is conceived and accomplished by the righteous and the wise.

Thus, the moral of the story, if one may address it to our age, is to view great scientific and technological inventions with great caution, and ensure that they are controlled by the right responsible people, who should view the invention not only with regard for its immediate benefit, but also in its overall human and cosmic implications. They must not be overawed by it, and should remain in control. For there is always the danger that the Golem will run amok, a point not to be lost in a generation weary about missiles "escaping" their electronic controls. The stress on the control of the wise and righteous over the powerful technology cannot be overemphasized in an era when it is feared that technology may fall into the hands of irresponsible, wicked agents. The example of the Golem being destroyed by the wise rabbi to prevent a catastrophe, while deserving emulation, can hardly be expected to be followed. For the reality in our nuclear age is that once the jinni is out of the bottle, it cannot be put back into it.

Doctor Faustus

Sharply contrasting with the legend of the Golem, though sharing with it some basic concepts, is the story of Doctor Faustus. It, too, expresses the quest for miraculous powers, for a meta-technological achievement. The wishful dream of humans to transcend their limitations is also in this case associated with mystery and magic.

Yet the similar medieval roots do not obliterate the pronounced differences. The creator of the Golem submits to ethical principles, while Doctor Faustus is an amoral adventurer. The Golem is created with God's help—be it through a magical use of the divine name or sacred letters—while

Doctor Faustus gains power by making a deal with the devil. The story of the Golem expresses a concern for a harmonious coexistence and even cooperation between religious faith and the quest for a human-made miracle, while the story of Doctor Faustus is the tragic collision between humans' reach for supreme power and the divine order which assigns humility and piety for humankind.

The story of Doctor Faustus originated in Germany and it reached its most famous literary perfection in Goethe's *Faust*. Between the origin and the apex one can find the English play of Christopher Marlowe, *Doctor Faustus*, published at the turn of the sixteenth century. Marlowe's work is a convenient text for our purpose, for it clearly reflects the juxtaposition of two opposite philosophies, the adoration of power and the commitment to piety—a collision which Goethe's *Faust*, a much more sophisticated and complex work, has transcended. This contrast and collision of divergent philosophies or ways of life, conveyed in Marlowe's drama, is closely related to the problem of the relationship between humans and technology.

The plot of the drama is fairly straightforward. Doctor Faustus, a scholar of high reputation, enters into a pact with the devil, in which he agrees to surrender his body and soul to Lucifer, the ruler of all the devils, in exchange for twenty-four years of life of unrestrained pleasure and unlimited power. And, indeed, Faustus is given a period of this kind of fulfillment, as Mephostophilis, Lucifer's agent, scrupulously serves Faustus and gratifies all his wishes, till the moment when the payment is to be exacted. Faustus is then torn to pieces by a pack of devils and his soul is doomed to eternal damnation.

The drama seems to suggest a clear choice between two ways of life—the Christian life of religious faith, piety and self-effacing humility, and the life of pride and human self-assertion, of the quest for joy and limitless power. The alternatives can well be regarded as expressing the medieval and the Renaissance ideals respectively, though in a way they embody a perennial choice in humans' quest for the right way of life. While Marlowe's play ostensibly sides with the Christian medieval ideal, it vigorously expresses the new rebellious outlook as well. To be sure, the juxtaposition of the two ways of life is not conveyed in a purely philosophical manner, but is clad in the beliefs of the age, which actually weakens the case which could be made by each side. Thus Christianity is linked to scholasticism and obscurantism, while the humanistic self-assertion is combined with belief in magic and with foolish pranks. Still, it is possible to see through the trivia and the irrelevant fantasies and superstitions, and to identify the salient elements of the work and their significance beyond the period of its composition.

Behind the commitment of Faustus to occult practices, for which he pays with his damnation, is the quest for power — power over nature and power over humankind. In the words of Faustus:

> O, what a world of profit and delight,
> Of power, of honour, and omnipotence
> Is promised to the studious artisan! [i.e., magician]
> All things that move between the quiet poles
> Shall be at my command: emperors and kings
> Are but obeyed in their several provinces
> But his dominion that exceeds in this [magic]
> Stretcheth as far as doth the mind of man:
> A sound magician is a demi-god![17]

This quest for power may well be regarded as a major psychological motivation for the ingenious technological inventions of later ages. In this sense, it could be said that the fantasies of Faustus foreshadow the modern era.

There is, however, an even closer affinity between Doctor Faustus and modern times. Though his dreams are linked to superstitions and black magic, scientific and technological elements are clearly discernible in them. Thus, there is a rejection of the speculative, scholastic studies in favor of magic, which is largely conceived as an applied, usable art and knowledge:

> Philosophy is odious and obscure,
> Both law and physic are for petty wits,
> Divinity is basest of the three —
> Unpleasant, harsh, contemptible, and vile.
> 'Tis magic, magic, that hath ravished me![18]

Magic seems to have distinct technological and scientific overtones. Thus Faustus speaks of "a bridge through the moving air to pass the ocean with a band of men"[19] and the Chorus refers to his explorations of the universe while flying in a miraculous chariot:

> Where, sitting in a chariot burning bright
> Drawn by the strength of yoked dragons' necks,
> He views the clouds, the planets, and the stars,
> The tropics, zones, and quarters of the sky....[20]

While one should resist the temptation of seeing in the chariot either an airplane or a spaceship, Faustus's involvement in scientific inquiry may well indicate the future course of his more sober followers. Indeed, Doctor Faustus himself, despite his involvement in the occult arts, occasionally exhibits clear rational-scientific traits which seem altogether incompatible with Faustus the magician. In his own words:

> Think'st thou that Faustus is so fond [foolish] to imagine
> That after this life there is any pain?
> No, these are trifles and mere old wives' tales.[21]

Though Doctor Faustus, in his quest for power, may still be groping in the dark, confusing magic with technology and science with the occult arts, the rational and scientific elements are clearly present in his approach, and, as we know, they were destined eventually to be separated from the alloys of superstition.

The Christian opposition to the Faustian quest is not merely due to Faustus's association with the devil and his practice of black magic. The fundamental issue is the anthropocentric endeavors of Faustus which cannot be reconciled with the theocentric philosophy of Christianity. This philosophy assigns to humankind a life of piety and faith in this world, which carries the promise of spiritual salvation in the world to come. The center of life is afterlife, the way to the future salvation is faith and piety now. Therefore humans' attempt to indulge in earthly passions and to find means for fulfilling desires, but above all their quest for power, become deadly sins. Their true meaning is turning away from the worship of God to the worship of humankind. In the words of the Chorus, commenting on Faustus:

> Till swoll'n with cunning, of a self-conceit,
> His waxen wings did mount above his reach....[22]

The allusion to Icarus is well chosen in order to emphasize the point that people overreaching themselves are doomed to failure and disaster. Indeed, Lucifer himself was once an angel and was cast into hell because of the sin of pride, which made him conspire against God. As Mephostophilis explains in response to Faustus's query why the beloved angel of God turned into the prince of devils:

> O, by aspiring pride and insolence,
> For which God threw him from the face of heaven.[23]

Addressing this philosophy to the issue of applied science and technology, the conclusion seems to be that these are futile endeavors at best, and sinful preoccupations at worst. People should focus on the salvation of their souls and on the spiritual afterlife rather than on material convenience in this world, and certainly not on amassing earthly power which is linked, or is bound to be linked, with *hubris*, the sin of pride.

The conflict between the Faustian philosophy and the Christian outlook is not resolved in Marlowe's play, or rather the resolution which presents Faustus as a sinner and Christianity as the embodiment of virtue leaves the impression of being arbitrary. The punishment in the play appears to be a mechanical device, not the intrinsic and necessary consequence of Faustian endeavors. It may fit the legend which intends to convey a moral, as it may — though less likely — satisfy some of the audience watching the play. Philosophically, the two outlooks merely face each other, without entering into a vigorous discussion, into a true dialogue. Even so, the mere confrontation of the two outlooks may have fulfilled the function of stimulating people to reflect on the fundamental choice between a religiously inspired humility and the power-seeking self-assertion of humankind, between spiritual life and scientific and technological materialism. While one need not necessarily see the alternatives in these terms today, this peculiar angle of looking at the problem may still be stimulating and thought-provoking.

4

Age of Reason

If the Middle Ages, in the framework of the present study, represent an age of superstition and belief in magic, which covers the attempts at discovering or forecasting novel means for human enterprise by means of mysticism and occult sciences, the following examples of speculative and literary works express a clear turning to reason and rationality. Even if close to the earlier works in time, they exhibit an entirely different spirit.

The trust in human reason, in reason as the best and most reliable human faculty, characterizes the new approach. It is *Homo sapiens* who can see and show the way to improvement, as well as to be able to criticize and pass judgment on the failings of human actions and institutions. Reason can be critical, as it can be constructive. In both capacities it offers a powerful means for the service of humanity.

One exponent of the building and constructive power of reason is Francis Bacon in his utopian composition *New Atlantis*. The representative of the critical — one could say, mercilessly critical — power of reason is Jonathan Swift in his famous book, *Gulliver's Travels*. The former is an optimistic picture of an ideal society, just as the latter is a devastating criticism of actual humanity. Yet the two are not necessarily contradictory, for as the actual and the desirable may stand far apart, the rational approach can consistently expose the failings of reality, while designing an ideal social order.

New Atlantis

New Atlantis was published only one generation after *Doctor Faustus*.[1] Indeed, it was written by a man who had been born in 1651, three years before Marlowe. Yet, in its philosophical maturity, Bacon's little unfinished composition was centuries ahead of Marlowe's drama. This need not surprise us, for Bacon, besides being a prominent statesman, was a distinguished philosopher.

The scientific and technological notions of Bacon are thoroughly emancipated and completely dissociated from magic. Unlike Marlowe's Faustus, or the Golem, Bacon's characters — at least those who express his views — look at nature and manipulate the forces of nature in a purely rational manner. They may pray to God, laud and thank him — they are Christians and there is even reference to the miraculous establishment of Christianity in *New Atlantis* — but these tributes to religion in no way affect the scientific and technological endeavors, rational human efforts and achievements.

There is no place for the occult arts, no mention of Lucifer or Mephistopheles, or, for that matter, no mysterious use of the holy name of God. Indeed, a New Atlantian smiles at the supposition of mysterious powers operating in New Atlantis, and condescendingly disparages the implication of his country being "a land of magicians."[2] Human affairs are explicable in naturalistic terms and the process of scientific inquiry is conceived in terms of reason and demonstrable truth.

To be sure, Marlowe too rejects magic and the occult arts — this, at least, is his professed stand — but he does it in the name of Christianity, and out of allegiance to the right faith: his rejection in no way diminishes his belief in the efficacy of magic. Bacon dismisses magic on purely rational grounds: it is an absurdity and not a powerful force of evil. As he puts it elsewhere, in an essay "Of Superstition": "In all superstition wise men follow fools."[3]

There is another profound difference between Marlowe and Bacon, or, to be more exact, between the respective images of their champions of science and technology. Faustus, Marlowe's protagonist, is a self-centered and self-seeking individual whose scientific, or pseudo-scientific, involvement is oblivious to society. He is a lonely individual hunting for his own fortunes and indifferent to the needs of other human beings and to the social order. The representatives of science and its application in *New Atlantis* are responsible members of society, aware of the needs and concerned with the well-being of other human beings. Indeed, Bacon is hardly interested in the individuals he depicts: they are for him no more than vehicles for ideas. His concern is with the system as such, the coordination between science and society, turning the achievements of science "into good and holy uses."[4]

The fable of *New Atlantis* is quite simple — indeed, it exhibits the impatience of the philosopher to cloak his ideas with a story. It is told in the first person plural, and occasionally singular, on behalf of a ship crew stranded on an unknown island. The authorities of this island extend hospitality to the Europeans, though not without some suspicion and reservations, due to the questionable character of various former visitors from Europe. The sailors, or some of them, exhibit curiosity about the island and its inhabitants, and, in the course of the narrative, are provided with information about the place, its history and social institutions, but, above all, about its main foundation, Salomon's House. It is the description of the institutions of New Atlantis — institutions which Bacon designs as models for the perfect state and society — that are the focus and the main substance of the book.

Salomon's House best reveals Bacon's appreciation of science and its social role, and thus is of primary relevance to our study. It could be best described in contemporary terms as a national academy of science and technology — "academy" in the French authoritative and imposing sense — but it is even more than that. The aim of Salomon's House is twofold: "the knowledge of Causes, and secret motions of things; and the enlarging of the bounds of Human Empire, to the effecting of all things possible."[5] This definition of purpose combines theoretical inquiry with practical objectives, science with its application to human needs and desires. As we now know, the combination of these objectives has proved to be of crucial significance in modern technological development. Applied science and technology could reach a high degree of sophistication and success because of the findings of theoretical science. Bacon seems to have had an intimation of this alliance between the theory and the practice, between science and its application to human objectives.

While "the enlarging of the bounds of Human Empire, to the effecting of all things possible" may sound like a more philosophical expression of Doctor Faustus's drive, the quest for "the knowledge of Causes" gives it a different coloring. The quest for theoretical knowledge has a civilizing impact on the drive to effect things; knowing affects and informs doing. A "father" of the House of Salomon — should we say, a member of the academy? — is not the ruthless seeker of power, the arrogant adventurer, but a kind and gentle man. Somehow Bacon sensed that the quest for knowledge does not usually go along with pride, and that scientific occupation — even if aimed at application and technology — gives people a degree of detachment which is rarely combined with hubris. The point may not be made explicitly by Bacon, but this is the unmistakable impression gained by the reader.

Bacon is not satisfied with declaring the ends of the institution. He also elaborates on the concrete means for the attainment of these ends, or, as he puts it, on the "Preparations and Instruments" of the House of Salomon.[6] These are imaginative, daring and diverse, and cover a wide spectrum of scientific inquiry and technological projects. They include experimentation in deep caves and on high towers. They are concerned with human health, with improvement of food quality and supply, with production of paper and silk, with sources of energy, with optical instruments (including telescopes and microscopes), with exploration and production of sounds and smells, with various instruments of motion ranging from clocks to the technology of flying, as well as "ships and boats for going under water."[7] It is the Promethean message reborn, only on a much more ambitious and sophisticated level. Indeed, it may be claimed as Promethean (endowed with foresight) in the literal sense, for much of what Bacon suggested was destined to become reality in the subsequent development of modern science and technology.

To be sure, what eventually proved to be scientifically feasible is mixed, in Bacon's story, with what is deemed today as fanciful or even absurd. Thus, besides improving on nature in food production, Bacon speaks of making "divers plants rise by mixture of earths without seeds."[8] Besides referring to "heats in imitation of the sun's" and instruments "which generate heat only by motion," he mentions "heats of dungs, and of bellies and maws of living creatures."[9] But then it must be realized that his blueprint for scientific and technological enterprise is not the end product of research, but a forecast or a design of a glorious future, the philosopher giving free rein to his imagination.

Even so, Bacon exercises a considerable degree of scientific control over his wishful thinking: though some of his ideas are without scientific foundation and many more must have seemed entirely unrealistic in his time, they are all intended to be rational and scientific endeavors. Though the spokesman of Salomon's House makes the patently unrealistic claim of making living creatures of putrefaction, he reveals the establishment's scientific spirit when he asserts: "Neither do we this by chance, but we know beforehand of what matter and commixture what kind of those creatures will rise."[10] The relationship between cause and effect, the condition of effective scientific technology, is insisted upon. Technology is not a concoction of Faustian gimmicks and tricks, but has to be based on predictable knowledge and thus become a body of reliable techniques. The list of scientific achievements and technological inventions may be partially unrealistic and intrinsically faulty, but the intent and spirit of the dream remain scientific and in this sense quite modern.

It is noteworthy that Bacon does not limit his description of Salomon's House to scientific and technological matters, but also speaks about the administration of scientific inquiry, about the social organization of science.

There are fellows of the House who collect information about scientific achievements in other countries, there are those who try new experiments, those who compile and classify these experiments, those who draw practical and theoretical conclusions from the experiments of others, those who design new and more significant experiments and so forth.

It is not the details which are of main interest here, but again it is the approach. Bacon's rationality, which governs his scientific approach, also dominates his social organization of science. It is his belief in reason which becomes expressed in the administration of the utopian academy, as it is revealed in his scientific dreams.

But reason, the cornerstone of scientific approach, goes beyond scientific affairs — whether the process of inquiry itself, or the administrative organization of the inquirers. Reason seems to affect, and possibly shape, the relationship between the scientists and the rest of society. Though this point is not stated in such explicit terms by Bacon and is not elaborated by him, it can be well inferred from the following passage concerning the activities of the House of Salomon: "And this we do also: we have consultations, which of the inventions and experiences which we have discovered shall be published, and which not: and take all an oath of secrecy, for the concealing of those which we think fit to keep secret: though some of those we do reveal sometimes to the state, and some not."[11]

It appears that it is not the society or the state that dictate to the scientists what to do, but the scientists decide what is good for the state and the society, and accordingly reveal or conceal their discoveries. The scientists and the technologists do not seem to be for hire, they are not commissioned with tasks, but remain their own masters, are sovereign in their collective endeavors as well as in deciding what may be divulged to society. It would seem that these decisions, as they are made by scientists, would be largely determined by rational procedures. Similarly, the society of New Atlantis proves its trust in reason and science when it considers Salomon's House "the noblest foundation that ever was upon the earth; and the lanthorn of this kingdom."[12] Reason seems to provide the overall unity and intrinsic harmony to New Atlantis.

The harmony is not only rational; it also involves benevolence and compassion. As already indicated, the scientific endeavors are at least partially concerned with the well-being of society. Besides the pragmatic advantages to society from the technological inventions of the House of Salomon, it also predicts "diseases, plagues, swarms of hurtful creatures, scarcity, tempests, earthquakes, great inundations, comets, temperature of the year, and divers other things," and advises the people what to do "for the prevention and remedy of them."[13] Thus, we get a picture of humanity achieving a good life, due to respect for reason and science, and because of the concern of the scientists for human well-being. The combination of these elements, implicit in Bacon's *New Atlantis*, precludes misunderstandings and conflicts. Society prospers and people thrive in a system rationally aiming at human welfare.

The title of Bacon's composition, linking it to the legend of Atlantis, may have been merely a convenient literary device. As Atlantis was an island that had vanished, it was tempting to have it resurrected as a place of an ideal society. The fact that the legend was given wide credence in the Middle Ages and later on meant that it could be expected to raise interest in *New Atlantis*.

Yet, there may have been a more profound reason for Bacon's choice of name for his ideal society than a mere literary convenience or a publicity gimmick. The story of the lost island of Atlantis originated in Greek mythology, but its only extant source is Plato's *Timaeus and Critias*. Conceivably, it was the Platonic connection that Bacon chose to point to — not the above mentioned dialogues, but *The Republic*. For it is *The Republic* that expounds the Greek philosopher's design of the ideal polity, and in some ways Bacon's *New Atlantis* bears the marks of Plato's political philosophy.

Plato designed an orderly and harmonious society ruled by philosophers. His Republic is the political embodiment of reason and is entrusted to the guidance and subject to the rule of rational and knowledgeable men. The rule of philosopher-kings, or king-philosophers, is the rule of reason. The idea must have had a strong appeal to the rationalist Bacon.

Yet, *New Atlantis* is not a copy of *The Republic*, and Bacon's ideal is not identical with Plato's design. We can clearly discern a difference between the Platonic philosopher-kings and the Baconian guiding elite. The latter are not speculative philosophers, but scientists and applied scientists. They do not think in Plato's cosmic terms about a perfect harmonious body politic, and show little concern for its human components. Bacon's scientists address concrete scientific problems and their practical application, and they aim at the concrete benefits accruing from science to concrete individual human beings. Bacon switches from philosopher-kings to scientist-rulers, and he aims not at the aesthetic harmony of the body politic, but at the well-being of citizens.

This may well be the reason why he chose to speak of the House of Solomon. Solomon was the king of Israel, who was said to be the wisest of men. In the words of the divine revelation, "Lo, I have given thee a wise and understanding heart; so that there was none like before thee, neither after thee shall any arise like unto thee."[14] Significantly, this wisdom is applied to concrete human affairs and conflicts, as in the famous judgment in the case of two women claiming to be the mothers of one child.[15] The use of wisdom to solve human problems is close to Bacon's heart. What may have been even more important is that, besides being the wisest of men, and excelling in knowledge of proverbs and songs, Solomon "spoke of trees ... of beasts, and of fowl, and of creeping things, and of fishes."[16] Here Solomon dons the mantle of the scientist of nature, the explorer aiming at the understanding of the surrounding world. This surely must have appealed to Bacon's scientific curiosity and to his ideal of scientific search.

Yet, with all these links to Greek antiquity and to the Bible, Bacon remains his own man. For he enlarges the tale of Solomonic wisdom and converts it into an institution in his utopian society. While following in the steps of Plato's rationalism, he translates it into the domain of science with its virtually limitless explorations and applications. And, as noted, his commitment to science, theoretical and applied, has a clear linkage to human welfare and well-being.

Thus, he is the prophet of salvation, offering a design for an institutional scientific order, forming the foundation of a good life for humanity. He becomes a latter-day Prometheus and an enthusiastic forecaster of science unlimited in scope and beneficial to humankind.

Gulliver's Travels

The hundred years that followed the appearance of *New Atlantis* witnessed the realization of the foundations of the Baconian dream. Modern science strode vigorously forward, as testified by the monumental achievements of such men as William Harvey, the discoverer of the circulation of blood; Antony van Leeuwenhoek, the maker of microscopes and discoverer of protozoa and bacteria; Robert Boyle, the chemist; and Sir Isaac Newton, the great physicist. It could have seemed that the Baconian utopia was on the way to realization: "the knowledge of Causes, and secret motions of things" was rapidly increasing, and one could well expect "the enlarging of the bounds of Human Empire, to the effecting of all things possible" (as, indeed, nearly proved to be the case in subsequent centuries). With the fulfillment of some of the prophecies of Bacon, could not one feel confident about the implementation of the rest of his predictions? With the successes of scientific achievements, was not humanity justified in being sanguine about social perfection?

It is a peculiar irony in the history of human spirit, therefore, that one hundred years after the publication of *New Atlantis* a book appeared which denigrated the fundamental beliefs of Bacon's utopia with devastating sarcasm. The book is no other than Jonathan Swift's *Gulliver's Travels*, published in 1727.[17]

To be sure, Swift is not opposed to the Baconian rule of reason and compassion. In fact, his ideal creatures' "grand maxim is to cultivate reason, and to be wholly governed by it," and "friendship and benevolence are the two principal virtues" among them.[18] And his criticism of humanity is rational and informed by compassion. If in this sense there is a basic agreement between the two writers, there remains a significant difference. For while Bacon implicitly believes in the realization of his ideal, Swift relegates it to the imaginary community of ... horses. Humans seem to be incapable of such an achievement. The optimism of Bacon, linked to the new rationalistic-scientific spirit, which was destined to revolutionize the life of mankind, meets in Swift its skeptical antithesis. The prophet of salvation confronts the prophet of doom.

Gulliver's Travels is a classic enjoyed by children as a fantastic and amusing travel story, as it is disconcerting to adults because of its sarcastic criticism of humans and human civilization. The book consists of four parts, each describing a separate voyage of Gulliver into a land of fantasy, the most famous being the first two parts, known to many children, namely the voyages to Lilliput and to its opposite, the land of the giants. The last two parts, notably the fourth one, describing a land of rational horses, have less appeal to children and are probably less well known, though their satirical punch is even fiercer.

The main concern of Swift's philosophy is not with the role of science and technology in human life, but with human morals and rationality. The key to human understanding, judgment, and, if it were at all possible, salvation, is not in external achievements, such as science and technology, but must be sought in human disposition and nature. While such a philosophy of humankind is not the theme of the present study, it has to be briefly outlined here, for when Swift introduces human achievements into his tale, and these include science and technology, his evaluation of these is closely bound with his view of human nature. Alas, this nature is, in Swift's judgment, the embodiment of vice and unreason. This view of humans runs through the entire book, but it is best represented in Swift's imaginative creation of the Yahoo.

Yahoos are abominable animals in the land of the rational horses, the Houyhnhnms, used by the latter as half-domesticated beasts. Swift almost indulges in describing the Yahoos as ugly, dirty, smelly, repellent brutes. But their main deficiencies are of a moral, rather than physical, nature. They are "malicious, treacherous, and revengeful ... of a cowardly spirit ... insolent, abject, and cruel."[19] They "hate one another more than they do any different species of animals."[20] They are absurdly greedy: "For if you throw among five Yahoos as much food as would be sufficient for fifty, they will, instead of eating peaceably, fall together by the ears, each single one impatient to have all to itself."[21]

While the Yahoo is no one else but humankind — or, to put it in other words, while Swift depicts *Homo sapiens* as no more than *homo Neanderthalensis* — Swift's satirical pen does not dry up with that. Swift attacks human deficiencies in a more specific way, presenting a veritable panorama of vice and folly. He criticizes the system of justice, he depicts history as "a heap of conspiracies, rebellions, murders, massacres, revolutions."[22] He exposes imperialism and colonialism without mincing words: "Ships are sent ... the natives driven out or destroyed, their princes tortured to discover their gold, a free licence given to all acts of inhumanity and lust, the earth reeking with the blood of its inhabitants: and this execrable crew of butchers employed in so pious an expedition, is a *modern colony*, sent to convert and civilize an idolatrous and barbarous people."[23]

Swift is equally vehement in denigrating wars and exposing their causes. Here are some of these: "Sometimes the ambition of princes, who never think they have land or people enough to govern; sometimes the corruption of ministers... Difference of opinions hath cost many millions of lives: for instance, whether flesh be bread, or bread be flesh; whether the juice of a certain berry be blood or wine...."[24] The examples could be continued on and on. Humans, both individually and collectively, are described as vicious, as well as foolish, to the point of absurdity.

Devastating as Swift's outright criticism of humankind is, it becomes fiercest when, using the invention of the Yahoo, he contrasts him with civilized people. It is in this connection that science and technology, important facets of human civilization, enter onto the stage. Gulliver, a civilized Yahoo — clothing his body, behaving in a civil manner and capable of using language and even learning a new one — likes to dissociate himself from the brutish

Yahoos and to emphasize human civilization and human institutions during his discussions with his host and master, the Houyhnhnm.

It is on one such occasion, while discussing the nature and causes of wars, that the Houyhnhnm expresses doubts as to whether the civilized Yahoos are capable at all of killing so many of each other in battle as Gulliver has claimed: "For your mouths lying flat with your faces, you can hardly bite each other to any purpose,[25] unless by consent."

These doubts are effectively countered by Gulliver:

> ... being no stranger to the art of war, I gave him a description of cannons, culverins, muskets, carabines, pistols, bullets, powder, swords, bayonets, battles, sieges, retreats, attacks, undermines, countermines, bombardments, sea fights; ships sunk with a thousand men, twenty thousand killed on each side... And to set forth the valour of my own dear countrymen, I assured him that I had seen them blow up a hundred enemies at once in a siege, and as many in a ship, and beheld the dead bodies come down in pieces from the clouds....[26]

Gulliver's description, far from impressing the rational horse, is received by him with indignation and abhorrence. For though he found the (wild) Yahoos hateful, "he no more blamed them for their odious qualities, than he did a *gnnayh* [a bird of prey] for its cruelty, or a sharp stone for cutting his hoof. But when a creature pretending to reason could be capable of such enormities, he dreaded lest the corruption of that faculty might be worse than brutality itself...."[27]

Thus, it would seem, that being endowed with reason has two consequences for the human condition: first, it makes people morally responsible for their deeds, unlike a bird of prey or a sharp stone, and, second, it makes people capable of inflicting harm on each other on a scale entirely different from that of a brute animal. It is the second point which Swift seems to emphasize most, when he points out the shortcomings of human reason, though the two facets are clearly intertwined, as one corrupts the other.

While reason, in the comprehensive and total sense, "is sufficient to govern a rational creature,"[28] a partial use of reason is worse than no reason at all. In Swift's words, humankind is "making no other use of reason than to improve and multiply those vices whereof their brethren in this country [the Yahoos] had only the share that nature allotted them."[29] The point is reiterated on several occasions, and it is also expressed in the plot of the story: Gulliver, who eventually becomes converted to the total rationality of the horses, has to be forced to return to "civilized" society. He would prefer to take a chance of living among some naked savages than "live with European Yahoos."[30]

Thus, if the Yahoos are initially a horrifying caricature of humans, they ultimately become, though not likable, the lesser of the two evil incarnations of humanity. The Promethean gift of civilization, far from proving the salvation of mankind, is its utter undoing. It is misused by people for their own moral degradation, as well as self-destruction. Technology, as a part of civilization and the product of that partial and distorted use of reason, only leads to effective killing, to mass slaughter. Human beings would have been much better off without it, for their mouths lying flat with their faces, they could hardly bite each other, unless by consent.

Swift exposes the failure of human civilization to abide by reason and he denigrates the attempts of science and technology to discover hidden truths and novel ways. Not that he is averse to rational endeavors in these realms of human activity, for he seems to approve of scientific approach applied to pragmatic objectives, mathematics "wholly applied to what may be useful in life, to the improvement of agriculture, and all mechanical arts."[31]

The more daring undertakings of science and technology, however, are ridiculed by Swift in Part III of *Gulliver's Travels*. There he describes absent-minded mathematicians on the flying island of Laputa, who seem to be cut off from present reality, and worry about cosmic disasters — one could say, another case of reason gone astray. In the Grand Academy of Lagado, another satirical invention of Swift, scientists engage in fantastic experiments, such as "extracting sun-beams out of cucumbers," "building houses, by beginning at the roof," as spiders do, "ploughing the ground with hog," etc.[32]

One scientist tries to improve "speculative knowledge by practical and mechanical operations through a machine which accidentally combines words: some verbal combinations being meaningful, they are expected to lead to significant books. Thus, eventually, "the most ignorant person ... may write books in philosophy, poetry, politics ... without the assistance from genius or study."[33]

The Swiftian Academy of Lagado is the very opposite of Bacon's Salomon's House. It also is a caricature of the emerging modern science and technology. His absent-minded mathematicians of Laputa may have represented Sir Isaac Newton and other theoretical scientists.

Though Swift's mastery as a satirist is admirable, the subsequent achievements of science and technology — and even those of his own times — have proved him wrong. To be sure, various theories and practical experiments have failed. Some, such as the mechanical (or computerized?) creation of philosophy or poetry border on the absurd. Skeptics may look askance at modern lunar and planetary explorations — especially when some practical benefits are expected from such explorations. Such projects as building a space station at a fantastic cost in order to find out the impact of weightlessness on various organisms, or to manufacture some drugs under these conditions, may be seen by some as worthy of the Grand Academy of Lagado.

Yet, by and large, it is obvious today that experimental science and technology have firmly established their viability and their practical worth. It is the Baconian Salomon's House, and not the Swiftian Laputa and Academy of Lagado, that has won the day. The overwhelming success of science and technology is here for all to see.

Yet, when we revert to the central point in Swift's satire — the failure of humankind to establish an overall rational and moral harmony in human life and social relations — the case for Swift becomes stronger. We do have the command over fantastic technology, but do we know to use it consistently to our advantage? We apply reason to the execution of scientific endeavors, but do we always apply reason to the determination of the goals of scientific and technological undertakings? Is the scientific civilization in which we live an overall rational and good way of life? Is *Homo sapiens* endowed with reason, or are people Yahoos, misusing the bit of reason they have? The questions were posed almost three hundred years ago; they seem today at least as pertinent as they were then.

Swift's central position might, in a sense, be regarded as akin to the medieval Christian philosophy as reflected in Marlowe's *Doctor Faustus*. Both seem to repudiate the notion that science and technology can solve human problems, both seem to view the human problem as being essentially a moral one. Indeed, in the concluding pages of *Gulliver's Travels*, pride is singled out as the most repulsive human vice.

Yet, the analogy has its limitations. For Swift's criticism is not waged in theological terms: faith, salvation of the soul, afterlife, piety do not form the ingredients of his argument. Swift speaks in the terms of reason and morals. Even his revulsion at human pride is moral-aesthetic, and not religious. He does not place faith above reason; he admires reason and deplores its absence in human relations. The trouble with Faustus, he might have said, is not his inquisitive mind and application of reason to difficult questions; his trouble is that he does not think to the end, that he does not apply reason to the overall problems of humans and civilization, including humans' pride and quest for power.

5

Science and Human Nature

The seventeenth century witnessed the flowering of modern science, philosophically foreshadowed by Francis Bacon, but translated into concrete and monumental achievements by such towering figures as Isaac Newton (1642–1727), Rober Boyle (1627–1691), and William Harvey (1578–1657). Newton's discoveries in physics offered a most comprehensive scientific presentation of natural phenomena, encompassing earthly experience and astronomy. Boyle laid the foundations of modern chemistry by making the distinction between element and compound and defining chemical reaction and analysis. Harvey's discovery of the circulation of blood, and the degradation, as it were, of human heart to a pump, addressed matters close to human concern. All these and such innovations were based on observation and experimental techniques rather than on the mostly speculative methods of earlier times. The innovations — and, even more, the new methodology — naturally awakened expectations of further progress, which indeed became manifest during the following centuries.

Moreover, the progress and innovation of the new science spread also into the field of the living world, including and culminating in humans. The work of Charles Darwin (1809–1882), whose *On the Origin of Species* made its appearance in 1859, revolutionized the self-perception of humanity. Humans became a part of the animal world, and the biological foundation of humanity tended to overshadow its spiritual distinctions and aspirations. At the same time, the idea of the improvement of the human race by approaching the issue in a scientific manner was propounded by a cousin of Darwin, Francis Galton (1822–1911), the founder of eugenics. Though these developments occurred only in the nineteenth century, the materialistic approach to the science of humans had been prefigured by Erasmus Darwin (1731–1802), the grandfather of Charles Darwin and Francis Galton.

The scientific trend of the new era, and its extension and application to the nature of humanity, affected the creators of literary works. While older perceptions and myths in no way disappeared from the world of letters—indeed, they thrived in the Romantic literature, even in Goethe's *Faust*—the new scientific approach made its appearance in various works of fiction. The impact of new approaches in science and technology on the condition of humanity and society turned into a pregnant theme for writers of imagination, for literary dreamers and speculators. They were intrigued by the idea of how machines or scientific innovations might affect society and humanity. Giving free rein to imagination, they introduced machines and innovations which may have seemed quite fantastic at the time, but often proved realistic subsequently. The most notable exponent of this kind was the French writer Jules Verne (1828–1905). The significance of this kind of literature is not merely in predicting and stimulating inventions and innovations, but also in depicting human and social scenarios affected by new scientific discoveries and inventions. Such depictions, whether based on realizable inventions or far-fetched discoveries, offered a focus of hope or concern for the future of humankind, and stimulated reflection on the destination toward which humanity was advancing.

Such concerns were particularly deeply felt when the nature of human beings themselves was involved. With the spread of science to the domain of life and humans, speculation about the potential developments in this sphere gave free rein to fantasy. Manipulation of the human body and the ancillary mind by physical, chemical, or biochemical means may have easily raised the specter of horrific consequences, though it may also have suggested hopes for making human life easier.

To be sure, fiction applied to this domain may have lagged far behind literature dealing with mechanical devices, as far as the eventual translation of fantasy into reality is concerned. Yet, we ought to bear in mind, especially in our own times when novel ways of engineered procreation are discovered and when cloning of living creatures is no more a fantasy, that biological and psychological fantasies in some forms may turn into reality — for better or for worse.

In the two examples offered below, the fulcrum of the story is in the scientific interference with human beings — even with the obviously far-fetched creation of a man. Yet, the stories also deal with the much more important discussion of the consequences of such interference for the individual and society. This theme, in turn, reveals the writer's perception of the nature of humankind, or some essential human qualities.

Frankenstein

Frankenstein is the title of a book by Mary Shelley (1797–1851), the wife of the famous English poet.[1] The book was first published in 1818, having been completed in the preceding year, before its author reached her twentieth birthday. While the novel bears the marks of youthful enthusiasm and sentimentality, it also reveals profound reflection and deep compassion in the face of human suffering.

Frankenstein has provided a theme and stimulus for a variety of creations — also in theater and film. Indeed, the name made its way into common English usage, as an invention which turns into a menace to its creator, or simply into a monster. Yet, all these ramifications and repercussions of the original story must not obscure or distort the novel itself, which is the subject of our analysis.

To put the story in the right perspective, it must be stated outright that Frankenstein, or Victor Frankenstein, the protagonist of the tale, is not a monster, but a young brilliant student who *created* the monster. The monster himself remains nameless in the novel. Moreover, the monster is not the embodiment of evil and wanton cruelty, as usually perceived in his later reconstructions. He is not a "congenital" monster, so to say. He becomes a moral monster only in consequence of his unfavorable experiences when encountering human beings.

The story itself is technically a story within a story. An English explorer of the Arctic, Captain Walton, rescues a man drifting on a fragment of ice. This man, a native of Geneva by the name of Victor Frankenstein, after recuperating from his ordeal, tells Walton his story — a very unusual story.

Interested in science from early youth, Frankenstein took up his studies in a German university and soon proved his brilliance. Enthusiastic about the achievements of modern science, especially in the field of chemistry, he is set on discovering the cause of life. Having succeeded in his objective, he is able to animate lifeless matter, to create some kind of a human being. As his creation comes to life, however, its horrible monstrous appearance revolts and terrifies even the creator, and Frankenstein regrets having made the being.

The monster, left on his own, wanders through the land, encounters rejection by every human being, and leads a lonely existence. Yet, by secretly observing human conduct, he acquires the skill of talking and develops a way of reasoning in human terms. Moreover, he is also endowed with emotions of kindness and goodwill to people, as well as with moral and aesthetic appreciation.

On top of it, he has superhuman power of endurance, physical strength, and capacity of locomotion. The only flaw is his revolting appearance.

Encountering misunderstanding and instant rejection by human beings, by people who appear good and compassionate, innocent and righteous, the monster's character changes: instead of compassion for human beings, he only feels anger and hatred. His vengeance is primarily directed against his creator, and he strangles the latter's young brother and cunningly makes an innocent young woman pay for the crime. Frankenstein finally comes face to face with him, and the monster argues that his rage is due to his loneliness. If Frankenstein created another creature, a female to offer companionship to the monster who is rejected by humanity, there would be no more atrocities.

Frankenstein initially agrees, despite the feeling of revulsion toward the monster, but then changes his mind. He fears that a pair of monsters may give rise to a new species which might eradicate mankind. Despite the threat to his own family, Frankenstein destroys the physical components of the second monster in the making. The living monster, however, fulfills his threats. He kills Frankenstein's best friend, and then Frankenstein's wife shortly after the wedding. He deliberately spares his creator to make him suffer.

Frankenstein pursues his creation through land and sea, intent on either killing him or perishing in the encounter. On his pursuit through the Arctic, he is rescued by Walton to whom he tells the story. As shortly thereafter Frankenstein dies, the monster makes his appearance to Walton and tells him that now he is ready to die, as well. He plans for himself a pyre on which he will be consumed by fire.

On the face of it, this is a story of horror and fantasy, which the afficionados of gothic fiction may relish. Whatever the merit of this genre of literature, it is not as such that the book is introduced here. It is certain elements of the story and various occasional remarks and comments in the text of the composition, related to our theme, that call for our attention.

While a story about an artificial human being who turns into a monster and threatens humanity may recall such old myths as that of the Golem, and while the achievements of Frankenstein may seem to belong into the category of Faustus's accomplishments, there is a crucial difference between the creation of Mary Shelley and its precursors. The latter are associated with magic — whether bent on selfish pursuits, or morally motivated and controlled. The creature of Victor Frankenstein, on the other hand, is the product of rational inquiry and experimental science. Not only the new scientific perceptions in general, but also the specific discoveries in physiology by such men as Luigi Galvani (1737–1798) and in chemistry by such as Antoine Lavoisier (1743–1794), evoked enthusiastic hopes about progress in life sciences and even life manipulation, which found their way to the fantasy of creating a human being. Here we face one of the early examples of the combination of science with fantasy, what the Italians call *fantascienza*, which more accurately represents this literary form than the English term "science fiction." For it is not the fictitious use of science which is the essence of Mary Shelley's tale, but the combination of science with fantasy. This is also the case of many another work of this kind, as long as the fantasy is intrinsically related to a scientific base, and not artificially linked to it, as is the case in many contemporary science fiction stories.

The positive and even enthusiastic attitude to the ever expanding science is clearly expressed in the story. Right at the opening of the book, Walton in a letter to his sister explains what motivates him to undertake a dangerous journey into the Arctic region. The reason for going on an expedition is not only the intent to discover a new part of the world, but also the potential scientific benefits of the enterprise. "I may there discover the wondrous power which attracts the needle and may regulate a thousand celestial observations that require only this voyage to render their seeming eccentricities consistent for ever."[2] In other words, the quest of finding a general scientific explanation of some mysterious phenomena is a major incentive for the voyage. The scientific discovery is intertwined with the geographical exploration which may lead to the discovery of a northern passage to the Pacific Ocean, which would be of "inestimable benefit" to mankind "to the last generation."[3] Thus, scientific curiosity and concern for humanity underlie the human search for the expansion of knowledge.

Frankenstein not only sings the praises of science, but also tries to outline, be it in general terms, its distinctive character.

Victor Frankenstein was initially attracted to medieval pseudo-science, to the dreams of alchemists, "when the masters of science sought immortality and power." By contrast, the modern scientists were set on destroying such visions. And so, on coming to the university, Frankenstein "was required to exchange chimeras of boundless grandeur for realities of little worth."[4] Finally he realizes that, while the earlier scientific speculations had set the foundations of knowledge, it is the new experimental scientists, who seemingly deal with petty things, "dabble in dirt" and "pore over the microscope," it is they who "penetrate into the recesses of nature" and "ascend into the heavens."[5] It is the meticulous scientific observation and experimentation, guided by the greater vision, that leads to the glorious achievements of modern science. *Per aspera ad astra*.

There is another characteristic of science which Frankenstein reveals. Scientific inquiry and progress have no limit. "In other studies you go as far as others have gone before you, and there is nothing more to know; but in a scientific pursuit there is continual food for discovery and wonder."[6] This dynamic nature of science carries the scientists into an enthusiastic never-ending pursuit.

This panegyric of science is not, however, unequivocal. For doubts, and even a reversal of attitude towards science, make their appearance. Thus, Frankenstein, having had his tragic experiences, tells his rescuer, Captain Walton: "You seek for knowledge and wisdom, as I once did; and I ardently hope that the gratification of your wishes may not be a serpent to sting you as mine had been.[7] While science is not discarded lock, stock and barrel, there is clearly a note of caution about the danger of scientific discovery. The metaphor of the snake used here may perhaps allude to the snake in the garden of Eden, enticing Eve to partake of the tree of knowledge. Thus the pursuit of knowledge would be both sinful and perilous.

The reversal of the attitude to science is much more vigorously expressed in depicting Frankenstein's revulsion to his scientific apparatus, to the room where his laboratory was located, and even to any discussion of science.[8] And this merely at the stage when he is disappointed with and revolted by the features of the man he created. Indeed, such a reaction can hardly be justified: a fantastic invention, even if not perfect, usually deserves and gets praise. Indeed, the hideousness of the creature and the fear and revulsion it produces, while a crucial element in the fable, may be judged to be the weak element in the story. For all the tragedy of Frankenstein and of his creature would not have developed, but for the latter's aesthetic monstrosity. Yet, there may be another explanation of this issue, as further suggested.

Be this as it may, the disillusionment of Frankenstein with science gets ample justification due to the subsequent murders perpetrated by the monster. Yet the issue is not merely that of change of attitude to science and its inventive application. There also emerges the fundamental problem of the relationship between the inventor and his invention. The monster has a will and power of his own and he cannot be dismissed or destroyed just because his creator so decides. In a confrontation of the two, when the monster wants Frankenstein to create a female companion for him, on the penalty of further murders, the monster exclaims: "You are my creator, but I am your master; obey!"[9] The humanity of the monster dramatizes this confrontation, but the epigrammatic statement of Shelley may well be understood, even if not so intended, as a reflection on the relationship between the inventor and his invention in general — notably when the invention has far-reaching consequences. The idea of robots taking over, of nuclear weapons overwhelming their human designers, of computers making decisions, may be foreshadowed in the pithy statement in *Frankenstein*.

The criticism of science leads to the problem of the scientist's responsibility. Mary Shelley does not offer a clear and simple verdict, but toys with a few ideas, sometimes in a merely suggestive manner. Thus, on one occasion she has Frankenstein voice a terrifying idea. Reflecting on the crimes of the monster, he considers the latter "nearly in the light of my own vampire, my own spirit let loose from the grave and, forced to destroy all that was dear to me."[10] While this may seem a Gothic touch, there are psychological overtones here, suggesting the existence of some hidden power in the human mind with destructive and murderous instincts. If such impulses do exist, their link to ingenious scientific inventions becomes a clear and horrifying danger to humanity. Do we face here another adumbration of a later era?

There is another kind of implicit criticism, directed not at some sinister impulses hidden in the recesses of the human mind, but at a more manifest trait. Though the following statement, coming from the mouth of the desperate Frankenstein, is addressed to a magistrate, an official in charge of legal matters, it may well convey a comment on the ambition of modern human to achieve progress through scientific endeavors. "Man, how ignorant art thou in thy pride of wisdom."[11] The sin of *hubris* pertains also to the trust in knowledge. Despite all the scientific knowledge, we remain essentially ignorant, as our knowledge inadvertently may be the cause of our misfortune.

Thus the scientist is cut down to size, with the full acknowledgement of Frankenstein. Moreover, he not only repudiates his daring scientific invention, but assumes responsibility for its future potential consequences. Realizing that the creation of a female companion to the monster might bring about "a race of devils ... who might make the very existence of the species of man a condition precarious and full of terror," he resolves not to do it, irrespective of the consequences for his own and his family's well-being.[12] To enlarge the conclusion, it can be said that the scientist as a human being must make a moral decision overriding any scientific interest, must be ready to put a stop to the momentum of scientific progress. This is in line with Bacon's *New Atlantis*, where the members of Salomon's House decide which of their discoveries will be published and which will be concealed.

The idea of science for the sake of science, let alone of a scientist for hire, is rejected. The notion that the designer of a guided missile need not be concerned as to what target the missile will be directed is emphatically rejected.

In the present story, the scientist bears responsibility not only *for* his creation, but also *to* his creation. At least this is the way the monster sees it. As God created Adam, so Frankenstein created him. But Adam was a perfect and happy creature, while the monster was hideous and miserable. Thus, the human creator failed and took no responsibility for his failure.[13] This element in the story may have little bearing on the issue of science and technology, unless some novel techniques in human reproduction are taken into account. Thus, if a child originating in an ovum of woman A is gestated by woman B, it may well face the problem of who is its mother, and thus raise the issue of medical responsibility for its creation. Some other problems of this kind may arise with the advancement and spread of biotechnology. A cloned human being, if such be created, may raise claims against the cloner. Thus, the responsibility of the creator to the creature may not be irrelevant two centuries after the publication of *Frankenstein*.

Though the monster makes a distinction between the divine creation of Adam, and Frankenstein's creation, it is possible to see in the analogy itself a comment of the author on the problematics of the God-human relationship. For the human-created being is initially at least morally acceptable, and only eventually turns vicious. Do not humans, initially perfect, fall into sin and disgrace? The unasked question of why God allowed the fall of humanity is addressed by the monster to Frankenstein: "Why did you form a monster so hideous that even *you* turned from me in disgust?" Moreover, when the monster exclaims in agony about the "hateful day when I received life," the outcry is reminiscent of Job cursing the day of his birth: "Let the day perish wherein I was born" (Job 3:3).[14] Conceivably, the story itself and much of the argument of the monster is an expression of Mary Shelley's dissatisfaction with the human condition, and expresses the dissatisfaction and anguish of humans as creatures, directed at their creator. Thus, the scientific and technological creation becomes a parable for the human plight. This reading of the argument has no bearing on science and technology, unless we choose to regard the divine creation as a scientific-technological act.

Frankenstein touches not only on the relations between the creator and his creation, but also on the issue of human relations. As noted above, the fundamental reason why Frankenstein's creature meets with rejection, which in turn makes a monster out of him, is his revolting appearance. The intelligent and tender-hearted creature becomes a moral monster for aesthetic reasons. Notably, it is good and kind people, including Frankenstein himself, who display this essentially unfair and foolish attitude. Could there be in this literary device some more profound intent?

A possible explanation which comes to mind is that Shelley wanted to convey the limitations of reason and of science in human conduct and civilization. While humans have made great strides in science and while Frankenstein has succeeded in creating a man-like creature, a relatively trivial factor such as external appearance is sufficient to create fear and hostility toward the remarkable creation — not only by casually encountered people, but even by the creator himself. Thus, whatever the role and power of science and knowledge in human endeavor, it becomes impotent when faced with an unaccountable impulse. The creation may be intelligent, powerful and noble — but its ugliness is the cause of its destruction and the eventual demise of the creator. If this is the law of nature ruling humanity, let humanity beware. For the most ingenious and efficient inventions will not protect humanity from the irrational elements inherent in human beings.

Indeed, Shelley wonders about the puzzle of the Janus-faced human civilization, a puzzlement which has not been resolved to date. She voices her perplexity through the words of Frankenstein's creature, as he reflects on human history: "Was man, indeed, at once so powerful, so virtuous and magnificent, yet so vicious and base? He appeared at one time a mere scion of the evil principle and at another as all that can be conceived of noble and godlike."[15]

Shelley's book may not offer a consistent view about science, humanity and civilization in their intricately intertwined relationships. Science may be beneficial and harmful, ennobling and destructive. The scientist may be wise and ingenious, but also blind and erroneous. Humans may be good and bad, wise and stupid. One can quote events and statements from *Frankenstein* to substantiate any of these positions. Yet, if one does not come up with a cohesive and consistent philosophy based on this book, the work remains stirring and stimulating. It tells the reader: "You think and reach your own conclusions."

Dr. Jekyll and Mr. Hyde

If Mary Shelley came to be puzzled by the contradictory nature of humanity, by the strange combination of good and evil in human civilization, this enigma becomes the focus of Robert Louis Stevenson's famous novella, *The Strange Case of Dr. Jekyll and Mr. Hyde* (1886). Stevenson (1850–1894), a Scottish writer, was born half a century after Shelley, and his book was published sixty years after *Frankenstein*. He also wrote it at a more mature age. Indeed, Stevenson's work exhibits greater intellectual and artistic command of the writer, as well as the greater sophistication of the Victorian age. The story is much shorter, and it focuses on the theme deliberately chosen by the author, as compared with Shelley's tendency to meander into sidetracks of tale and description. At the same time, both stories combine a tale of horror with a philosophy of human nature as revealed through the human search for knowledge and self-experimentation.

Dr. Jekyll and Mr. Hyde has had a great fascination for the reading public to date, and transformations on screen and television, often with crass distortion. It is important, therefore, to keep our eye on the original text when expounding and analyzing its meaning and message. The novella, a mystery and horror tale, can be viewed as structurally divided into two parts. Of the seventy-eight pages in the present edition,[16] fifty-nine contain the events of the tale as seen by the external writer and the various characters, including the protagonists; while the concluding nineteen pages are the testimony of Dr. Jekyll. Thus, the first three quarters are a tale of mystery and horror, while the last quarter unravels the mystery, but retains the horror. Clearly, it is the second part which is of primary concern and interest to us. Yet, it has to be preceded by a brief outline of the first part.

The "external" story tells of an unpleasant or even revolting man, by the name of Hyde, who, having collided with a little girl, is seen to trample over her without any concern or attention to her screaming. Strangely enough, the same Edward Hyde is named as the sole beneficiary in the will of Dr. Henry Jekyll, a prominent and wealthy doctor and scientist — this to the bafflement of the latter's attorney and friend, Mr. Utterson. When subsequently Hyde is seen clubbing to death a kind and respected public figure, Sir Danvers Carew, without any provocation, the horror and mystery escalate. While the search for the murderer produces no results, the behavior of Dr. Jekyll toward his friends becomes odd. He secludes himself and refuses to see Utterson. At one point, Dr. Jekyll's butler becomes alarmed by some strange occurrences in the doctor's laboratory, and with Utterson's assistance and authorization, they break into the laboratory, only to find there the dying Hyde, who apparently took some poison. There is no sign, however, of Dr. Jekyll. A letter of Dr. Jekyll's diseased colleague and one time friend, Dr. Lanyon, which is opened by the attorney, reveals a startling fact: Mr. Hyde by drinking some kind of potion changed into Dr. Jekyll in Dr. Lanyon's presence. The two are but one person. The written testimony of Dr. Jekyll, offered in the concluding chapter, "Henry Jekyll's Full Statement of the Case," explains the mystery.

Born into fortune, naturally gifted and industrious, Dr. Jekyll had the prospect of a distinguished career. Yet, there was a flaw in his character, namely, a duality of disposition which, though common in humanity, was exacerbated in his case. Contrasting with his earnestness and dignity was "a certain gaiety of disposition" and love of pleasure. While these would have been accepted as normal by other men, Jekyll, because of his high standards, "regarded and hid them with an almost morbid sense of shame." Still, by looking objectively at the situation, he reached the conclusion "that man is not truly one but truly two." Indeed, he even suspected that, with the progress of inquiry in the field, "man will be ultimately known for a mere polity of multifarious, incongruous and independent denizens."[17]

Reverting to the basic duality of human personality, Dr. Jekyll set an objective for himself to separate the opposing tendencies naturally intertwined with each other. Such a separation would enable people to enjoy themselves without remorse on the one hand, and to pursue noble objectives unhampered by base instincts on the other hand. Instead of struggling "in the agonized womb of consciousness," they would be dissociated from each other.[18] This objective is achieved by Dr. Jekyll by the use of a chemical mix. Though taking the potion had painful physical and mental side effects, they were temporary and the result proved extraordinary. In Dr. Jekyll's testimony: "I felt younger, lighter, happier in body; within I was conscious of a heady recklessness..., a solution of the bonds of obligation, an unknown but not an innocent freedom of the soul." He also felt wicked, "sold a slave to my original evil." He diminished in physical stature, and his features changed and became distorted, as "evil was written broadly and plainly" on the face of Edward Hyde.[19]

Hyde enjoys his new freedom, which he can attain at will through the chemical formula. As Hyde, he indulges in depravity, "drinking pleasure with bestial avidity from any degree of torture to another." The murder of Sir Danvers was one example of such wanton cruelty. Yet Dr. Jekyll continued to live in accordance with his virtues, dissociated from the evil of Hyde.[20] This seemingly placid coexistence of Dr. Jekyll and Hyde is shattered as the transformation starts occurring spontaneously, without the use of the drug. Moreover, whereas the potion would effect the change in either direction, the spontaneous transformation was from Jekyll to Hyde. The way of return was becoming increasingly more difficult. The coexistence of the two personalities turned into a struggle, and with all the resolve of Dr. Jekyll to fight Hyde, the latter got the upper hand. Indeed, a successful period of repressing Hyde, only led to his invigorated reappearance. "My devil had been long caged, he came out roaring."[21]

Thus Hyde took over and became the dominant force in the personality of Dr. Jekyll, as he disintegrated into his hideous alter ego.

There are certain salient features in this story which are of special interest for the present study. One major point is the interest in the scientific exploration of the human mind and personality, what came to be known as the discipline of psychology. To be sure, modern psychology cannot be dissociated from its ancient antecedents and subsequent philosophical speculations, but Stevenson's story clearly has some modern features and is, in a way, a fictional precursor of some later insights and theories.

Thus, the idea of conflicting elements in the human mind, of a pleasure-seeking and selfish force facing a controlled and conscientious personality, clearly adumbrates Freud's psychoanalytic theory. Mr. Hyde may well represent Freud's id, while Dr. Jekyll is the ego, guided by a strong superego. Indeed, it is the vigorous control of the superego that leads to the unfettering of the id. The stress on the conflict in the human mind, the inner struggle which poses a fundamental problem for humans and their peace of mind, is pointed out by Stevenson in a clear and forceful manner, forecasting a major characteristic of the psychoanalytic perception of the dynamic turbulence in the human mind.

That the uncontrolled and selfish seeking of pleasure turns into pure evil, and that thus the story focuses on human depravity, may not be an innovation — either psychological or literary. The numerous stories about the devil and such literary characters as Shakespeare's Iago exemplify the age-old concern about the primary force of evil. The perception of the evil inclination in man is manifest already in the Bible: "For the imagination of man's heart is evil from his youth" (Genesis 8:21). In subsequent rabbinical literature there appears the term *yetzer hara*, the evil inclination or impulse in humans,[22] occasionally juxtaposed with *yetzer hatov*, the good tendency. We find this perception also in Plato's *Phaedrus*, where he divides "each soul into three — two horses and a charioteer: and one of the horses was good and the other bad... The latter is made of insolence and pride." The control of the soul and its right direction can be achieved only with great effort after a hard conflict.[23]

Yet, there is a difference between the perennial notions of evil and good and their place and role in human personality and the modern approach. The ancient approach, though evidently based on observation and introspection, was speculative, general, philosophical. The modern approach addressed the issue by a more careful observation, exploration, experimentation, and therapeutic involvement. Significantly, Freud started with the treatment of psychological disorders, and only through attempts at therapy advanced to his psychological theory. Other psychological schools have also been involved with experiments or medical treatment, with scientific exploration followed by theoretical conclusions. Thus, modern psychology has followed the general principles of modern science.

This trend is clearly manifest in Stevenson's tale. Dr. Jekyll, starting with an introspective notion of the duality of personality, endeavors to explore this phenomenon by scientific experimentation. Whether his approach would be approved by modern psychologists or not is immaterial. After all, this is a tale of fiction. Yet, what *is* significant is that Dr. Jekyll's method is within the range of modern science, and his conclusions follow the logic of scientific inquiry.

Dr. Jekyll's conclusions lead him to the belief in the duality of personality, and in an inner conflict which can assume terrifying proportions. This seemingly testifies to literary license. Yet, even in this respect the story foreshadows the psychoanalytic view of man, which stresses the inner conflicts and which points to the precariousness of maintaining a harmonious balance within one's personality. The manifestations of the loss of such balance and the consequent mental and emotional disorder, even without the sad drama of our story, can still be serious and devastating to the well-being of an individual. Here again Stevenson reveals an uncanny foresight.

Another aspect of the story's modernity is the ease with which Dr. Jekyll is ready to divide and dismember, as it were, the human soul. The recognition of the incongruous duality may well echo the Platonic and the ancient Jewish perceptions. Yet the idea of separating the two elements — to allow the baser individuality freedom and the higher one a separate lofty existence — is a loan from the mechanical world which is alien to ancient notions insistent on the unity of personality. Indeed, it also contradicts the psychoanalytic approach which aims at the reconciliation of the conflicting elements as a way to mental well-being. It may, however, agree, in a broad sense, with behavioristic psychology which allows the individual to be conditioned to a diversity of opinions and behavior without a cohesive unity among these. Such a fragmented personality is explicitly suggested by Dr. Jekyll when he says, as quoted above, that "man will be ultimately known for a mere polity of multifarious, incongruous and independent denizens."

To be sure, Dr. Jekyll does not have in mind the creation of such a personality, split in many ways — an apparently feasible objective from the perspective of the behavioristic psychology — but only its revelation and discovery. Still, this does not mean that he considers the human soul a sanctum which must not be invaded and interfered with by scientific or technoscientific endeavor. On the contrary, his fundamental idea is such an involvement, namely, to separate the two aspects of human personality.

That this led to ultimate disaster is a caution against such undertakings, and a cardinal moral of Stevenson's tale. Yet, to proclaim such a warning, the possibility of interference had to be assumed or foreseen. And, indeed, Stevenson's cautionary tale can be addressed to the dehumanizing implications of perceiving a human as a conditionable or programmable being, and the employment of techniques which would make human beings behave according to someone's design in one sphere of conduct or another, even to the point of turning from free individual to controlled puppet.

To be sure, Dr. Jekyll does not experiment with others, but with his own self. But then in medical and psychological inquiry this may well be the first step to a wider experimentation and application of treatment. It may also be pointed out that Dr. Jekyll *releases* the elements in the human personality, in accordance with the psychoanalytic approach, and does not *instill* attitudes, in line with the behavioristic school. Still, once human mind is tampered with, it is hard to impose limitations on the "treatment." Thus, Dr. Jekyll's approach opens Pandora's box of potential abuse of human personality by scientific techniques, or techniques which are believed to be based on scientific findings. The consequences implicit in Stevenson's story may well deserve to be heeded, if not necessarily taken as a definitive conclusion in this domain of scientific inquiry and practice.

Our story introduces another element of subsequent scientific techniques, namely the use of chemical ingredients to influence human mind and personality. Here Dr. Jekyll, alias Stevenson, touches on the mysterious and baffling issue of the connection between the material element and the mental and emotional disposition, between body and soul, or, in a broader philosophical sense, between matter and spirit. Indeed, Dr. Jekyll, or Robert Stevenson, is aware of the intricacy and mystery of the problem, as he extols the "virtue of transcendental medicine" in contrast with "the most narrow and material views."[24] Yet, the means to which Dr. Jekyll resorts to influence and to play with the human mind or soul are chemical, material. He finds a chemical formula which affects the spirit through a physiological channel.

That human mind, emotions, and disposition can be affected by a material substance has long been recognized with regard to alcoholic beverages, specifically wine. The religious frenzy in the worship of Dionysus was apparently at least partly induced by wine. The Bible contains stories of the stupefying impact of excessive drinking, as in the story of Lot and his daughters.[25] Yet wine is also mentioned as beneficial, as it "maketh glad the heart of man."[26] Such stories and comments merely reflect a common human experience from times immemorial to date. Yet, the endeavors to affect the human disposition and mind have gone beyond wine and its various effects, and reached into the realm of the fantastic. One such example is the myth of a love potion, *l'elisir d'amore*, producing the desired passion in a person affected by it. In the words of Shakespeare:

> Fetch me that flower; the herb I shew'd thee once:
> The juice of it on sleeping eye-lids laid
> Will make or man or woman madly dote
> Upon the next live creature that it sees.[27]

Dr. Jekyll experiments with a scientifically concocted compound which, through physiological link or channel, affects the mind of his experimental subject — which happens to be his own self. The experiment, as we have seen, produces striking, but eventually uncontrollable, results. This facet of the tale both reveals foresight and carries a warning. It predicts the feasibility of the technique, but it also points to its dangers.

Casting a bird's-eye view on the actual development in this regard, we have to acknowledge a diversity of beneficial uses. People facing surgery may be given drugs which allay their anxiety. People suffering from certain mental and emotional disorders are in certain cases treated with drugs which apparently prove beneficial. Yet, drugs — even prescribed drugs — may have adverse side effects, and they can be addictive. Stevenson in his story points to these manifestations. What is much more serious as a social phenomenon is the tendency of people to look for enjoyment, ecstasy, new psychological experience, with the help of chemicals, drugs of a different kind. Such trends are in no way novel, and Stevenson must have been well acquainted with these trends, if not from other sources then from the famous testimony of Thomas De Quincy in *The Confessions of an English Opium Eater*, published in 1822. Dr. Jekyll's case can well serve as a prescient warning against such use of drugs, as in the story it leads to the degeneration of the protagonist, to horrid crime, and finally to the disintegration of the experimenting doctor himself. The technique of chemical manipulation with human disposition is a domain of science or applied science about which humanity must remain extremely cautious.

The last point which characterizes Stevenson's insight, or an attempt at insight into the science of human soul, is the description of evil. It is not simply the censure and rejection of evil. It is not the age-old and venerable moral judgment. That is implicitly taken for granted. But Stevenson tries to define, or at least describe, the intrinsic nature of evil, which is so often baffling to normal people. Edward Hyde is the embodiment of this evil and his wanton acts of cruelty to a child and unprovoked murder exemplify the irrationality of evil — evil in its quintessential nature. The author, however, not only tells the story of the wicked deeds of Hyde to convey the nature of evil, but tries to explain these acts in a clinical way.

Dr. Jekyll, using introspection and accepted moral judgment, describes the frame of mind of his alter ego, Hyde: "This familiar that I called out of my own soul, and sent forth alone to do his good pleasure, was a being inherently malign and villainous; his every act and thought centered on self; drinking pleasure with bestial avidity from any degree of torture to another; relentless like a man of stone."[28] This kind of incomprehensible evil, of evil for the sake of evil, goes beyond the explanations of psychoanalysis, beyond the fall of humanity, or the fall of Satan. For it is not evil due to some mishap, disappointment, or mental crisis, let alone circumstantial pressures. It is evil which has no known origins, and must be taken as an initial force. It may be hidden, but it is real nonetheless. Though usually under control, once let loose it knows no bounds and restraints. Modern psychology may point to sadists and psychopaths who mirror the image of Hyde. Yet modern science of the human mind has not progressed beyond the description of such manifestations of evil.

The limitations of psychology in explaining the baffling manifestations of evil — at least in its ultimate forms — do not obviate the importance of this problem. For we witness the sporadic manifestations of criminal behavior perpetrated by individuals with sadistic and psychopathic characteristics. We have had also the experience of such acts of evil performed in the framework of political conflicts and even masquerading as expressions of religious beliefs, political ideals and scientific theories. Wars, inquisition, and genocide are clear examples of the rampage of evil, which still waits for an explanation, and, if possible, for a cure or an effective counter-action. These have been slow in coming, despite the early warnings in the works of fiction, such as Stevenson's story.

6

The Machine Prophet

The nineteenth century witnessed the steady progress of the Industrial Revolution from its early stages in England in the late eighteenth century. This advancement was expressed in a variety of ways. First, there was the expansion of the novel means of production, both in the country of their origin and outside it — especially in Europe and North America. Then there was the vigorous attempt, in England and elsewhere, to add new inventions and make use of them for economic and other objectives. All this was a cause of great enthusiasm about technology specifically, and about the scientific endeavor in general, the underpinning and stimulant of applied technology. The new machines, such as the steam engine, which became the source of motive power in factories and which was adjusted for mechanical transport in the form of railways, were transforming the way of life of an ever-growing number of people. As new inventions sprouted during the century, the trust in the machine and the anticipation of ever novel means for improving human lives and expanding the horizons of the possible gained momentum. With it grew the admiration for great inventors and respect for professional scientists, scientists in any field of inquiry, whose work was associated with the optimistic perception of the new age.

It is understandable that these new developments affected the literary creation of the era. Perhaps the most prominent example of literary fiction informed by the spirit of the new technology and suffused with the scientific approach is the work of the French writer, Jules Verne (1828–1905). Most, if not all, of his prolific writing abounds in scientific exploration or technological invention, interwoven into stories of adventure. Characteristically, the actual and the fantastic are intertwined in Verne's fiction. Anyone not familiar with the stage of scientific development at the time of the publication of one of Verne's novels, would be often at a loss to decide what in his narration reflects reality and what fancy, or, to be more exact, where the dividing line between these two should be drawn. The reader may go through pages of detailed scientific explanation, which may reflect the scientific knowledge of the time, and then imperceptibly enter a world which was fanciful at the time of Verne's writing, though it may not be fanciful today. For Verne, even though not lacking in fantasy, did not usually embark upon the impossible or even improbable, but rather on the not yet attained. True, a voyage to the center of the earth remains technologically questionable, but sending men to the moon exceeded in reality his fantastic story. Verne's powerful submarine roaming through the oceans is but a pale shadow of modern nuclear submarines. The balloon flights in Verne's works seem predeluvian in the age of popular jet transportation.

It is Jules Verne's restrained fantasy, controlled science fiction, which makes him the spokesman, the prophet, of his scientific-technological age. "Prophet" is a more appropriate designation than "spokesman" in this instance, for a spokesman announces the state of things as they are, while the prophet's vision reaches beyond the present into the future. The view of the prophet extends beyond the horizon, perceiving the present from the perspective of the future, and the future from the vantage point of the present. It has been the nature of the scientific-technological age that it cannot be confined to strict time limits, as its dynamic nature continuously propels it onward. A faithful representative of such an age must be endowed with a great measure of futuristic perspective, or even with a predictive genius. Such a capacity entails both prophesying in the narrow sense by foreseeing the future, and carrying the mantle of a prophet in a wider sense, namely by being a person endowed with a comprehensive vision. Jules Verne combines these two qualities. He displays an uncanny capacity for making specific predictions, and he has the more important quality of discovering some general trends, some moral characteristics of the new age, and conveying them in his writings.

The biblical prophets not only presented their view of the reality of their age, and their insight into its nature. They also passed judgments and offered advice and warning. Verne too is a prophet also in the latter sense, even if his judgments are not always as explicit and emphatic as those of his biblical prototypes. For he not only points to the achievements and potentials of science and technology, but also to their benefits and their dangers. Spectacular human achievements do not appear in a vacuum. They become manifest in a social or political context and they may affect human affairs — for good and for ill.

The analogy between Verne and the biblical prophets is also relevant in another sense. The prophets viewed their own times as sinful and consequently leading to catastrophes; yet they extended the hope of a blissful future, often in "the last days." Verne, too, sees the blissful consequences of science and technology, as well as the dangers inherent in new daring inventions. Thus, in a manner of speaking, he too is a prophet of doom and boon. But in his case the forebodings are characteristic of his later work, while the earlier novels, those generally perceived as his basic message, are essentially optimistic. The impression gained from the biblical books of prophecy, on the other hand, is that the gloom and doom are their basic message, and the hope and redemption are a postscript destined for the remote future. Needless to say, the analogy between Verne and the prophets does not extend into the sphere of religious fervor, moral tenor and poetic sublimity, which remain a distinctive characteristic of ancient Hebrew genre of literature.

I will not attempt to present a comprehensive account of the place of science and technology in Verne's works. Instead I offer a sampling of these elements in his writings, dividing the analysis into thematic chapters.

Of Science and Scientists

Verne's perception of science, as well as his image of the modern scientist, is vigorously expressed in his book *Voyage to the Center of the Earth*[1] (1864). Even though the idea of traveling to the center of the earth is one of the least feasible in Verne's works, in the context of such an implausible adventure his perception of science and his profile of a scientist are conveyed with deep insight and clear understanding.

The story starts in 1863, when Professor Otto Lidenbrock, a prominent geologist from Hamburg, finds a parchment in runic letters which states that the sixteenth-century writer of that note descended to the center of the earth through the crater of an Icelandic volcano. This whets the professor's appetite to repeat the adventure. He recruits his nephew Axel to accompany him, whether willingly or not, and the actual descent into the entrails of the earth necessitates the company and assistance of an Icelandic guide by the name of Hans. The descent into the deep recesses of the earth is filled with surprises and dangers, moments of anxiety and despair, as well as of elation and virtually miraculous delivery. The voyage ends with the ascent of the travelers to the surface of the earth through the crater of another volcano — Stromboli, in the Lipari islands off Sicily.

One somewhat surprising perception of science in Verne's story is the admission or claim of connection between modern science and some antecedents in earlier centuries. In view of the novelty of scientific approach in the modern era, starting with the seventeenth century, earlier historical connections could well be deemed irrelevant. Surely Galileo's experiments proved Aristotle wrong. Science in the modern era, with its rigorous pursuit of eternal laws, could have little consideration, let alone respect, for its vague antecedents — least of all of those formed in or around the Middle Ages.

Yet, when Professor Lidenbrock discovers that the runic parchment is linked to an alleged "sixteenth-century scholar who was a famous alchemist," he waxes ecstatic and sings the praises of the medieval pseudo-scientists. "Those alchemists, such as Avicenna, Bacon, Lully, and Paracelsus, were the real, the only scientists of their time."[2] Thus, modern science is seen as originating from earlier endeavors to penetrate the mysteries of nature. It is a manifestation of a perennial human quest, and not a revelation of the lucky generation of advanced humanity. Thus, Verne pays tribute to civilization in its broad sense, as the framework within which new and important advancement of science can take place.

Still, the respect for the past and for the wider endeavors of humans to define their place in the general order of things in no way diminishes the importance and stature of science and the strict and disciplined scientific approach which is characteristic of the modern age. This becomes clear when one goes through Verne's disquisitions about one or another field of science in one or another of his stories. It may be an elaboration on geology, on the animal kingdom, on the manifold sea creatures, on calculations of the velocity required to overcome earth gravity by a missile, and so on. Whether traveling through the depths of the earth or the sea, whether encountering known creatures or invented ones, Verne dons the mantle of the modern scientist and does it with ease. It does not matter whether his scientific information is correct or stretched to fit the story. Nor is it easy for anyone who is not familiar with the branch of science discussed to ascertain this. The point is that the description adheres to the basic principles of a scientific account, including factual detail, reference to classification (especially in biology), wide range of information, and authority of knowledge. Verne clearly intends to convey to the reader the prominent and reliable place of science in the strict modern sense (no alchemy here), in his own advanced times.

Nor is Verne satisfied with mere descriptive details produced by scientific inquiry. He hints at higher levels of scientific formulation and speculation. He drops such names as that of Poisson, whom Professor Lidenbrock considers a "real scientist," who applied mathematics to various fields of physics. It is the sophisticated levels of scientific inquiry which are hinted at, and indeed some scientific speculations based on alleged calculations of Poisson about the interior pressure of the earth are put forth. In a similar vein, Humphry Davy, the English scientist, is mentioned, with whom our protagonist has supposedly discussed the hypothesis that the earth's core is liquid.[3] The notion of the intricacy and great insights of science, due to its sophisticated methods, is deliberately conveyed. This is not done to overwhelm, let alone intimidate, the lay reader, but rather to impress on readers the grandeur and the wisdom inherent in scientific inquiry.

At the same time, Verne points to the nondogmatic and dynamic nature of science. Professor Lidenbrock conveys this in an explicit and clear statement: "Science is eminently perfectible, and accepted theories are always being destroyed by new ones."[4] This means that new information or a new argument can modify and change accepted notions and theories, and this laborious process leads to the advancement of science. Therefore, science never rests on its laurels, but always continues to inquire. It is not a static, complete, final body of knowledge; it is a continuous process which requires initiative and energy for the expansion of knowledge. The character of Professor Lidenbrock perfectly represents this perception of science. Eager and purposeful, he embarks on his scientific adventure with singular determination.

Though modern science proceeds according to strict rules of reason and logic, Lidenbrock is not, as might be expected, as cool as a cucumber. Verne's scientist is anything but a dispassionate, detached, emotionless human being. Professor Lidenbrock combines rigorous scientific discipline with passion and even ecstasy in his scientific pursuits. Though Verne describes the behavior of the professor with deliberate exaggeration, in order to add a comical touch to his story by presenting the image of an eccentric scientist, there is clearly an intent to show the emotional driving force behind the systematic and rational pursuit of scientific truth.

As Professor Lidenbrock attempts to decipher the old parchment which will lead him to the adventurous exploration, he discovers that his nephew Axel is in love with his ward, Grauben. The professor's reaction is barely human. "So you love Grauben," he repeated distractedly. 'Well, let's apply my method to the document in question.'" The comment of Axel, who is the narrator here, about his professorial uncle is that "the head of the scientist could not comprehend matters of heart." Yet, the professor was in no way devoid of emotions. "As he was about to make his crucial experiment, his eyes flashed behind his glasses, and his fingers trembled when he picked up the old parchment. He was deeply moved."[5] Clearly, the professor is in love with science, as much as — if not more than — Axel is in love with the girl. When finally the parchment is fully deciphered, the behavior of the professor is thus described by his nephew: "Having read this, my uncle started as if he had unexpectedly touched a Leyden jar. He was a magnificent picture of daring, joy, and conviction."[6]

The image of the enthusiastic scientist enraptured in his inquiry is contrasted with the personality of his laboratory assistant nephew who, if a budding scientist, is evidently not of the same stature. While Professor Lidenbrock is enthusiastic, Axel is very much down to earth. The projected expedition, with its inherent risks, fails to appeal to Axel's imagination, let alone fire his enthusiasm. While the professor reaches for the stars, his assistant carefully watches his steps. Indeed, the pair is reminiscent of Don Quixote and Sancho Panza. The nephew's comments about his uncle are characteristic in this respect. On their trip from Hamburg to Copenhagen, when a passenger points to a big building which is a madhouse, the following thought occurs to Axel: "No matter how big it is, it's still too small to hold all of Professor Lidenbrock's madness!"[7] If Verne deliberately followed the model of Cervantes, he clearly favored his Don Quixote, the mad professor. For the "madness" is the emotive power which propels the scientist, and thus assures the progress of science. It becomes a kind of a holy madness, just as science becomes a new religion in this and various other books of Verne.

The reluctant, down-to-earth assistant gets a psychological and moral boost from Grauben, to whom the professor explained his venture and of which she wholeheartedly approves. And so she exclaims: "Oh, dearest Axel, it's so noble to devote oneself to science like that! What glory is waiting for Lidenbrock and will be reflected on his companion!"[8] Scientific venture holds out the promise of glory. Science becomes a new object of what could be likened to patriotic feelings. It is the new frontier to be crossed so that the territory of knowledge may expand. The fact that Verne's scientific heroes in his various books belong to different nationalities may well express his sense of the impending switch in human civilization from patriotic to scientific pursuits which ignore national borders. Thus, in the present book he refers to scientists of different national origin — German, French, English, Danish. In *From the Earth to the Moon*, the three travelers to the earth's satellite are two Americans and one French citizen. Implicitly the new science is a testimony to a new epoch in human history, characterized by its international orientation and by its new objectives and new fields of glory.

The lofty nature of science does not obliterate the pedestrian requirements of the scientist embarking on a scientific expedition. Thus, Verne does not hesitate to remind us that the professor prepares an exact list of instruments, weapons, tools and food needed for the expedition. The instruments include a thermometer, a manometer, a chronometer, two compasses, a night telescope, and two Ruhmkorff devices for providing a portable source of light.[9] That the last may be elementary by our standards does not matter. The preparations convey the perception that, however sophisticated and ambitious the scientific enterprise, however quixotic it may even be, it must take care of the practical technical needs. These include also the Icelandic guide, Hans, a man of considerable experience in his field, of sang-froid and resourcefulness, a man of deeds and not words, who succeeds in extricating our travelers to the center of the earth from unforeseen menaces and impending disasters. Scientific endeavor, especially when involving exploratory expeditions, must be linked to ordinary human experience and common sense. Science and scientists cannot be separated from the earthly and human limitations. For Verne, science, however lofty and sublime, must also be practical.

Yet, the overall result of scientific inquiry and consequent knowledge is its overwhelming impact on human consciousness and on humans' philosophical perception of—or perhaps puzzlement about—their place in the cosmos. Significantly, this almost metaphysical realization is conveyed as the experience of Axel, the down-to-earth and unimaginative nephew of the professor. After an encounter with some living creatures, known only from their fossilized remnants, Axel experiences a paleontological dream in which he travels to prehistoric times among wondrous creatures. Then the evolutionary history of the world is vividly witnessed in his dream, only that he pursues it backwards: from living beings, through plants, to a solid empty globe, turning liquid and then gaseous. "My body becomes rare, purifies itself in its turn, and blends like an imponderable atom in those immense mists which mark their fiery orbit through infinity."[10] Scientific observation leads to far-flung theories and speculation which, when reaching a comprehensive view of cosmic evolution, cannot but lead to bewilderment or inspire awe, result in total alienation or spur a mystic quest for union with the mysterious forces. In the case of Axel, it is awe and mysticism which dominate his experience. Indeed, it is conveyed as virtually a religious experience, only that the quest of union is directed at matter, which may be even more mystifying and elusive than God. This is so much more startling, as Axel, in his dream, mentions the Creator too.

What was Verne's intent in introducing this dream? As it traces evolution backwards, it can hardly present an actual craving of Axel to dissolve in the primordial form of matter. Moreover, the experience is presented as a hallucination, which may be an indication that it does not have to be taken seriously. Yet, the fact that such a scientific-philosophical dream is introduced points to some serious intent on the part of Verne. Apparently, he wanted to express a philosophical notion of humankind's tiny place in the order of things, a notion which could be inferred from paleontology and the cosmogonic speculations related to it. That this led to a sense of awe is quite understandable. That it did not result in a sense of alienation may well be a matter of temperamental choice — of Axel or of Verne. That it is presented in a lofty, poetic style testifies not only to Verne's genius, but also to his perception of the mystery of being.

In summation, Verne's perception of science ties it to both the rational and the emotional attitude of the scientist. It combines theoretical speculations and the practical approach in inquiry and experiment. It is down to earth and it reaches for the stars. It is prosaic and it is poetic. It is concerned with factual reality and it turns mystical. The new age of science seems to hold out a promise of boundless human involvement and endless gratification. Science answers questions, but also widens the horizons of puzzlement and wonder.

The Power of Technology

While the overwhelming power of the new technology is expressed throughout most of Verne's fiction, which vigorously conveys the sense of the newly gained means of the inventive era, we shall focus here on two sources for the documentation and analysis of Verne's perception of this theme and reflection on it. One is his story *From the Earth to the Moon* (1865).[11] The other is *Twenty Thousand Leagues under the Sea* (1869).[12]

The plot of the first novel is quite simple. The frustration and malaise of the members of the American Gun Club in Baltimore, a malaise due to a prolonged period of peace, is cured by the dramatic proclamation of its president, Impey Barbicane, to design and construct a gun which will fire a projectile to the moon. The announcement is followed by worldwide enthusiasm and financial support. Another dramatic step in the developing story is the appearance of Michel Ardan, a young Frenchman who wants to be put inside the shell and thus go to the moon. His daring desire is accommodated, and when the shell is fired it contains three humans: Ardan, Barbicane, and Barbicane's former adversary Captain Nicholl, a proponent of the efficacy of armor against the advocates of projectiles.

While the shot from the supergun is fired, with the three adventurers inside the projectile, the expedition fails to achieve its declared aim. For the astronomic observatory reveals that rather than land on the moon, the projectile has gone into an elliptical orbit around the moon, turning into its satellite. The great project ends, if not in a fiasco, at least in an enigma. For there are two scientific hypotheses about the future of the projectile: it may eventually land on the moon or orbit it to the end of time.

Was this intended by Verne to caution against overconfidence in technological capacity, to point to the need to take new human powers with a grain of salt? Was it intended to warn against the new age hubris? Or was it merely a literary device to end a story, without going into all-too-fantastic tales about lunar life, or the frustrating alternative of the emptiness of the lunar surface? The question remains unanswered, even if in another novel, *Round the Moon*—the sequel to this, published four years later, in 1869—Verne rescues the three voyagers and sends them back to earth. Whatever the motives of the writer, it is up to the reader to interpret the works, and an enigma only enlarges the scope of interpretation and reflection.

The drama of *Twenty-Thousand Leagues under the Sea* is of a different kind. Here it is human conflicts which form the axis of the basic plot. Some kind of a monster having allegedly collided with or attacked various ships, the United States puts to sea a frigate on an expedition to find the monster and deal with it appropriately. The U.S. secretary of the navy invites Pierre Aronnax, professor at the Paris Museum of Natural History, to join the expedition. Aronnax is the narrator of the story.

After a wild goose chase, the frigate encounters the monster and attacks it, with disastrous results. There is a collision and three men are thrown overboard by the impact. After some harrowing hours, they find themselves inside the monster. This proves to be not a biological creature, however, but a submarine. The three are Aronnax, his devoted Belgian servant Conseil, and Canadian harpooner Ned Land, who joined the expedition in expectation of an encounter with a superwhale. The three men find refuge in the submarine, but are regarded as prisoners, destined to stay there indefinitely. The commander of *Nautilus*, as the submarine is called, is Captain Nemo, an enigmatic person heading a crew of anonymous men. The name "Nemo," meaning in Latin "No Man," may well have been intended to separate him from humanity, to point to a unique personality of the captain. And, indeed, Nemo is a very unusual human being.

He is a scientist, a scholar, and a sea captain of enterprise and courage. He is deeply humane and compassionate, risking his life to save a stranger. Yet, he is also ruthless, vindictive, and successful when encountering navy vessels bent on his destruction. He chose to live on board a floating ship — over and under water — because of his resentment of humanity, which had caused the death of his family — wife and children. These sentiments are apparently shared by his crew. After a fascinating journey round the world in *Nautilus* for ten months, the three guest-prisoners are thrown ashore during a maelstrom, and land on the Lofoten Islands. The lot of *Nautilus* and Captain Nemo — whether they survived the storm or perished — is not known.

It is into this story that Verne weaves accounts of adventure, scientific exploration and above all technological ingenuity, which made it possible to make and sustain an autarchic and independent, comfortable and powerful submarine, a self-contained state floating where it will through the seas and oceans of the earth.

While technological achievement seems to be the overwhelming impression made by these two books, they are not divorced from the domain of science. In the first place, pure scientific curiosity, the mark of the civilized human, may be a motivating factor for an enterprise facilitated by a technological invention. It is such curiosity that turns Professor Aronnax into a willing prisoner of Captain Nemo. Of course, Verne's choice of the French professor of natural history as the voyager on the *Nautilus* and the narrator of the story is not incidental. For only such a narrator can give justice to the wonders of the sea which can be observed from the submarine — equipped with glass windows to facilitate such observation.

The scientific speculations of the learned professor about the possibility of a maritime monster, prior to its identification, are a splendid example of a detached logical argument based on a limited factual knowledge. That the speculation, which remains guarded, proves wrong, does not detract from its worth. Indeed, it shows that science, at least biology, is neither exhaustive nor infallible. Still, appreciative as Verne is of the academic nature of Aronnax's science, he depicts it with a touch of irony — the professor is concerned not only with truth, but is also careful in his presentation to protect his scholarly reputation.[13]

No such doubts are voiced about Captain Nemo, who is both a scholar-scientist and a man in command of a marvel of technology. Clearly, it is the combination of the theoretical and the practical, of knowledge and its application, of science and technology, that is Verne's ideal.

Indeed, science may play a direct and indispensable role in a technological enterprise. Thus, the expedition to the moon is linked to and dependent upon the scientific advice of the Cambridge (Massachusetts) observatory. The latter responds in detail and with quantified statements to the queries of the Gun Club as to the feasibility of transmitting a projectile to the moon. An excerpt from the answer will exemplify the nature and quality of the scientific report, a fundamental element in the technological planning. The project is deemed feasible, provided the projectile

> ... possess an initial velocity of 1,200 yards per second.... In proportion as we recede from the earth the action of gravitation diminishes in the inverse ratio of the square of the distance.... Consequently, the weight of a shot will decrease, and will become reduced to zero at the instant that the attraction of the moon exactly counterpoises that of the earth ... and, if it passes that point, it will fall into the moon by the sole effect of the lunar attraction. The *theoretical possibility* of the experiments is therefore absolutely demonstrated; its *success* must depend upon the power of the engine employed.[14]

The scientific evaluation is in no way Verne's discovery, but the fact that it is incorporated in the story testifies to his recognition of the role of science in contemporary and future endeavors of complex technological projects.

The gist of these works is to point to the power of technology — of the application of science, engineering and skill to some daring and ambitious project. While remarkable achievements in this respect had been recorded by the time Verne wrote these novels, he makes a big leap forward in the trip to the moon and in the creation of *Nautilus*. The fact that eventually these two fictional projections were realized within a century testifies not only to his visionary capacity, but also to his correct evaluation of the overall power and significance of modern technological development. To focus on such fantastic achievements in his time may have provided entertainment for children — mainly boys — for many decades. Yet, eventually the innocent adventures turned into hard reality, as not only men orbiting round the moon, but landing on the moon and returning to earth, and interplanetary spacecraft turned into virtually regular enterprises. As to the singular, powerful submarine, it turned into an established kind of ship, with immensely greater power, in the arsenals of major navies in the second half of the twentieth century. Indeed, Verne's *Nautilus* turned to be the fictional link between Robert Fulton's primitive *Nautilus* of 1801 and the first nuclear-powered submarine in the United States Navy, launched in 1954 and also assuming that name.

To be sure, Verne's projectile to the moon was all too simplistic a design, both as to its propulsion and the life-support systems of the travelers. Similarly, Verne's submarine did not have the benefit of nuclear propulsion. After all, Verne was not a scientific designer or an inventor of new technology, but a writer of fiction. Still, he had an uncanny insight into the shape of the machines of the future. To encapsulate three men in a projectile sent to the moon comes very close to the twentieth-century experience of the actual thing. His *Nautilus* is a very powerful warship, even if it destroys enemy ships simply by goring them. And, of course, Verne's submarine has no nuclear rockets. Still, it is a marvel, pointing to its entelechy. It runs on electric power—a daring assumption at the time the book was written; it displaces about 1,500 tons; it can go down to great depths and be submerged for a long period. Curiously, it managed to travel under the ice cap of Antarctica, just as the USS *Nautilus* did under the ice of the North Pole.

It is noteworthy that Verne himself hints—be it ambiguously—at the potential developments of his fictional technologies in future reality. Thus, Captain Nemo says: "It took many centuries to discover the mechanical power of steam! Who knows if we will see a second *Nautilus* within a hundred years!" Professor Aronnax is no more optimistic when he responds: "Your boat is one or maybe several centuries ahead of its time."[15] Verne underestimated his predictive capacity. From his *Nautilus* to the American *Nautilus*, the time span was a mere eighty-four years.

In speculating about the trip to the moon, the planners envisage eventual contacts with the lunar expedition by sending it provisions once a year. Moreover, the lunar travelers expect regular news from the earth, and plan, in turn, to communicate with their friends on earth.[16] While we have here no chronological prediction, we are facing a scenario of transportation and communication between the earth and the outer space, which, of course, has been exceeded far beyond Verne's vivid imagination.

Besides Verne's vision of new technology and its tremendous power and achievements, he makes some observations about the men who are able to actually invent the new machines. Clearly, Captain Nemo is the ideal of a creative engineer: he designs the submarine and its vital systems, acquires its components from the best sources, and navigates it. His scientific knowledge, technical ingenuity, practical skill, intelligence, and common sense combine to make him an accomplished example of the champions of the new technological age.

Besides depicting such a comprehensive ideal, Verne makes broader comments in *From the Earth to the Moon* about some of the qualities of the technological inventor and entrepreneur. These comments may be straightforward, though occasionally tinted with irony. They may also become outright critical and caustic. Thus, the success of the Americans in devising big guns is attributed to their naive national characteristic: "The Yankees, the first mechanicians in the world, are engineers ... by right of birth."[17] Another quality of the Americans which favors technological invention is their optimism and trust in their capacity to overcome difficulties. "Nothing can astound an American... In America, all is easy, all is simple; and as for mechanical difficulties, they are overcome before they arise."[18] Indeed, Verne conveys here an attitude familiar to date: positive thinking. Expect good results and solutions to a problem, and it will be solved. While Verne may have made these observations with some reservations, he still appears to wish to convey the idea that this kind of optimism is an important factor in finding solutions to technological difficulties.

Verne also realizes the absurdity of technological and scientific enthusiasm when people's zeal make them forget the basics of the human condition. Thus, the members of the Gun Club, in their enthusiasm for improving the technology of artillery, disregard human casualties, including those of the members of the club. Verne's criticism extends to the penchant for cold statistics—another perennial inclination of the Americans. Thus, it was calculated by a great American statistician "that throughout the Gun Club there was not quite one arm between four persons, and exactly two legs between six."[19] The irrelevance of statistics, scientific a tool though they may be, is brought to light here with Swiftian sarcasm. The implication of such an exposé is that scientific tools have to be related to the purpose at hand— whether scientific, technological, or other. Just waving some findings attained by scientific tools, such as statistics, and claiming for them a special status because attained by such means, does not indicate their relevance or add to their importance.

Yet, if Verne criticized misapplied science, because of the essentially irrational nature of such misapplication, it does not mean that he considered technological ventures as the pure and exclusive extension or corollaries of the rational scientific approach. Thus, the expedition to the moon includes the systematic, scientific, rational Barbicane and the adventurous, bohemian fantast, Michel Ardan, for whom "the love of the impossible constituted his ruling passion."[20] This strange combination may well symbolize the need in bold technological enterprises to link reason with fantasy, science with enthusiasm, logic with emotion. The point was conveyed in the profile of Professor Lidenbrock in *Journey to the Center of the Earth*, as noted above.

Not only do technological breakthroughs require other than purely scientific foundations, but the achievements themselves have to be perceived in the broader framework of human civilization. This, at least, seems to be the ideal of Verne. Technology for the sake of technology only, or technological enthusiasm which ignores other facets of human, or perhaps European, civilization, would be a biased and questionable commitment and achievement. This stance seems to be implicitly adopted by depicting Captain Nemo as a man of high culture, who makes a point of carrying in his floating state some of the illustrious products of human spirit. The *Nautilus* has a large collection of books, including poetry, fiction and science, with emphasis on the latter category. Then there is a collection of paintings, including ones by Raphael, Leonardo da Vinci, Murillo, and Holbein. Scores by composers like Rossini, Mozart, and Beethoven, and a large organ on which Captain Nemo occasionally plays, are added to the cultural scope of the submarine. Rarities of nature, personally collected by Nemo from the seas and oceans, amount to a collection exceeding that of any European museum.[21]

These cultural riches of the Nautilus, as well as the overall impression of the ship, suggest that the refuge of Captain Nemo represents Verne's image of a utopia — a perfect state, or at least a human niche. The Latin "Nemo" ("no man") parallels the Greek "utopia" ("no place"). Nemo, in a certain sense, is the ideal human, as Thomas More's Utopia was the ideal place. The *Nautilus* represents a utopia in that it is technologically powerful and thus free and independent. It has the accoutrements of culture, with strong scientific components, apparently representing the philosophy and taste of Verne. It is cosmopolitan: Nemo's nationality is not revealed, and his library contains books "written in every known language," which is no problem for the polyglot captain. Significantly, the library contains not "a single book on politics or economy," which points to an apolitical and non-economic ideal of society.[22] It is science and art, in their variety of expression, and not accumulation of riches and power, which are extolled as worthy objectives of humanity, even if Nemo happens to be both immensely rich and powerful. Apparently his riches and power are necessary for his goals, and are not aims in themselves. Technological power assures *Nautilus*'s existence and comfort, but is not an objective in itself.

Indeed, technology as a means of power for the sake of power is derided by Verne. He conveys his criticism by depicting the enthusiasm of the Gun Club members for the science of gunnery, frustrated by peace. "'Ay! and no war in prospect!' continued the famous James T. Maston, ... 'Not a cloud in the horizon! and that too at such a critical period in the progress of the science of artillery!'"[23] The immoral use of technology is expressed in more general terms, when the rivalry and competition between the power of gunnery and the protective armor of ships is discussed. As the guns grew heavier, the armor became thicker. The U.S. Navy used these technological improvements to advantage by making heavier guns and thickening the armor of ships. In doing so, "they did to others that which they would not they should do to them — that grand principle of immorality upon which rests the whole art of war." Twisting the Golden Rule, as formulated in the New Testament, and earlier by Hillel, Verne conveys his abhorrence of war in an epigrammatic statement.[24] This is also clearly criticism of the use of technology for such sinister purposes as warfare. Verne would rather have it serve the well-being of humanity.

Captain Nemo, by contrast, though wielding enormous power, is not intoxicated by it, but treats it from the perspective of overall human goals. He certainly abhors using power for its own sake. This is well expressed in his refusal to let Ned Land, the harpooner, go for a hunt of black whales. That would be "killing for the sake of killing," explains Nemo. Aronnax agrees with the captain, musing that "the barbarous, unthinking way these animals are hunted down will one day wipe the last whale from the ocean." Interestingly, Nemo goes beyond the ecological concern, when he makes *Nautilus* attack a herd of sperm whales, in order to save the harmless black whales from annihilation.[25] This human and humane interference with nature may well be another facet of Verne's utopia, reminiscent of the biblical picture of the last days, when "the wolf shall dwell with the lamb" (Isaiah 11:6). For Captain Nemo interferes with nature, guided by ethical principles.

Still, this does not necessarily turn Captain Nemo into an unquestionable paragon of virtue. For though technology remains subservient to higher human goals and to the principles of right and wrong, what he deems as right is not always above dispute. While he shows humanity and compassion in the face of human danger and suffering, he is dedicated to a war of revenge against some unidentified sector of humanity, which is accused of inflicting disaster on his own family. Here his anger flares up in righteous indignation, and his fury shows no pity. On facing a ship pursuing the *Nautilus,* he cries out: "O ship of an accursed nation, you know who I am! I do not need to see your colours to recognize you.'"[26] Soon he sinks the ship with all hands. Professor Aronnax is shocked at the sight of the sinking ship, though he cannot pass judgment on Nemo's punishment for his terrible grievance.

Thus, we are left with no clear ethical resolution, despite the fact that Nemo is extremely sensitive to moral judgment. The problem whether the awesome technological power of *Nautilus* is used justly is not resolved — perhaps because the enigma surrounding the mysterious captain and his crew offers a convenient framework for the story. What is clear, however, is Verne's stand that technology ought to be subservient to human purpose, which must be judged by ethical considerations and concerns. This point will be made crystal clear in some of the later works of Verne, as will be further seen.

The Danger of Technology

The alternative use of science and technology for the good of humankind or for the service of evil is presented with crystal clear simplicity in Verne's novel *Les Cinq Cents Millions de la Bégum* (1879), translated into English under the title *The Begum's Fortune.* The alternatives of good and evil in this story are presented the way they appear in folk fables, children's stories, or religious morality tales. There is good and it can be all perfection, a virtual paradise, and there is evil and it can be an evil without a touch of goodness, a pure devilish conduct.

Into this perennial dichotomy Verne introduces the factor of power offered by modern technology, which is particularly menacing when combined with evil — perhaps such dangers outweighing the benefits which science offers to the good. In some ways, the scales are weighted in favor of evil. To anticipate the story, the good Frankville might have perished in the attack by Stahlstadt, had not the ruler of the latter miscalculated the trajectory of his missile.

One must add a historical note. Verne presents the story in the shadow cast by the Franco–Prussian war of 1870–1871, in which France suffered a humiliating defeat. Verne, in a patriotic gesture, glorifies the nobility of the French founder of Frankville and blackens the character of the German founder of Stahlstadt. The Frenchman is a virtual angel, while the German is the incarnation of devil. Moreover, another major character in the story, an ingenious and resourceful angel, Max Bruckmann, is a native of Alsace, which France had to cede to Germany, who remains an ardent French patriot and becomes all but the savior of Frankville. Making allowance for Verne's patriotic ardor, which makes him glorify his compatriots in the story beyond reasonable judgment, and turns the German professor into a caricature of evil genius, it has to be borne in mind that a monster of the ilk of Verne's German chauvinist is not a stranger to the twentieth century. In this sense, the French author could be seen as manifesting a singular prevision.

The story introduces Dr. Sarrasin, a selfless, dedicated physician, who inherits an enormous fortune from a relative who married a begum, the widow of an Indian rajah. Overwhelmed by the enormity of the sum of money, Dr. Sarrasin does not even consider using it for his personal gain, but decides to put the money at the disposal of science and human progress. The abstract ideal is translated into a practical project, namely building "a model city, based upon strictly scientific principles." Such a city, worthy in itself, would "present to the world ... a practical illustration of what all cities ought to be."[27]

However, as soon as the news of Dr. Sarrasin's great inheritance reaches the press, Professor Schultz (elsewhere referred to as Schultze) — a pedantic and authoritarian bully, though a man of great intellectual capacity — makes a claim for the fortune, too. He appears to be related to the millionaire, as well. Through the services of a British solicitor, and not least because Dr. Sarrasin does not really mind dividing the inheritance, Professor Schultz gets one half of the inheritance. Even so, enough is left to each to embark on the project of a model city. For Schultz follows Sarrasin's example, though his city has an entirely different character and purpose. It is called Stahlstadt, City of Steel, built in Oregon, and rather than pursuing the establishment of a humane and rational community, it is bent on the production of guns of superior quality. It markets its products to various countries and accumulates great profits. Yet the purpose of the enormous enterprise is not wealth and riches, but the assertion of power, aimed at achieving German supremacy over the entire world, through some mysterious, cataclysmic weapon. "The general opinion was that Professor Schultz was working at the completion of a terrible engine of war of unprecedented power, destined to assure universal dominion to Germany."[28]

Stahlstadt, a city built like a fortress, is closed to outsiders and controlled like a military base. Yet, Max (elsewhere called Marcel) Bruckmann, the brilliant, resourceful, energetic and courageous friend of Dr. Sarrasin's family, succeeds in infiltrating this forbidden and forbidding city. Posing as a steel worker, he makes a rapid advancement and becomes Schultz's trusted assistant. As such, he succeeds in provoking Schultz into showing him the inner sanctum of the establishment and the supergun and powerful missiles which would make it possible to annihilate a city like Frankville and its one hundred thousand inhabitants, thirty miles away with one shot. As a matter of fact, this is what Schultz intends to do, and he sets the date and the hour of the attack. To the query of Max as to why Schultz would attack people who did him no harm, Schultz replies: "Right — Good — Evil are purely relative, and quite conventional words. Nothing is positive but the grand laws of nature. The law of competition has the same force as that of gravitation." It is in the name of this law that the Germans of Stahlstadt will annihilate the weaker Frankville.[29] Thus we face here a crude variety of social-racist Darwinist gone mad — though not a fantastic creature for a generation with the twentieth-century experience.

Schultz having opened all his cards to Max, the latter is condemned to die, so that the Professor's grand design will remain secret. However, through a series of clever maneuvers, Max succeeds in escaping and makes his way to Frankville. Here he designs ways of defense, sending women and children out of the city and organizing shelters and fire-extinguishing teams. Then he figures out that the projected missile will fortunately be subject to such propelling power that it will go into orbit around the world and miss any terrestrial target — which proves to be the case.

Frankville having escaped destruction, there follows the demise of Stahlstadt. Though Schultz plans a maritime expedition against Frankville, in order to destroy it in a more conventional manner, he falls victim to an accident caused by his ingenious devices. With his disappearance, the city, ruled by the iron hand of a devilish genius, collapses like a pack of cards. Max Bruckmann, with the help of Frankville, takes over Stahlstadt and reestablishes it as a productive enterprise. It will offer an arsenal to Frankville, which will protect it from any attack. In the words of Dr. Sarrasin: "And as we shall then be the strongest, we must at the same time endeavor to be also the most just, we must spread the benefits of peace and justice all around."[30] Thus, the moral of the story seems to be that the ideal of peace and justice cannot ignore the factor of power. It has to arm itself in order to be able to survive and to thrive.

While references to scientific principles and technological marvels have been made in recounting the story of *The Begum's Fortune*, the aspects of science and technology manifest in the book ought to be highlighted. The relative importance of wealth and science, and the possible relationship between them, is addressed directly by Dr. Sarrasin. There is no doubt in his mind that science is of great worth in that it can advance the well-being of humankind, while immense riches, are superfluous and may be even dangerous, unless they are turned to scientific enterprise.

Indeed, Sarrasin senses the destructive effect his immense riches have on the way his friends see him. "He, himself personally, appeared to dwindle into insignificance before the imposing figures which denoted his wealth. He was inwardly conscious that his own personal merits ... were already, even in the eyes of those who knew him best, sunk in the ocean of gold and silver. His friends no longer saw in him the enthusiastic experimentalist, the ingenious inventor, the acute philosopher; they saw only the great millionaire."[31] The personality of the scientist all but disappears in the glitter of material possessions. This is a reflection not only on the predicament of the afflicted millionaire, but also on the failing judgment of people.

Dr. Sarrasin, alias Jules Verne, clearly asserts the true value of wealth and science, elevating the latter and seeing the former only as a means for advancing it. In a letter to his son, Dr. Sarrasin expresses his concern and forebodings about the impact of his great fortune on his life as a scientist, "unless this same fortune were to become in our hands a new and powerful engine of science, a mighty tool in the great work of civilization and progress!"[32] The fortune is not a source for personal gratification, but a trust which obliges the scientist to get involved in great scientific endeavors for the benefit of mankind.

This stance conveys not merely the subservient relationship of wealth to science, but also the unequivocal belief in science — at least science addressed to human well-being. It is noteworthy, therefore, that in the course of the story, when Frankville is threatened with annihilation by the attack of Herr Schultz, and Max tries to find ways of salvation at the last moment despite the poor odds, Verne makes the following comment. "In Europe Max would have been thought mad. But in America it is unwise to refuse to believe in any miracle of science, however unexpected; so ... the young engineer was listened to and believed in."[33] Verne may be writing tongue in cheek, alluding to the naivety and credulity of Americans. Yet, he may express a genuine admiration for such virtual religion of science, the mark of the modern and future world, which he so eagerly describes in many of his works.

The city of Frankville is a perfect expression of rational design and of scientifically guided precautions for securing the best possible existence for its inhabitants. Verne elaborates on various details, such as the quality of the construction material, the outlay of homes and gardens, the reduction of the risk of illness allegedly caused by carpets and painted papers. Washable walls would assure that "not even a germ of anything harmful can be harbored there." For "individual and collective cleanliness is the great idea of the founders of Frankville." Due to these and other rational-scientific arrangements, the citizens of the city are exceptionally healthy and mortality is much lower than in the outside world. An even greater hope is expressed for the future, as a German journal puts it: "It will be interesting to follow the development of this attempt, and ... to discover if the influence of this scientific regime may not in the course of ... several generations weaken hereditary and morbid predispositions."[34] Whatever one may think about all these scientific techniques and beliefs, there is no doubt about Verne's picture of well-being and progress resulting from properly directed science.

Science is also manifest in the organization and working of Stahlstadt. It is expressed in the supremely efficient organization of the city, as well as of the system of industrial production which is perfectly coordinated. Here is how the steel production system is described: "It was all executed with such wonderful precision that just at the appointed time the last crucible was emptied and flung into the vat. The maneuver seemed rather the result of a blind mechanism than the cooperation of a hundred human wills."[35] The description implicitly forecasts automation, a blind mechanism which succeeds cooperation of a hundred human wills.

Besides this rational-scientific organization, there is, of course, the ingenuity of Schultz, who invents and constructs new guns, missiles and explosives. His scientific knowledge, combined with inventive genius, produces tremendous results. His failure, due to an error in calculation, and his accidental death, are not consistent with his scientific stature. Indeed, they are a kind of deus ex machina, necessary to provide a happy ending to the story.

Thus, the warning of Verne stands. Science can be effectively used for evil designs, as it can be used for human benefit. It offers promise and menace. Humans must beware and not only work for beneficial science, but be on high alert against the dangers of sinister uses of science and technology.

7

Evolution: Natural and Designed

The nineteenth century witnessed not only a spectacular development of technology and its industrial application. It was affected not only by the Industrial Revolution and its growing momentum. It also saw profound changes in the perception of nature and humanity, due to a novel scientific perspective, namely the theories of evolution. Human self-image has a profound impact on human consciousness, self-esteem and confidence. People created in the image of God tread more securely on this earth than humans evolved from primitive forms of life. In this sense, it can be argued, theories of evolution do not serve the interests of human psychology and, if anything, undermine our sense of security and basic satisfaction with ourselves.

Yet, science and bold scientific theories pursue truth, as best they can, without regard for human pride or self-confidence. The scientist, as a human being, may prefer to have been created in the image of God. The human being, as a scientist, cannot but follow the principles of logic and mental discipline, irrespective of the consequences. The result were theories of evolution, developed by such men as Charles Darwin (1809–1882), Herbert Spencer (1820–1903), and Thomas Henry Huxley (1825–1895). We need not go into the differences among the ways evolution was perceived by its various proponents. The important fact is that this new perspective had a tremendous impact on the outlook of educated men and women of the age, as well as in subsequent times.

One example of a writer open to such influence was Herbert George Wells (1866–1946), or H.G. Wells, as he is usually referred to. The fact that T.H. Huxley had been one of his teachers may explain the important role evolution played in the writings of Wells, fictional and other. Wells, a novelist as well as an English version of the eighteenth-century French *philosophes*, was essentially a writer with a message — even if the nature of the message changed due to the vicissitudes of the turbulent times of his life.

On the face of it, the theory of evolution leaves little for speculation or fantasy. If humans are a product of a long process of natural selection, there is nothing for them to do, but accept their place — whether as the ultimate stage of evolution, or an intermediary between the present species and some future development. Yet, this has not actually been the case. For there is always the possibility of speculating about future evolution and where it is likely to take humans and other creatures. Then there is the more challenging endeavor of turning *Homo sapiens* from a passive manifestation of natural evolution into an active agent of his own development and of the progress of human society. If evolution can be likened to an automated train, moving in a predetermined though unknown direction, people who are on this train may try to take over the controls and decide on the direction of travel.

H.G. Wells, impressed and affected though he was by the new science of nature and mankind, became caught in this antinomy of the evolutionary doctrine. The new theory and approach had a strong hold on him and his imagination, but the active and creative element in his personality would not acquiesce in mere waiting for the slow, hardly noticeable, biological development. Naturally, he was eager to either predict the eventual significant transformations, or speculate about human attempts at modification, change, acceleration of the process of evolution, or even at designing human progress. In the words of Wells, pointing in the latter direction, in the introductory chapter to *The Outline of History*: "Since man has existed as a self-conscious social creature for only a few tens of thousands of years, this gives him illimitable opportunity for the attainment of knowledge and power."[1] It is noteworthy that Wells seriously contemplates such a possibility in a comprehensive outline of history which, in an unconventional manner, starts with an account of the earth in space, continues through emergence of life and evolution — reptiles, mammals, humans — to the history of human civilization, as we know it. The findings of astronomy, paleontology, and biology are incorporated into the story of humankind. Wells starts with the stars, before eventually dealing with the vicissitudes of human history. One could say that his trail leads, to reverse the Latin saying, *per astra ad aspera*, "Through stars to hardships."

For, pace the optimistic statement quoted above, Wells is not actually committed to such a beneficial outcome. Such may be the opportunity of humans, but there is no assurance that they will take advantage of it. They may misuse it, abuse it, relinquish it. Well's fictional stories explore some such diverse possibilities, as well as give an expression to some fundamental doubts about the desirable direction of the evolutionary process itself. Such doubts were entertained by his teacher, T.H. Huxley: "The cosmic process gives rise to what is evil in man's moral life, and in the long run will get the best of the contest, and 'resume its sway' when evolution enters on its downward course" (*Essays*).[2] Wells, too, is caught in the dilemma of evolutionary prediction and moral judgment, as his writings testify.

While I will not pursue the development of Wells's thoughts in this respect, I will single out two works which exemplify his treatment of evolution and the relationship of humans to its forces and dominance. The analysis will pay attention to the scientific theory of evolution, that is to say, to the biological determinant of the human condition, as well as to humans' active involvement in their place in the framework of evolution. The latter issue may be linked to the science of social planning — social engineering, as some may call it — which is clearly guided by human norms. The interplay of these two issues may be discerned in both of the following works. Still, in the last resort, one represents an essentially resigned acceptance of the scientifically discovered imperatives of evolution, while the other may express humans' active involvement in assuring desirable progress.

Thus, the Wellsian imagination hovers between resignation and action, passive acquiescence and active design, determinism and freedom, evolution and resolution — even if he does not necessarily draw the line between these alternatives clearly and deliberately.

Contending with Evolution

Challenged by the theory of evolution, *Homo sapiens* could try to interfere with it and reap the benefits of such interference. As humans, though part and parcel of evolutionary process, are also the discoverers and formulators of this scientific perspective or even truth, does not this offer an opportunity, be it a slight one, to interfere in the process, manipulate and modify it, according to our chosen goals? Must evolution remain a theoretical, descriptive science, or can it be translated into scientifically-founded techniques, which would enable humans to use them to their own purpose and advantage? This is essentially the scientific problem which underlies Wells's novel, *The Island of Dr. Moreau* (1896).

The story itself strikes the reader as a tale of horror. Edward Prendick is shipwrecked and finds refuge on a small island in the Pacific Ocean. Prendick, a former student of the Royal College of Science, who did "some research in biology under Huxley"³— not an accidental name dropping by Wells — is rescued by Montgomery, a physician, and encounters Dr. Moreau, a biologist. Thus, biology is the common ground of the three Englishmen, which should establish some basic understanding among them. Yet, this proves far from being the case. For Moreau, who is in charge and exercises an unquestionable authority over the island, is a controversial figure.

A prominent physiologist, he was compelled to leave England on allegations of some cruel experimentation with live animals. Yet, committed to his scientific work, he engages in vivisection in his laboratory on the island, thereby driving the humane Prendick out of his wits. Eventually the latter discovers that the endeavor of Dr. Moreau is to convert various animals — apes, pigs, dogs — into human creatures. The result is creatures with quasi-human appearance and some human characteristics and behavior, but not fully human beings. Moreover, the various beast-people retain their specific animal traits: a swine-human differs from a dog-human. In their humanoid stage, the creatures are strictly ruled by Moreau, who is a kind of god to them.

This transmutation of species by ingenious, though cruel, techniques comes to an end with Dr. Moreau's death; he is killed by a wild puma on which he was experimenting. With his demise, though Prendick succeeds for some time to control the creatures, eventually Moreau's community disintegrates, and the various creatures gradually lose their human traits and revert to their original animal form and nature. Prendick, eventually back in England, lives under the cloud of his horrific experience. This is magnified by his sense of the possible degradation of humanity into some animal stage. "I feel as though the animal was surging up through them, that presently the degradation of the Islanders will be played over again on a larger scale."⁴ It may be a delusion, it may be a foresight. It is noteworthy that the sentiment expresses the forebodings of Huxley, above.

The conclusion, even if it points to Prendick's pessimistic view about the future stature of humanity, remains deliberately vague. No definitive and clearcut answer is provided, allowing the reader to muse about alternative developments. This approach characterizes the novel throughout. While Prendick, who presumably represents Wells, does not hide his attitude, Wells allows other points of view to be expressed, thus preserving a hidden dialogue within the story. The topics of this dialogue are the application of scientific techniques to biological organisms, the nature of evolution, and the consequent philosophy concerning the relationship of humans, nature, and the universe.

The application of scientific knowledge to humans, the use of biological and physiological discoveries for developing a technique for affecting or controlling living organisms, including people, is at least as old as the practice of medicine. However, developing a technology for the modification or transformation of living beings, let alone humanity, to a model transcending their nature, turning one being into another, changing a beast into a human, or human into a superhuman, is another matter. True, the idea of some kind of biological technology was explored in *Frankenstein*, as well as in *Dr. Jekyll and Mr. Hyde*, not to mention the early myth of Golem. Yet, to do so in the era of the theory of evolution, and in the context of evolutionary ideas, is in a way an even bolder step, for such a technique seems to become more feasible than in the thoughts of its crude precursors, and therefore its consequences more frightening. For humans to step out of the evolutionary chain and reorder it, is to play God. *Deus ex evolutione* may well aspire to become deus ex machina, resolving the perennial human tragedy, but it may also be the cause of just another tragic twist in the sad story of mankind.

Today we have a presentiment of such developments, in view of the transplantation of organs, cloning of sheep, and genetic manipulation. Some of the impending or actual techniques may be beneficial and life-saving; some may in the future facilitate biological control by an authority, benevolent or vicious, wise or foolish. An inkling of such problems is conveyed in Wells's story, which exposes the controversy concerning such practices. While these practices may be hypothetical or even fantastic, the fundamental issue and controversy remain relevant to date, and possibly more so in the future.

Dr. Moreau offers a cogent explanation of his experiments with animals, which he justifies as scientific procedures built on past precedents but systematized and anticipating greater achievements. Surgery has practiced the transplantation of skin from one part of the body to another. Grafting from one animal to another is also possible. From here to an attempt to change the nature of an animal by suitable surgical procedures is only another logical step. He sums it all up: "You begin to see that it is a possible thing to transplant tissue from one part of an animal to another, or from one animal to another, to alter its chemical reactions and methods of growth, to modify the articulations of its limbs, and indeed to change it in its most intimate structure."[5] Thus, the progress from established curative surgery to creative surgery, from people helping people to people creating people, is established. The creation of humanoid animals paves the way for active human participation in natural evolution.

Moreover, the physiological experimentation can be complemented by psychological molding. "A pig may be educated... In our growing science of hypnotism we find the promise of a possibility of replacing old inherent instincts by new suggestions, grafting upon or replacing old inherent instincts by new suggestions, grafting upon or replacing the inherited fixed ideas. Very much, indeed, of what we call moral education is such an artificial modification and perversion of instinct; pugnacity is trained into courageous self-sacrifice, and suppressed sexuality into religious emotion."[6] Dr. Moreau plays here with psychoanalytic concepts (formulated in the concluding years of the nineteenth century), but he not merely suggests them as explanatory principles of human mind, but insinuates the potential use of this scientific revelation for shaping the minds and conduct of humanoid creatures, and evidently of human beings. From the understanding of the mind to the manipulation of it is only a small step. And thus Moreau implants in his people-beasts certain fixed ideas which control their imagination. "They were really hypnotized, had been told certain things were impossible, and certain things were not to be done."[7]

The objections of Prendick are fundamentally the reactions of a decent civilized human being. As he cannot avoid hearing the screamings of the puma, which is vivisected by Dr. Moreau, he is driven out of his wits. The result was that "in spite of the brilliant sunlight and the green fans of the trees waving in the soothing sea breeze, the world was a confusion, blurred with drifting black and red phantasms."[8] This description insinuates — though it does not prove or even argue the point — that the natural world is pleasant and soothing, while human scientific interference is cruel and upsets the cosmic harmony.

Yet Moreau remains indifferent to Prendick's concern about the pain and suffering of the vivisected animals. Pain is for Moreau, the man of science, a minor issue in his pursuit of knowledge, or of the limits of applied science. In his own words: "Was this possible, or that possible? You cannot imagine what this means to an investigator, what an intellectual passion grows upon him. You cannot imagine the strange colorless delight of these intellectual desires. The thing before you is no longer an animal, a fellow-creature, but a problem."[9] The ethical consideration is deliberately disregarded by Dr. Moreau, who states, rather cynically: "The study of Nature makes a man at least as remorseless as Nature."[10] Prendick, alias Wells, taking the humane stance, cannot acquiesce with the amoral, or immoral, attitude — or the cruelty of nature, for that matter.

The opposition to the scientific technology of manipulating and shaping the living world finds its most emphatic expression if we interpret the story of Dr. Moreau's island as a parable of human society and human civilization. If the humanoid beasts turn into human beings, and the ape-humans, swine-humans, hyena-humans, turn into human beings displaying the traits of ape-like creatures, swinish types, and hyena characters, we face an even more repellent zoo. If it is human beings who can be manipulated, surgically or psychologically, into shapes desired by a godlike leader commanding the tools of modern science, we face a society on the verge of the extinction of its human characteristics, as we like to think of these. Thus, Wells seems to warn us against the menace of applied physiology and psychology — a warning eventually brought to perfection by Aldous Huxley. In a more concrete, but not less frightening way, the specter of the totalitarian state of the twentieth century, shaping people in its chosen image, rises from the island of Dr. Moreau.

However, the caution against applied, or misapplied, science is, in a way, reversed, when Wells casts doubts about its efficacy. For if the humanoids reverse to their beastly nature, and if Prendick seems to see in his fellow human beings in England "patient creatures waiting for prey,"[11] then there is no hope, not merely for improving the human species, but even from keeping it from sliding back to a lower, morally inferior, stage of evolution. The theory of evolution comes not only to lower the barriers between humans and other creatures, but actually destroys them, as humans respond to the call of the wild inside themselves. The great scientific discovery, the monumental theory of the century, only points to the disillusionment of humans with themselves. Wells, the enthusiast of science and the popularizer of knowledge, presents here a dismal picture of humanity and a futile effort of the scientist. Thus, humanity loses both ways — whether by interfering with evolution, or submitting to it.

This philosophy of disillusionment, incomprehension and despair is expressed in other ways in the novel. Thus, Montgomery, the alcoholic physician, puts it in a nutshell: "What's it all for, Prendick? Are we bubbles blown by a baby?"[12] And if this might be dismissed as raving, as Prendick does, here is his own conclusion. "A blind fate, a vast pitiless mechanism, seemed to cut and shape the fabric of existence, and I, Moreau (by his passion for research), Montgomery (by his passion for drink), the Beast People, with their instincts and mental restrictions, were torn and crushed, ruthlessly, inevitably, amid the infinite complexity of its incessant wheels.[13] Thus, neither quest for knowledge, nor addiction, nor the blind instinct and stupidity of the bulk of humanity (the Beast People), offer a solution to, or escape from, the grinding mechanism of the blind fate. Neither knowledge nor ignorance, neither wisdom nor stupidity, offer a way out. The mood of Ecclesiastes overwhelms any hope of purpose, any trust in knowledge.

Yet Wells offers us a ray of consolation. As Prendick withdraws from men and society, he still finds solace in wise books, which make life "lit by the shining souls of men." Then he studies astronomy, and finds some peace of mind there. "There is, though I do not know how there is or why there is, a sense of infinite peace and protection in the glittering hosts of heaven. There it must be, I think, in the vast and eternal laws of matter, and not in the daily cares and sins and troubles of men, that whatever is more than animal within us must find its solace and its hope."[14] The conclusion of hope is cautious and circumspect. It remains inexplicable. Yet, it offers something to clutch at. Humans, or some of them, are ultimately offered a way of escape from total despair, and it is an escape into scientific contemplation. Yet, this is not the science of humankind, nor the science of biology, nor knowledge of the laws of life. It is the inanimate world and its amazing laws of matter that is the stuff on which rational humans can lean. It is going back from the nineteenth century to the seventeenth century, from Darwin to Newton. In a strange way, Wells becomes here a materialistic mystic.

Accelerating Progress

If in *The Island of Dr. Moreau* the human effort to tamper with evolution fails, and evolution itself is marked by a regressive trend, *A Modern Utopia*, published in 1905, takes a reverse attitude. It is based on the assumption that evolution, as it applies to humans and society, points to improved conditions and institutions, to progress, and it considers the possibility of speeding up the process by a deliberate and willful human involvement. If the former book is horrific and gloomy, the latter is suffused with hope and optimism.

The literary form of *A Modern Utopia* is somewhat questionable. It is neither a tale of fiction, nor a systematic treatise on a perfect society, but a strange combination of the two. The story almost exclusively involves two men, one a botanist, who is an emotional man living in a world of his own romantic but hackneyed imagination, and another, the major character who is also the narrator, a man of an intellectual fancy and whose dream is presented as a cogent image of the good world, the utopia in question.

7—Evolution

The two men are on a vacation in the Swiss mountains, when they imperceptibly step into another world, a planet in the deeps of space, which happens to be an exact geographical parallel to the earth, but where human beings, technical facilities and social institutions are the embodiments of a much superior civilization.

The miraculous transition is a mere technical device, and the utopian world is eventually explained as the dream, a waking dream, of the narrator. Yet, its being a dream does not detract from its potency. For, when the botanist, at the conclusion of the utopian dream, comments, "It spoils the world of everyday to let your mind run on impossible perfections," the narrator reacts: "I wish I could *smash* the world of everyday." And he adds: "You may accept this as the world of reality—not I!"[15] Clearly the ideas which entail the potential of realization are more than a dream; they may become the new reality, the future reality. They are a good dream which can be realized. This clearly is the intent of Wells in propagating his ideas. Indeed, he puts it in an unambiguous way in "A Note to the Reader," when he says that his *Utopia* represents "a state of affairs at once possible and more desirable than the world in which I live.[16]

As the visitors from the earth to the parallel locations in Switzerland and London encounter the new civilization, the narrator outlines in vivid detail some of the material and social manifestations of the utopian world. Broadly speaking, it has to fulfill the notion of utopia, "where men and women are happy and laws are wise, and where all that is tangled and confused in human affairs has been unravelled and made right."[17] Yet, such a broad perception is common to all Utopias, and Wells points out that his design is different also in some of its basic assumptions.

One such assumption is that "the Modern Utopia must be not static but kinetic, must shape not as a permanent state but as a hopeful stage, leading to a long ascent of stages."[18] Unlike Plato's ideal state, and other designs for a perfect society which, when realized, would put an end to further development and improvement simply by having achieved perfection, Wells's acceptance of the evolutionary theory precludes the assumption of such a final station in human development. However perfect society may become, there is further improvement ahead of it.

Another assumption is that the utopia has to be worldwide, universal, for the simple reason that any good society, if geographically limited, may be threatened by less perfect and more bellicose neighbors. Thus, we are forced into one world, or a world state. A further corollary, perhaps not absolutely necessary, but preferred by Wells, is the establishment of a universal language, a coalescence of "a dozen once separate tongues."[19] Such unity of language will abolish the bar of misunderstanding and hostility, which has plagued multi-tongued humanity.

The utopian cities are clean and pleasant. People are civil. Local transportation is efficient. Transportation over long distance is fast and smooth, due to the very comfortable trains traveling at the speed of two hundred miles per hour. Accommodation is provided for all in clean and pleasant apartments, which are designed to be virtually self-cleaning by reducing adornment and introducing efficient designs and devices. Food is provided in communal kitchens. Rich people have the choice of having their own houses, but personal service is eliminated.

The cheap and efficient transportation and ubiquitous hotel accommodation facilitate geographical mobility. This fulfills two objectives. One is travel for enjoyment. Another is travel from one region to another as economic circumstances require: the unemployed in one country may easily move to another where working force is needed. Migration is not a hardship. It is a manifestation of the "loosening of the fetters of locality,"[20] and thus a new dimension of freedom is created for people, who are citizens of the world.

The problem of freedom touches on the issue of the relationship between the individual and the social organization, or the state. Wells deals with this problem in the context of the theory of evolution and the consequent, as already mentioned, kinetic nature of his utopia. It is the function of the world state to provide the foundation and the framework for individual initiative, which is the agent of progress. The state will provide a humanizing element to the otherwise ruthless competition for survival and domination. The state will assure everybody housing, nourishment, health protection, and education. Yet, it will be individuals who will introduce innovation in various spheres of life and thus offer a path to advancement and progress, which cumulatively will affect the entire society. "The factor that leads the World State on from one phase of development to the next is the interplay of individualities."[21] Thus, we have a welfare state, combined with individual ambition which, in turn benefits the progress of the state.

The management of the world, of humanity, involves more than securing welfare and facilitating initiative and competition. There is the problem of the rational and efficient use of the workforce. As noted above, geographical mobility and abolition of borders will facilitate the mobility of labor. The allocation of workers requires indexing humanity and classifying it with regard to professions, health, crime, etc. Such central information about each individual will make it easy to send people where they may be needed. This need not be seen as policing the people by a sinister authority, for the government will be well intentioned, and must not be seen as intrinsically inimical to human freedom. The indexing of the world population, with thumb-marks if necessary, is a matter of administrative efficiency.

The functions of the state naturally include the protection of society from undesirable elements, such as lunatics, cheats, and drunkards. Such misfits are to be removed from the community to a variety of secluded islands, each with its own kind of misfits, where they can lead an autonomous existence. This is more humane than prison and in no way a vindictive policy: it only protects society from incurable asocial elements. These kind of people are forbidden to have children, so as not to increase the numbers of misfits.

Indeed, the restrictions on propagation imposed by the state go much further. For it is the function of the state or its government to assist natural selection, to design a guided selection of the fittest, by restraining the birth of inferior humanity and encouraging the natural increase of superior human types. Wells is not in principle opposed to eugenics, but, realizing the complexity of individual genetic antecedents, he is satisfied with following some general guidelines for preferential breeding, namely the evidence of successful and productive life and accomplished personality. Indeed, this approach is based on the assumption of human inequality, which is manifest in the division of humanity into four categories.

Wells, or his protagonist, divides humanity according to four "temperaments": the Poietic, the Kinetic, the Dull and the Base. Such classification is considered preferable to occupational or social-class differentiation. The Poietic types are creative people — in whatever field of endeavor. The Kinetic are intelligent and efficient organizers and executives — whether in administration or research. Unlike the Poietic, they are not innovators. The Dull are the stupid, the incompetent, the imitative. The Base may be any of the former three categories, though most likely the third one. They are essentially morally flawed — narrow-minded, devious, overly egoistic, sometimes cruel. The dividing lines between these groups are not always clear. Nor are these classes self-perpetuating. Yet the society at large, and the state, want to increase the numbers of the first two classes — essential, respectively, for innovation and progress, and for good management of public affairs — and to reduce the numbers of the last two. This can be gradually achieved, as many of the Dull will fall below the income level which is required for having children, and presumably many of the Base will find themselves in the prison islands, where no procreation is allowed.

Thus, by accepting the social reality, which points to the inequality of humans, and by imposing suitable laws, the state lends a helping hand to the natural evolutionary process. Indeed, it not only helps evolution, but humanizes and civilizes the process. "The method of Nature ... is to degrade, thwart, torture, and kill the weakest and least adapted members of every species in existence in each generation...; the ideal of a scientific civilization is to prevent those weaklings being born."[22]

The actual running of the world state and the various institutions and establishments is done by the samurai — a kind of self-perpetuating elite. It is the involvement and work of the samurai which over a few hundred years achieved the utopia, and did it by a social evolutionary process. The samurai, though a distinctive class, are not jealous of their position and status, nor do they wish to exclude others from participating in public affairs. They may be somewhat similar to the class of Guardians in Plato's *Republic*, but they are volunteers, and accept "any intelligent adult in a reasonably healthy and efficient state" to become one of them, "and take a hand in the universal control."[23]

Still, the samurai have certain distinctive traits in common. They are concerned not only with their own individual well-being, important as such concern may be. They go beyond it, and work for some impersonal interest to which they are dedicated. This is natural to humans in general, but has often been wasted on destructive activity, such as patriotic conflicts or religious controversy. In the case of the samurai, their idealism (as we would put it) is devoted to the "good of the society." To assure their faithful work, they must adhere to certain strict rules. They must take care of their health, including cold baths in the regimen. They are forbidden tobacco, alcohol and narcotic drugs. They eat no meat, like the rest of the population. They are not engaged in commerce (exchange of goods for money), though they may engage in manufacturing industries and are occasionally, but not typically, rich. Essentially, money must not become the focus of their interest. Women samurai must keep to rather simple dress and not concentrate on alluring appearance. Samurai women must also choose to bear children, to promote selective breeding.

The samurai not only fill public offices and vital professions, but are the only voters, except for the supreme legislative assembly where some seats are reserved for members outside the select order.

Thus, Wells, like Plato, is not an enthusiast of democracy. In utopia, "the tendency is to give a practically permanent tenure to good men."[24] Yet this meritocracy must not be confused with a tendency of the class to perpetuate its elite status and its grip on power. For anyone, subject to the rules of conduct, can join the samurai, and thus the caste has been increasing, "and may indeed assimilate almost the whole population of the earth."[25] Meritocracy may become democracy, if and when all the people are meritorious. Yet the crucial factor for political participation is not popular *will*, but individual *merit*.

Interestingly enough, the samurai are not only concerned with social issues and public responsibilities and the rational and efficient management of human affairs. They have also a religious life, which essentially belongs to their private feelings, to their personal relationship to God. This religion must not be linked to any cult — no altars, music, incense; it is some kind of a mystical experience, without human organization or a collective church. Yet it gets state encouragement in the form of a requirement that each *samurai* devote one week a year to solitary withdrawal into some wilderness. This kind of mystical requirement, as one is tempted to characterize it, is rather odd in view of Wells's overall rationalism, but it testifies to his acknowledgement of spiritual dimensions which transcend simple reason and pure logic.

Having presented an outline of *A Modern Utopia*, let us focus on the elements of technology and science in Wells's work. These features, whether already noted or not, will be highlighted, and a direct assessment of their role in his scheme will be made. While some manifestations of these factors are obvious, others may be implied and hidden, but their significance is in no way diminished thereby.

Wells puts great store in technology and its potential impact on the mode of human life. He expects a steady increase in reliance on mechanical power and consequent "emancipation of men from the necessity of physical labour. There appears no limit to the invasion of life by the machine."[26] He welcomes such an invasion, for he prefers people to engage freely in artistic production, say, than be obliged to toil for sustenance. Technology is an emancipating force, which may facilitate such choice.

We have noted the convenient transportation system and accommodation facilities in Utopia. Wells enlarges on the technical provisions, which secure convenience while reducing work. There is no fire place in the hotel lodgings, but there is a thermometer and six switches to heat floor, walls and mattress, according to one's wishes — as close an approximation to a thermostat as Wells's imagination could get. He elaborates on doors and windows impervious to draft, and mentions shafts for soiled towels. The principle followed is the use of technology and rational arrangement for the ease of getting one's basic needs.

Wells is aware of the criticism of the mechanical aspects of industrial civilization, which often contrasts the beauty of nature with the ugly face of mechanical devices, which opposes art to engineering. While he admits the actual ugliness of the contemporary scene, he vehemently denies the notion of an inherent connection between technology and absence of aesthetic consideration, and points to little difference between utopian and terrestrial engineering. He elaborates: "The tramway, the train road, the culverts and bridges ... will all be beautiful things." For "in utopia a man who designs a tram road will be a cultivated man, an artist craftsman... He will make his girders and rails and parts as gracious as that first engineer, Nature, has made the stems of her plants and the joints and gestures of her animals."[27] Artifact and nature, human design and natural surroundings, innovative technology and the perennial setting of man, can coexist in perfect harmony, and humanity can benefit from both.

Technology in utopia will not just happen, or be left to the chance of invention of some ingenious eccentric, on the assumption that "fools make researches and wise men exploit them." Technology and scientific research which may be applied to human needs must be pursued systematically and public institutions provided to facilitate such experiments and inquiries. "Bacon's visionary House of Salomon will be a thing realised, and it will be humming with business."[28] Wells pays tribute to a utopian precursor, and — need one point out?—clearly foresees things to come.

The factor of science, or rather of scientific theory, impinges on Wells's utopia in another, more fundamental way. Utopia, by its very nature, aims at a design of a perfect society and an ideal world. Yet such a design, however perfect and beautiful, can have no claim on science. It is merely a wishful dream, whose realization is not contained in its nature, nor made probable or plausible in any other way. When the prophet announces that the peoples of the world "shall beat their swords into plowshares, and their spears into pruninghooks" and that "nation shall not lift up sword against nation" (Isaiah 2:4), he offers no scientific evidence of the realization of the prophecy. It must be taken on trust. For that matter, if Plato, Thomas More, or Francis Bacon present their versions of the perfect state or community, there is nothing in their design to assure its realization. The implementation of utopia depends on human resolution, will, capacity.

7—Evolution

This is not the case of Wells's utopia. For, as he puts it, it is a kinetic utopia, and the kinetic element is linked to the scientific theory of evolution, or the theory of evolution transplanted to and adjusted for the evolving of human society. If the social evolution is a continuous development toward an ever-improving society, and if such a development is built into the nature of things, into the nature of the human society, then progress is as inevitable in human society as the survival of the fittest is in the realm of biology. Yet, while Wells seems committed — at least in this stage of his writing — to this stance, he does not discard his own ethical notions of a civilized human. He cannot simply identify himself with the cruel biological or social contest and see himself and humanity as merely a stage between a lower and a higher level of success and form of existence. He realizes the nature of the objective process, but he extends a helping hand, provides a guiding light.

In the first place, Wells wants to make the process kinder and gentler, without however interfering with its basic aim and nature. His utopia provides guidance for a humane evolution, for a charitable way for the survival of the fittest, or rather the best. (For the social evolution itself seems to be guided by human-social, rather than purely biological, objectives.) The utopian state makes provisions for all, but within this framework individuals compete, and thus push society forward to ever higher levels of accomplishment and perfection.

Moreover, Wells wants to improve and accelerate the ways of social progress by assuring the formation of suitable elites to work on this kinetic process. The samurai are the moving force of social evolution, and harnessing their energy and initiative to the objectives of evolution makes its progress smooth and easy. Thus, in the last resort, humans cooperate with nature, civilization works along with the laws of biology (or bio-sociology), will helps necessity.

Ingenious as this approach is, the question may be raised whether it makes sense. Wells clearly intends to be scientific in relying so heavily on the theory of evolution, but is it good science? Indeed, it can be argued that we face here not definitive scientific conclusions, but merely a scientific theory. The Darwinian notions of evolution transposed and adjusted to social development raise some serious problems. As is well known, evolution as a biological process works at a very slow pace, whereas social evolution is incomparably faster, if indeed it occurs at all. Wells himself makes the samurai achieve the modern utopia over a few hundred years. This may appear rather slow by historical standards, especially when technological changes are involved; yet it is extremely rapid when compared with slight biological changes in, say, the class of Mammalia. Thus, social change becomes an evolution sui generis. As such, its validity cannot be compared with or inferred from Darwin's biological evolution.

Once such a speculation is degraded from the level of a substantiated scientific theory, it becomes open to questions and doubts on various scores. What is a good, or a better, society? What are the yardsticks of progress? What is the foundation, in the first place, for assuming social advancement? Perhaps society advances and deteriorates in cycles, perhaps it degenerates and declines. Indeed, as we have seen in *The Island of Dr. Moreau*, Wells himself had doubts about the progress of humankind at one stage of his intellectual exploration. Such doubts again clouded his mind as he aged into the catastrophic decades of the twentieth century. (He died in 1946.)

To sum up the issue, it can be concluded that even if the idea of social evolution is a questionable scientific theory, it was believed by Wells, at the time of writing about his utopia, to be a valid theory. For we must bear in mind the powerful influence of Darwin's theory on socio-historical speculations. It may also be apposite to recall that Hegel's and Marx's explanation of history relied on theories or philosophies of historical progress, which leads from "lower" to "higher" levels, and culminates in one or another kind of utopian fulfillment, even if not called so by name. To explain is not to justify, but it helps to understand the shortcomings of a sincere thinker.

If Wells can be criticized for his affiliation with the theories of social evolution, he can be lauded for his incisive analytical examination of some important aspects of human society and of the widespread misunderstanding and misinterpretation of these aspects. As a common-sense analytical sociologist he displays considerable scientific acumen. This becomes evident from his observations when building his utopia, as further exemplified.

Wells deliberately and consciously points to sociology as the discipline which provides the understanding of social grouping and the emotional attitude related to social divisions. In his own words: "The study of aggregations and of the ideals of aggregations ... is the legitimate definition of sociology...."[29] Unfortunately, sociology is open to abuse, due to common bias of people who, without foundation, generalize and attribute all kinds of deficiencies and flaws to "others," whether they are working people, Hindus, French citizens, etc. Such blatant misjudgment even assumes scientific authority when racist theories come into the picture, each race claiming for itself superiority over other races and justifying imperial rule over others in the name of such principles. Wells points to the actual mixture of various European races, and rejects the claims of one nation or race to rule over others as manifestations of prejudice and pride. For, to put the sociological deviation of humanity in the broadest terms, "crude classifications and false generalizations are the curse of all organized human life."[30]

Therefore the politician in utopia "must be a sociologist," that is to say, a true follower of the science of society. Yet the politician's commitment must be not merely theoretical, but also and foremostly practical. Sociology becomes an applied science, as the tasks of "sociologist-statesman" are defined. Politicians must study the "science of aggregations" to promote the world state, or the unity of humankind, and must devote themselves to overcoming the divisions of humanity and the effacement of divisive ideas which promote prejudice.[31]

Though the goal of the "sociologist-statesman" is to oppose the divisions of mankind and to strive for its unity — one state, one language — the sociology of utopia is not doctrinally committed to the abolition of all human aggregation. We have to bear in mind the samurai caste, as well as the division into the four types of humanity — Poietic, Kinetic, Dull and Base. The Wellsian sociology does not ignore differences, which it regards as objective, or organization, which it sees as beneficial. It objects to divisions which are patently based on mistaken assumptions, such as racial prejudice, and to divisions which enhance strifes and wars, such as nationalism.

Bold and perceptive as Wells's sociology is, it can be argued that it is guilty of at least one mistake. Blaming nationalism for warfare — justly and prophetically, as the two world wars following his *Modern Utopia* show — he may have prescribed a cure which is too radical, as well as impractical. One can envisage a world consisting of various nationalities, each nation speaking its own language and adhering to its own culture, which overcome their political and military aggressiveness and coexist in peace. Western and Central Europe today offer such an example. The demand from nations to disregard their cultural traditions and group-identity, and merge with the rest of humanity, seems to contradict some deep sentiments and emotional attachment. It may prove as impractical as it is undesirable. One must bear in mind that though nationalism has been a major factor in international strife, wars have been waged also between non-nationalist aggregates — religious wars, dynastic wars, even civil wars.

The most audacious application of scientific approach in Wells's utopia is resorting to reason and logic, the fundamental tools of science, for the design of a perfect society. This, indeed, is not peculiar to Wells, for every utopia as a literary genre is based on a design, claiming to be rational, of an ideal state or society. Wells follows this pattern, but his attention to the many facets of the good society and to various details is perhaps an exceptional testimony to a scientific design.

There is no point of reiterating, or enlarging on, the various facets of the utopia which reveal the rational design, or the intent of rational design, of its author. Transportation, housing, city planning, social organization, government, are all meant to be the product of careful rational reflection and planning. The limitations of people and their aspirations, economic needs and individuality, material conditions and spiritual yearning, are among the issues touched upon and resolved in a rational, "scientific" way. Indeed, reason is the ultimate arbiter of every institution and established practice.

This approach would be expected to produce perfect results. The design being rational and scientific, it ought to bring as good consequences as people can possibly expect. Yet, as one reads *Modern Utopia*, one encounters a variety of projections which do not awake one's enthusiasm, and some which one may find outright objectionable. This may well be a matter of personal opinion and individual sentiment. Yet, the fact that such attitudes can be raised against Wells's utopia, indicates that the scientific validity of various elements in his design is not above reasonable doubt. A few examples will illustrate the point.

We have already expressed doubts about the sacrifice of national identity, as well as language and culture, for the sake of world unity — a high, and neither necessary nor necessarily effective, price for peace. Promotion of geographical mobility for an effective distribution of the working force may be economically sound, but it undermines local ties to community and environment, an imponderable asset for emotional gratification and social stability. The political institutions which greatly limit popular participation, while entrusting all the responsibility to an elite, could meet with a sympathetic response from Plato, but with reservations from Aristotle, who, while favoring a political elite, remained attentive to the need of all the people to express their will in political institutions. Needless to say, Wells's constitutional design runs contrary to contemporary democratic sentiments — which does not necessarily prove him wrong.

Wells imposes cold baths on the samurai, to mention an oddity. Was it a puritanical streak, or spartan atavism? Perhaps he was not aware that the Japanese, from whom he borrowed the name for his elite, were taking daily *hot* baths. On the other hand, Wells shows blatant disregard for tradition and good taste when he replaces "the squat temple boxes of the Greek" with architecture relying on "steel and countless new materials." The utopian town buildings "will have flung great arches and domes of glass..., the slender beauty of the perfect metal-work."[32]

The obvious limitations of the above examples, and many more that could be adduced, are that they are not scientific, though they are intended to be so. Wells's various proposals and designs may be criticized as expressing no more than their author's opinion, sentiment, or bias. Architecture which is entirely modernistic or futuristic, and detached from some established and cherished forms, may deprive us of a certain dimension of aesthetic enjoyment. London emptied of old and distinguished buildings, including the "temple boxes of the Greek," may be aesthetically poorer, even if glistening in steel and glass.

The crux of the issue is that a good many of the utopian innovations of Wells offer a simplistic rational response or design to matters which are too intricate in nature to allow such facile solutions. It is not reason or science which are flawed here, but their inadequate sophistication. Aesthetic judgment is one example of such simplistic approach. Attachment of people to place and community, to national identity and culture, is another manifestation of very complex feelings which ought to be taken into consideration by any rational designer of an ideal world order. Humans, in social attachments, in historical awareness, in emotional experience, cannot be manipulated by a simplistic, seemingly rational design. If they are, the design may fail for having ignored the intricacy of the human mind. Or, if it succeeds, it may create a paradise which is not human, and therefore amounting to the very opposite of a utopia. Such a false paradise was depicted by Aldous Huxley in *The Brave New World*.

Having said this, one need not disparage the efforts of Wells and others to design a utopia. For they express an urge to repair the state of human affairs, which certainly could do with improvement. They may even contain many correct and sensible — in a way, "scientific" — proposals, which offer solutions to grave problems and deserve support. Moreover, where they fail, or appear to us to fail, they can provoke criticism and become a catalyst to a new and better-founded proposal in one matter or another, based on a better argument, deeper understanding and more sophisticated human and social science.

8

Mind Control

While the idea of interfering with, manipulating, or controlling the human mind by a deliberate human action was entertained in such stories as Stevenson's *Dr. Jekyll and Mr. Hyde* and H.G. Wells's *The Island of Dr. Moreau*, this notion came into full bloom later in the twentieth century under the impact of various psychological theories, experiments and practices. In other words, the development of psychology as a science, both theoretical and applied, gave rise to works of fiction in which this new discipline was accorded a major, or even a central, place. The possibility, real or imagined, of applying the techniques of the new science to human and social situations, and even to the human condition, challenged the imagination of some writers, and produced some ingenious results.

The new psychology, as distinguished from the philosophical speculations about the human mind, whether in ancient Greece or in modern Europe, was not satisfied with enumerating and explaining the basic faculties of the mind and the actual or desirable relationship among them. The new schools of psychology did not deal with the issue of the confrontation of reason with emotion. Nor did they dwell on the various sentiments with which humans are endowed. They were not satisfied with the simple, perhaps simplistic, distinction between good and evil impulses in people, so central to the monotheistic religions. The new science, as it claimed to be, ventured to go deeper and unravel the inner mechanism of the working of the human mind, the basic laws and principles according to which people act and behave, which underlie and can explain the manifestations of reasoning, feeling, and judging. It tried to turn the human mind and behavior into a legitimate, explorable and explicable field of inquiry.

Once this was accomplished, it was only natural to expect that factual findings and their theoretical explanation could lead to the application of scientific conclusions to human problems — whether problems of individual people, or problems of human society. Once the human mind and its working was well understood, any problems related to human behavior could be addressed, and conceivably resolved or set right. Understanding of human psychology would be the key to solving the issues, big and small, temporary or perennial, of humankind. If people were the agents — witting or unwitting — of their own misery, once they understood themselves, they could get rid of their predicaments.

As we know, this was a tall order and these were great expectations. Psychology, skeptics may argue, is not, strictly speaking, a science. There are various psychological theories, often incompatible with each other. Psychology of one kind or another may have offered important insights into the human mind, but it is far from providing a comprehensive and scientifically founded picture of the working of the mind, and the reflection and expression of such working in communal, social, and political conduct. Despite new findings and new insights, humans, to a large extent, remain a mystery to themselves.

Yet, despite epistemological reservations and even doubts, modern psychology has established its niche among the scientific disciplines. Moreover, it has applied its theoretical conclusions to the treatment of specific practical problems, such as the treatment of various mental disorders, or improving training and teaching techniques. These two fields are, indeed, vast areas of activity comprising great numbers of clinical practitioners, as well as educational approaches, especially those addressed to early years of training. The reliance on certain psychological techniques in commercial advertising and in political propaganda is well known.

Bearing in mind the theoretical claims of psychology, and the practical application of the new science, it is not surprising that writers with the power of imagination would see great potential for resorting to psychological techniques for objectives transcending their actual usage. They already had real examples for applying psychology to political objectives in the Soviet Union and Nazi Germany, and their fictional conclusions were in some cases an enlargement or extrapolation of ugly experiences into even more nightmarish scenarios. Yet, not all saw in the psychological techniques a sinister means. Psychology could also be used for human well-being and for harmonious social relations. The understanding of the human mind and behavior, like the understanding of various domains of reality revealed by science, could be used for good and for ill. One way or another, here seemed to be a new powerful means placed in the hands of humankind.

The conclusions reached by various writers focusing on psychological means — psychological technology — may well have been exaggerated. For one thing, people in authority and power resort to an unrestricted reliance on psychology less consistently and persistently, and perhaps not as imaginatively, as some writers of fiction suggest. They try it for some time, but then regimes and fashions change, and a modicum of common sense and decency takes over. Also, psychological techniques have proved so far to be less perfect and less efficient than originally believed. Some people retain their own independent judgment despite, and in total disregard for, propaganda and advertisement. Some individuals have refused to be psychologically controlled by totalitarian regimes, and some refrain from consuming Coca-Cola after half a century of advertising. Not all people can be fooled all the time, or even most of the time.

Still, even if creative writers exaggerated the power of psychological techniques, they pointed to the entelechy of the processes they had witnessed. The techniques did not proceed to the goal set for them all the way, but they did go a considerable way, and they threatened to go further. This was the case of the sinister goal, as well as that of the well-intended aim, which could turn sinister too. The writers saw the threats or promises which the experience had suggested.

This chapter will examine three books in which psychological techniques play a major role (even if some other aspects of science and technology, as well as scientific social organization, may complement the picture). One was written by a prominent psychologist, of a certain school, another by a prominent novelist and essayist, and the third by one of the most distinguished philosophers and mathematicians of the twentieth century. In their literary art they obviously differ. So they do in the appreciation of psychology. The attitude of the psychologist to psychology is, not surprisingly, positive — even enthusiastic. The attitude of the other two is anything but rapturous.

Behavioral Engineering

"Behavioral engineering" is not my ironic invention, a metaphor intended to point to the inner incongruity of molding human conduct with techniques usually applied to inanimate matter or mechanical inventions. "Behavioral engineering" is a phrase deliberately used, without the slightest doubt as to its propriety, by B.F. Skinner in his utopian novel *Walden Two* (1948). The fundamental idea conveyed in this phrase is that it is possible to shape human conduct and thereby assure human happiness through the rational and skillful management of society and the psychological control of the mental development of individuals. Daring as such an approach must sound, it is in the nature of utopias that they constitute bold intellectual forays.

The title of the book is clearly and intentionally chosen for its linkage with Henry David Thoreau and his Walden experience and testimony in *Walden; or Life in the Woods* (1854). In the words of Frazier, Skinner's spokesman in the novel, and the founder of the community known as "Walden Two," "We chose our name in honor of Thoreau's experiment."[1] If Thoreau's was an *individual* attempt to withdraw from society and live close to nature, Walden Two is a *communal* detachment from the surrounding world, and aims at creating a model for society at large. Thus, in a sense, the two Waldens are worlds apart. Moreover, Thoreau was primarily a poet, while Skinner was an experimental psychologist; the accomplishment of the former primarily depends on intuition, while the work of the latter is strictly connected to rational analysis. Still, both looked for the realization of an ideal.

The story in Skinner's novel is recounted in the first person by Burris, a professor of psychology, who — accompanied by a philosophy department colleague (Castle) and two younger couples — pays a visit of a few days to Walden Two. This is a community of one thousand people, planned and established by Frazier, once a fellow graduate student with Burris. The substance of the book, only thinly intertwined with the actions of the various persons, is a description of how the community works, accompanied by a fierce discussion of the principles involved, chiefly between Castle and Frazier.

The community is a cooperative venture. The members are all required to work, and they have an equal share in the fruits of their labor, as well as in enjoying the collective amenities of the community. The working hours are adjusted to the kind of work performed: pleasant work is accorded more working hours, while unpleasant labor has a reduced load. Thus, all necessary functions are fulfilled without coercion: people choose between more hours on the job they like, against less leisure time, or more leisure time at the cost of harder labor. The accommodation is modest but adequate. Women are equal with men, and their child-rearing duties are relieved by a communal arrangement for child care, and the accommodation of babies and children in collective dormitories. Beside the labor-saving advantages, this strengthens the community ties, as all the adult members develop affection for all the children, even though family ties are not abolished.

All these provisions are clearly reminiscent of the kibbutz, a form of cooperative settlement in Israel preceding the establishment of the state, though continuing after the achievement of political independence. One can also discern echoes of platonic communism in *Walden Two*. Curiously enough, Skinner makes no reference to the kibbutz, possibly because this distinctive experiment in communal living didn't get the attention of scholarly studies until a few years later. Then, there is a difference of focus between the kibbutz movement and Walden Two. The former aimed at the realization of socialist and national ideals, while the latter is concerned with the efficiency of economic performance, happiness, and harmonious human relations. There is an overlapping of the two philosophies, but they are not identical.

Walden Two elaborates on the efficiency of communal life and functions, starting with the architectural plans and ending with serving tea in high glasses, each glass in a kind of basket, one of the advantages being that it will not spill. Though some of the details are bizarre, and many are tedious, the purpose of the author seems to be to convince the reader of the practical significance of such arrangements, which result in increased comfort and reduction of labor at the same time. Indeed, the inhabitants of Walden Two work, on the average, only four hours a day. Women's participation in the workforce, facilitated by collective child care, is of great help in this respect. The short workday facilitates all kinds of leisure activities, including classical music, scientific pursuits and the like.

A community, even though it is essentially apolitical and withdraws from the affairs of the national society and avoids its ways, needs its own governing or managing institutions. Walden Two has a Board of Planners, consisting of six persons, usually half of them men and half women. Their term of office is restricted to ten years. While the planners are in charge of the community, its outside relations and some judicial functions, the diverse day-to-day functions are in the hands of trained specialists, who are the managers. There are plenty of these, heading such services and enterprises, as health, supply, education, arts, and diverse industries. The managers, being professionals, are not elected. Nor are the planners elected by the members: they are coopted by the Board from candidates suggested by the managers.

Thus, Walden Two dispenses with internal democratic institutions — unlike the *kibbutzim*. The platonic notions of the rule of the knowledgeable seem to have won the day, though the community is ruled not by philosophers, but by technocrats. Significantly, the planners and the managers, though exercising control over the community, and thus forming a kind of elite, enjoy no special benefits, economic or other. If anything, they carry a heavy burden, and eventually become ordinary citizens again. Thus, despite the absence of popular will expressed in elections, the basic equality within the community is preserved.

The general well-being and sense of economic security, coupled with the absence of competition motivated by the quest of economic gain, make Walden Two residents happy and satisfied. The long leisure hours enable people to pursue artistic and other interests in an active way. "Walden Two has demonstrated very nicely that as soon as the simplest necessities of life are obtained with little effort, there's an enormous welling up of artistic interest." Similarly, scientific interests persist. For while the scientist may be thinking of the needs of others, "his own motives are clearly cultural."[2] Thus, the utopian community, while satisfying material needs, and avoiding wasted energy and effort for the superfluous creation of wealth and its attendant ills, facilitates cultural progress in its limitless diversity of expression.

The story virtually ends with the conclusion of the visit to Walden Two by the inquisitive outsiders. Of the six people of the party, one young couple is enchanted with the community and the prospective ease of starting their married life in the cooperative setting, and decides to join. Another young couple is divided and does not join. The philosophy professor, critical throughout the visit, is not convinced of the overall worth of the experiment upon leaving the place. The narrator, Professor Burris, hesitating throughout the visit, makes his way to Walden Two again, leaving his college and academic career for good.

What is the place of science in the scheme of *Walden Two*? In what way does the scientific approach make its impact on the design and working of Skinner's utopia? It is clear that the fundamental idea and its translation into institutions and practice are guided — deliberately and emphatically — by rational thinking and science. Strictly speaking, it is the *application* of reason and scientific findings to the needs of humans and society which is relied upon. For it is applied, practical science that Frazier, alias Skinner, is interested in. It is noteworthy that such applied science is used not to cure undesirable situations, but to construct a perfect, or as nearly perfect as feasible, society. The reason for such use is inherent in the construction of a utopia, which designs the good community in contrast to the criticized reality, but does not suggest how to change what *is* into what *ought to be*, save by presenting the model of the good community to potential converts.

One way in which reason is resorted to is in applying strictly rational, and thus scientific, principles to the organization of the community in all its aspects. This applies to such trivial issues as the "engineered tea service" referred to above, which is perfected after "application of scientific method" to the problem of efficiency in serving this function.[3] The use of these terms is characteristic of Skinner's penchant for addressing every problem in a scientific manner and for engineering an improvement. A staggered schedule for meals (in the communal eating rooms), for bathroom use, for entertainment, is another "amazing piece of cultural engineering." The benefit is that the community can "get along with limited installations quite conveniently." This is, as we would put it today, cost-effective: "Our equipment is used fifteen or eighteen hours a day without undue hardship." And if this sounds like turning life into a factory, operated in shifts, Frazier assures us of the psychological benefits of his system, which avoids uniformity, with everyone "doing the same thing at the same time."[4] Pedestrian as all this engineering may appear, it has clear benefits for the community.

The social design, the cooperative egalitarian community, a grand-scale engineering of society, has much deeper influence on social relations and on individual peace of mind. For it makes certain well-established emotions all but obsolete. Thus, jealousy, related to competitive struggle in traditional society, is withering away in a cooperative community. Jealousy fulfilled a useful function in human evolution — especially by promoting competition and progress. Yet jealousy is an unsettling emotion and to get rid of it without harm to social progress is a clear advantage. In a cooperative society there is no individual struggle for existence, and therefore "there's no need for jealousy." A rational, scientific social organization promotes the mental comfort of the members of the community. Rational organization promotes, inter alia, psychological benefits.[5]

Skinner also links his utopia to science in another way. As is well known, the nature of modern science, at least in many of its domains, is predominantly experimental. This is usually pointed out when comparing it with the largely speculative science of ancient Greece. A characteristic of experimental science is that it does not reach absolute, final conclusions, but is always ready to enlarge knowledge and modify practice based on such knowledge, by new findings and discoveries. This must not be confused with scientific relativism — a liberal acceptance of diversity of truths on matters pursued by scientific inquiry. Science is in pursuit of strict truth, and applied science is committed to acting on the scientific findings at any stage of scientific endeavor. However, as scientific conclusions change, due to new experience or experiment, the application of science will change accordingly.

Walden Two consciously and emphatically takes this scientific attitude into consideration. This becomes evident in seemingly minor matters, as well as in issues concerning the very soul of the utopia. In commenting on what we would call an efficiency-analysis project by some community members, concerning the tea service, which brought useful, practical results, Frazier says: "The actual achievement is beside the point. The main thing is, we encourage our people to view every habit and custom with an eye to possible improvement. A constantly experimental attitude toward every thing — that's all we need."[6] Thus, the minor improvement, based on a technical trial and its scientific evaluation, serves as a model and symbol for a constant and widespread application of systematic reasoning toward every habit and custom. Social usages established in Walden Two are not merely rationally justified, but are continuously subject to further improvement with the help of scientific reasoning.

Scientific research proper is supported by the community, too. "Experiments are in progress in plant and animal breeding, the control of infant behavior, educational processes of several sorts, and the use of some of our raw materials."[7] The choice of fields is clearly weighed in favor of the practical needs of the community, and pure science is notably absent. Significantly, besides material concerns — use of materials and improvement in breeding — applied psychology and its educational corollaries are singled out. This is not surprising in view of Skinner's professional interest and commitment. More about this aspect of *Walden Two* will follow.

Frazier attributes utopian failures mainly to communities' unscientific approach. They were established on religious belief, or on a philosophical notion of perfection. "The community wasn't set up as a real experiment, but to put certain principles into practice." It "was usually a matter of revealed truth and not open to experimental modification."[8] It is the notion of experimental science which must be the guide of Walden Two. To be sure, the community was planned, and did not emerge out of nothing, out of a social tabula rasa. Frazier admits that he conceived and created Walden Two. Yet such a creation was not intended to be a final and unalterable design, but a process, subject to development. In his words: "I did not plan Walden Two — not as an architect plans a building, but as a scientist plans a longterm experiment." Thus, if in one sense Walden Two is predetermined, in another sense it remains adjustable and improvable with the help of the active intelligence of its members.[9] The experimental social science and engineering retain their importance in the utopian society.

By far the most prominent and most startling application of science in Skinner's utopia is manifest in the field of psychology and education, or, strictly speaking, in the application of certain psychological techniques to educational purposes. Here Skinner relies on his own experience as an experimental psychologist, and expresses his belief in the power of psychological techniques to shape and control human behavior.

The principle resorted to is fairly simple and well known. In order to make people — in this case primarily children — behave in a desired way, one has to associate such behavior with a pleasant sensation or experience. "When he [a person] behaves as we want him to behave, we simply create a situation he likes, or remove one he doesn't like... Technically it's called 'positive reinforcement.'"[10] Frazier prefers encouragement of desirable behavior to discouragement of undesirable conduct (punishment), even if the latter has historically been relied upon. To be sure, the psychological training of children may not be devoid of certain hardships, as youngsters are trained to self-control and discipline by being deprived of pleasures, unless abiding by certain rules which are intended for individual and social benefit. All this "ethical training" is completed by the age of six. Evidently, psychological experience puts a premium on early training. As children grow up, they require less and less supervision, as they will have acquired the capacity of self-control. Consequently, they are happy by having been saved from temptation, and the society benefits by the reduction, or even elimination, of unruly and antisocial behavior. For clearly, the ethical engineers educate their wards in accordance with beneficial principles.

All this is the task of the science of behavior which relies on techniques "which will shape the behavior of the members of a group so that they will function smoothly for the benefit of all."[11] The vision of such a science, not yet perfected, informs Frazier's innermost hopes. Indeed, he even speaks of controlling people's temperament and designing personalities. Shaping people to specifications and cultivation of special abilities is also foreseen — producing mathematicians, artists and the like.[12] In his zeal for psychological engineering of human responses, Frazier uses even an example from religious ethics to make his point. Here is his interpretation of the teaching of Jesus to love one's enemies. The famous injunction, according to Frazier, was "a psychological invention for easing the lot of an oppressed people." The suffering induced by the impotent rage at the loss of freedom and subjection to oppression is reduced by practicing the opposite emotion of love. Thus the love of enemies becomes a psychological device to reduce one's suffering.

"What Jesus offered in return for loving one's enemies was heaven on earth, better known as peace of mind."[13]

The moral imperative aimed at the relationships among human beings, whatever one may think of its validity, turns into a psychological device contrived for the release of mental anguish.

While Frazier, or Skinner, may have scored a point in indicating the psychological benefit from the Christian attitude under certain political circumstances, he completely misses the ethical intent of the doctrine. "Jesus Christ super-psychologist" is a twist which is difficult to accept, not only by a Christian believer, but also by an adherent to the principle of ethical independence of—and even supremacy over—psychology. Religion and ethics become here subservient to psychological engineering.

Yet Frazier cannot avoid the cardinal question about the place and role of moral judgment in the scheme of human affairs. For he readily admits that he has no monopoly on behavioral engineering. He offers an honest testimony about the use of and reliance on psychological techniques by sinister agents. "Look at their frightful misuse in the hands of the Nazis! ... What about education? Or religion? Or practical politics? Or advertising and salesmanship?" These techniques are in the wrong hands. They ought to be taken up "for the good of mankind."[14]

Yet, if a fundamental value judgment is imperative for establishing the aim and the yardstick for behavioral engineering, Frazier seems to be on shaky grounds when he deals with such issues. For "good of mankind" as the supreme goal is one thing, and the determination what it consists of is another matter. A moral philosopher would determine such good by rational analysis, or by resorting to an innate moral sense, or some other universal principle. A theologian would seek it in divine commandment and in holy scriptures. All of them would look for an absolute moral law, as does Castle, the philosophy professor in the story. Frazier, however, refuses to embrace such an approach. He advocates "an experimental ethics," which will "profit from experience in working out an agreement for the common good." Such an experience will include experimentation with modifying basic human psychological characteristics and creating new ones and shaping the behavior of individuals, "so that they will function smoothly for the benefit of all."[15] Thus Frazier pushes the psychological techniques beyond the confines of human nature. Psychology seems to offer the promise of changing humankind.

Whether this is a realistic expectation or not, the questions remain what modifications the psychologist *should* aim at, how human nature *ought* to be changed, and what is "benefit." These questions are ethical questions and cannot be resolved by psychology. In his zeal for experimental psychology and psychological engineering, Skinner seems to overlook the distinctive perspective and logical structure of ethics, or moral philosophy, which must be approached in its own terms and modes of inquiry. Skinner's scientific bias for experimentation makes him oblivious of the distinctive ways of reasoning in another dimension of the human condition.

Indeed, Skinner's perception of the human condition, or human nature, is cavalierly simplistic. "We have no truck with philosophies of innate goodness — or evil, either, for that matter. But we do have faith in our power to change human behavior."[16] Yet, if humans are morally tabula rasa, then the inscription of values in their minds become so much more important. By the same token, the definition of such values becomes more elusive. From where will such values be derived? And how will people be able to determine what is good and what is evil? Surely, the technique of psychological implantation of values has no inherent capacity to determine their nature. Indeed, such a technique threatens to become a means in the hands of arbitrary decision-makers. We are back at the problem of ethical determination, which is independent of psychological engineering, programming, and conditioning.

Skinner's weakness of argument when the realm of ethics is concerned is linked to his notion of determinism and freedom. He shows clear preference for the former — for reasons which Frazier makes quite clear. "I deny that freedom exists at all. I must deny it — or my program would be absurd. You can't have a science about a subject matter which hops capriciously about." Yet the requirement of the postulate of determinism for the behavioral control of people does not *prove* that humankind is not free, as Frazier himself admits. He merely thinks that his success makes it increasingly plausible.[17] Still, even if the resolution of the problem of freedom is not definitive, behavioral engineering relies on the deterministic laws of psychology, while trying to accommodate such determinism with imaginary feeling of freedom. "Our members are practically always doing what they want to do — what they 'choose' to do — but we see to it that they will want to do precisely the things which are best for themselves and the community."[18] In other words, the members of Walden Two are conditioned to behave according to the planner's design, but, at the same time, they are programmed to believe that they do so out of their own will and decision. A critic of the system would formulate the condition in a different way. He would say that they are forced to behave in accordance with the planner's design, and are not even given the freedom to know that they are forced. They are deprived of the freedom of thinking for themselves about what is or is not the right behavior.

Being deprived of such freedom, they lose their individual sovereignty, which is a condition for a conscious moral behavior. One cannot act morally as a human being, if one has no capacity to think — freely and independently — about the rightness of action. Skinner argues that such a stance "is incompatible with the observed fact that men are made good or bad and wise or foolish by the environment, in which they grow."[19] If so, there is no source for authoritative judgment, unless some people are endowed with extra intellectual or spiritual powers, and set the way for the rest of humanity.

Conceivably, Frazier — or Skinner — saw himself as such a true leader. Yet, he failed to inform us what is the source of his wisdom and goodness. If he too was born with a moral tabula rasa, and subsequently subject to common, largely mistaken, notions of what is right and wrong, how did he overcome the environmental social influences and reach the truth? Evidently, he must have retained some freedom of sovereign thinking and judgment, or else there would be no place for a new idea on the crucial issues of mankind. And if he retained a measure — a crucial measure — of such freedom, why couldn't some other persons retain such freedom? But if they do, behavioral engineering encounters significant limitations.

It is the scientific zeal, mainly in his own psychological domain, which leads Skinner to disregard, or to invade, domains outside its rightful application, such as ethics. Skinner seems to overlook the fact that the realm of experimental psychology and its application does not encompass all the facets of human life and social institutions. The issue of right and wrong, a perennial consideration of humanity, cannot be resolved or determined by his discipline, even if it can be affected by it. There is a niche of ethical inquiry — whether it be called moral science or not — which requires a different approach, an approach sui generis. And perhaps there is a dimension of human existence, a dimension of a certain inner freedom, associated with what we call the human soul, which eludes scientific inquiry.

Indeed, Skinner's ardent commitment to science and rational order makes his utopia an all too facile construction, missing some important, though not clearly discernible, elements of social existence. Let us look at one example. The rational and ostensibly scientific arrangement of collective child-rearing may overlook some important emotional and social ties which children develop in conventional family households. Dispensing with the virtually universal traditions of millennia, which may well be rooted in experience, and replacing them by a few rational arguments is a simplistic rationalism which, though indulged by venerable philosophers like Plato, may be fundamentally faulty.

While there have been various social designs which were unquestionably evil and vicious — the totalitarian regimes being the most outstanding recent examples — there may also be serious flaws in social planning sincerely intended to improve human lot. Utopias, even when motivated by the noblest intentions, may involve some dangers. Scientific reasoning, even when trying to be scrupulously honest and faithful to accepted notions of inquiry, is not necessarily flawless. Behavioral engineering, however ingenious, must not be left to the exclusive discretion of such engineers.

At the Service of Power

George Orwell's novel *1984* was published in 1949, one year after the appearance of Skinner's *Walden Two*. In some ways there is an affinity between the two works. Both present imaginary societies in which rationally planned institutions and applied psychology are the salient features of the new order. Yet, despite these common characteristics and in some ways because of them, the books are polar opposites..

Walden Two describes, or intends to describe, an ideal community where people live happily in perfect harmony. *1984* describes the very opposite: society based on ruthless repression of the many by the few. The book depicts the very opposite of utopia: dystopia. Skinner's book presents, or was meant to present, paradise as it can be achieved on earth, while Orwell's novel takes us into hell. Bliss and horror face each other from the pages of these contemporary works.

The books also differ in their literary worth. Skinner's book is only marginally a work of fiction; the scientific and philosophical arguments and the often tedious description of the institutions and practices of Walden Two dominate the narrative. Orwell's book is clearly and deliberately a work of fiction, and the nature of the society he describes takes shape in the reader's mind while reading the horrific story. Yet, despite its fictitious character, *1984* is a realistic book, much more so than *Walden Two*. This is due to the artistic talent of Orwell, as well as because the society he describes had its concrete precursors in Nazi Germany and the Soviet Union. Thus the dystopia cannot be easily disregarded as a morbid fantasy of a pessimistic artist.

8 — Mind Control

The title of Orwell's book, a date set thirty-five years after the publication of the novel, may have been intended to add concreteness and urgency to the menace envisaged in it. Specifying the time of the future occurrence may have added the weight of historical event, should it come to pass, to the prophecy. Still, this does not mean that Orwell considered the development and the date as inevitable. In my opinion, the book should be considered a cautionary tale, as indeed some of the biblical prophecies were meant to depict catastrophes, that the people to whom the prophecy was addressed might experience if they did not repent.

As we know, 1984 came and passed, and the nightmare of Orwell had not been realized. The precedents of Nazi Germany and of the Soviet Union under Stalinism vanished into history, leaving horrible memories, but no grand emulators. On the contrary, they remained a warning to future generations, so far largely heeded. Totalitarian regime, in which the state assumes an intrusive and absolute control over the individual, is generally rejected — not least in the countries which were subjected to such an experience.

Still, a menace of this kind cannot be regarded as no longer relevant, as a thing of the past. What did not happen in 1984 could still happen at some point in the future. Indeed, totalitarian regimes and ruthless government techniques in some less prominent countries than their European predecessors have displayed their viability even at the end of the twentieth century. Consequently *1984* remains relevant, pointing to the actual emulation of its horrific picture and warning against its possible wider revival at some unspecified date. The book may make a significant contribution to the prevention of such an eventuality.

The protagonist of *1984* is Winston Smith, a rather inconspicuous man of 39 who is living in London. It is essentially through his eyes and his experiences that the reader faces the world depicted by Orwell. It is a very different world from 1949, or the world as we know it now. The old political boundaries have been abolished, and the world is divided into three major powers: Oceania (including the Americas and the British Isles), Eurasia (including the former Soviet Union and continental Europe), Eastasia (including China and the rest of the Far East). These political entities are militarily balanced and no one can overcome and subdue another. Yet, they are constantly at war, a kind of a limited war, with the adversaries changing from time to time without any clear reason. While the wars are conducted about the control of territories in Africa and the Middle East, which are outside the three superstates, the real reason for the wars is to destroy the surplus production of modern economy and to sustain the atmosphere of crisis and tension which the state needs to perpetuate the system. The inner structure and ideology of the three powers is essentially identical, though the story deals with Oceania only. The implication is that the political divisions, as well as the internal unity of each state, are arbitrary. They seem to be merely convenient for the rulers of each political entity.

The inner structure of the state is deliberately hierarchical. "At the apex of the pyramid comes Big Brother. Big Brother is infallible and all-powerful." He is the inspiration of all that is good. His picture is everywhere and his voice is on the telescreen. Yet, nobody has seen him, and perhaps he does not exist. He symbolizes the party, and his function is to be a focus "for love, fear, and reverence, emotions which are more easily felt toward an individual than toward an organization." Below him comes the inner party (the brain of the state), whose numbers are less than two percent of the population of Oceania. Next is the outer party (the hands of the state), comprising about thirteen percent. Below the party, about eighty-five percent of the population, are the dumb masses, usually referred to as "the proles" (proletarians).[20]

The proles, though the overwhelming majority, do not count for much, as they are not considered a threat to the regime. They are left uneducated, and they lead their passive lives without interference — simply because they are intellectually unable to perceive an alternative to the status quo. If some gifted individuals appear among them, who might stir discontent, they are simply eliminated. The relative laxity towards the proles does not extend to the party. Here the strictest supervision and control are exercised, as "a Party member lives from birth to death under the eye of the Thought Police." The control is total. "Wherever he may be, asleep or awake, working or resting, in his bath or in bed, he can be inspected without warning and without knowing that he is being inspected.... His friendships, his relaxations, ... the expression of his face ... are all jealously scrutinized." A party member should have no private emotions, but be continuously enthusiastic about public affairs, as dictated by the Party.[21]

The state exercises its functions through four ministries. The Ministry of Truth deals with news, entertainment, education, and the fine arts. Of course, truth is the last thing the ministry is concerned about. Essentially, it is a ministry of propaganda, which has nothing to do with truth. The Ministry of Peace concerns itself with war. The Ministry of Love is in charge of maintaining law and order. It enforces the policy of the state with utmost ruthlessness, including torture and killing. The Ministry of Plenty is responsible for economic affairs, which are not guided by concern for the economic well-being of all. Deliberate destruction of surplus production through warfare, as mentioned above, and the drab living conditions of the proles, offer evidence of concerns other than economic.

In the midst of this system there appears to exist a mysterious clandestine movement, directed against the regime, and founded on straight thinking and liberal principles. It is headed by a renegade by the name of Goldstein, who is the object of well-engineered public hatred. A recent book of Goldstein, exposing the sinister nature of the ruling oligarchy, is secretly circulating and testifies to the existence of the underground. In fact, as it transpires in the story, the book is a fake designed to attract potential renegades and thus lead to their arrest and elimination. The state control is absolute and foolproof.

This conclusion is, as a matter of fact, forcefully conveyed in the opening paragraphs of the story. As Winston Smith was climbing to the seventh floor of a building to get to his flat, on each landing a large, colored poster with the face of a man gazed from the wall. "It was one of those pictures which are so contrived that the eyes follow you about when you move. BIG BROTHER IS WATCHING YOU, the caption ran."[22] An instrument called the telescreen announced information deemed important by the state, and, at the same time, watched and listened to everything Winston, or anyone else, did. One lived exposed to continuous propaganda and to unrelenting spying.

Winston, a member of the outer party, works in the Ministry of Truth, in the Records Department. His function is to readjust earlier printed material to the present policy. As the present announcement of the Big Brother was by definition true, all earlier statements which did not square with it had to be revised or rewritten. History had to be rewritten to fit the current policy. This would go on indefinitely, as policy changes were made in one matter or another. "Day by day ... the past was brought up to date... All history was ... scraped clean and reinscribed exactly as often as was necessary."[23]

Though involved in this task of official falsification of records, and though raised from childhood by the present regime, Winston retains some vague memories of his mother, and deep in his soul has doubts about the whole system. In his mind he is asking heretical questions and even develops a hatred of the Big Brother. He is a rebel in the making.

It is this stance that makes him respond to the invitation of Julia and start an illicit affair with her. She too is a member of the outer party, and she too hates the regime. The relationship between them is forbidden, because

Winston is married, though separated from his wife, and because the party discourages sex, for psychological-political reasons. Sexual repression is supposed to facilitate the hysteria of warfare and focusing emotions on leader worship. While lovemaking is for them first a subversive political act, eventually Winston comes sincerely to love Julia.

The next step of Winston, joined by Julia, is far more radical and dangerous. On the intuitive feeling that O'Brien, a member of the inner party, is also a member of the clandestine organization, Winston approaches him and declares his intention to join in the conspiracy. O'Brien asks him whether he is ready to commit any crime, if instructed to do so, and Winston readily agrees. O'Brien lends him the subversive book of Goldstein, which Winston reads when he trusts he is not being watched.

Then the thunder strikes. Winston and Julia are arrested and separated. Winston undergoes a series of questioning, accompanied by all kinds of physical and mental torture. His investigator is no other than O'Brien. There is, of course, no doubt as to Winston's guilt, but O'Brien, or the party, insists on having their victim's mind reformed and made conform to the party discipline. This is symbolized by making Winston admit that two and two make five. After initial resistance, Winston complies. In other words, he gives up his individual capacity of intellectual judgment.

Yet this is not enough. The personality change must also encompass total moral degradation. Faced with a torture which he dreads more than anything — the inquisitors are clever in identifying the personal revulsions of their victims — Winston exclaims: "Do it to Julia." He is saved from the torment and then actually rehabilitated and restored to health. Having been reformed, he is now ready to be eliminated. As he is being shot by an armed guard behind him, he watches the image of the Big Brother, whom he came to love.

While throughout the story Winston comes to understand the complex ways in which the party assures its position and control over the state and society, he remains puzzled as to *why* it does it. What is its motivation? Is it the good of the people who are not capable of governing themselves? O'Brien, during the investigation, disillusions him about the possibility of any such high motives. The reason for all its action is quest of power, pure power. Some oligarchies pretended that their rule aims at establishing a paradise on earth. Some may have even believed in it. "We are not like that... Power is not a means; it is an end. One does not establish a dictatorship in order to safeguard a revolution; one makes the revolution in order to establish the dictatorship. The object of persecution is persecution. The object of torture is torture. The object of power is power."[24]

What is the place of science or technology in this horrific story? Surely, there is no quest for knowledge and truth in a human organization whose exclusive objective is power — power for the rulers, attained by the humiliation of the humanity subjected to their rule. Yet, there is a place for organizing government and policy, control and subjection of people, in an effective and unassailable manner. This requires the use of reason and the exploitation of techniques — political, administrative, ideological, psychological — for securing and maintaining the aim. Thus, we face here a political science, combined with other systematic knowledge, in its most Machiavellian and ruthlessly consistent form. As we shall see, the focus of these rational-systematic attempts is controlling and shaping the human mind.

One major category of control is the efficient use of intimidation and spreading of fear among the population. This is perfected to a science of intimidation, an interdisciplinary or multidisciplinary science. There are the Thought Police, constantly watching and listening to people, who have no way of knowing when and where they are spied upon. Then there are the Black Guards, a constant threat of physical violence against any person deemed suspect or undesirable. Purges and disappearances of people frighten others. Spy organizations of children, modeled on former scouts organizations, instruct them to spy on their parents out of loyalty to the party. Technological means — print, radio, television — are the most useful ways for controlling and intimidating the people. The omnipresence of the Big Brother, mentioned above, remains the clearest symbol, and perhaps the most emphatic means, of universal intimidation.

Then there is a plethora of psychological techniques for controlling the minds of the citizens. Some are aimed at mass psychology, the control of reaction and behavior of a group, aiming at unifying and solidifying the emotions of the community. To put it in other words, mass hysteria is used to suppress individual cogent reflection and to create unity of opinion, decided on by the party. A "Two Minute Hate" meeting of the people working in the government office exhibits the notorious Goldstein on the screen and elicits a frenzy of hateful reactions, whether genuine or simulated. A "Hate Week" is an organized promotion of war hysteria, in which the proles are stirred to participate.

Then there are techniques aimed at the individual. Writing a diary is a transgression which may lead to the death penalty, or at least a long prison term. The apparent objection is that the writer of a personal diary may develop his own thoughts, rather than remaining a blank slate on which the party imprints its guidelines and policies. Moreover, the notion of "thoughtcrime" prevails, "an essential crime that contained all others in itself." Such a crime "could not be concealed forever ... sooner or later they were bound to get you."[25] Winston, who conveys these thoughts, is deprived of even a modicum of self-confidence, the trust of keeping his thoughts to himself. The party succeeded in stifling individuals' freedom of thought — not merely speech. The concept of "thoughtcrime" indicates the effectiveness of thought control.

The ultimate in mind control exercised by the authorities is achieved in the technique of personality replacement, employed to "rehabilitate" the deviant Winston. Such restoration of his personality is, of course, nothing less than its total destruction. Whatever the techniques used — a combination of torture, psychology and what not — the aim is clearly spelled out by O'Brien. "We shall crush you down to the point from which there is no coming back... Never again will you be capable of ordinary human feeling. Everything will be dead inside you. Never again will you be capable of love, or friendship, or joy of living, or laughter, or curiosity, or courage, or integrity. You will be hollow. We shall squeeze you empty, and then we shall fill you with ourselves."[26]

The party not only strives to control the minds of the citizens by psychological and other techniques. It also aims at shaping the truth, controlling reality, and twisting the logical process of thinking. Characteristically, while the party pursues its objectives in a thoroughly rational and scientific manner, science as such, empirical science, is virtually ruled out, so that technological progress is arrested. The exceptions are warfare and political espionage where techniques may be improved. Otherwise, "the empirical method of thought" is considered a danger to the rigidly imposed ideology.[27]

A guiding logical principle, which essentially is antilogical, is "Doublethink." This means holding "simultaneously two opinions which canceled out, knowing them to be contradictory and believing in both of them." Thus, one would believe "that democracy was impossible and that the party was the guardian of democracy. To forget and to recall things as needed, consciously to repress ideas from one's mind and not to be aware of having done it are among the possibilities of 'doublethink.'"[28] Clearly, doublethink goes beyond what we call doubletalk. For the ambiguity in doublethink becomes a virtue, and is elevated to the status of a supreme principle in allegedly logical thinking. It trains people for crooked thinking and intellectual dishonesty — even to the point that they may no more be aware of the flaw. It turns antilogic into logic.

Of course, it is doublethink which justifies calling the ministry in charge of producing lies the "Ministry of Truth," or the branch of government practicing torture "Ministry of Love." Doublethink comports with the system of the constant revision of history, mentioned above, in which the past as documented, suddenly disappears, or is changed. In the case of Winston, charged with updating past events, the logic of doublethink has to be constantly employed. As he retains some doubts about the validity of the approach, he is doomed to get into trouble.

In other words, this manipulation of logic destroys truth, and even the very notion of truth. If truth is manufactured to the order of authority, and not subject to rational inquiry and logical thinking, it stops being truth — unless one has become a doublethinker. Without the notion of truth, and human right and capacity to inquire into it and seek it, the entire fabric of intellectual pursuits and common sense judgment becomes distorted and destroyed. The efficient technique of manipulating the rules of mental processes destroys the integrity and viability of these processes. Consequently, it is all too easy to proclaim and make people believe in any kind of absurd slogan, such as War is Peace, Freedom is Slavery, and Ignorance is Strength.[29]

Orwell goes even one step further, if possible, in devising a thorough and devilishly ingenious technique, employed by the party to secure its absolute control over the minds of the people. It is a system of controlling the concepts and ideas which people can form, by the control of language — for it is linguistic usage that carries ideas, or the potential for forming ideas. In the "Newspeak" which gradually replaces "Oldspeak," the language becomes a dry, allusion-free, oversimplified means of communication. A man working on this project waxes eloquent on how hundreds of words are destroyed each day. "We're cutting the language down to the bone," he says, and adds ecstatically: "It's a beautiful thing, the destruction of words." The whole literature of the past will be destroyed, for its version in Newspeak will change it into the opposite of the original. Even the party slogan "Freedom Is Slavery" will have to change, for the concept of freedom will be abolished.[30]

Indeed, the purpose of the reduced, skeletal language is not only to offer the desired guidance toward right notions, but to deprive people of any residue of independent thinking as such. The reduction of the vocabulary was aimed at the reduction of thought. "Ultimately it was hoped to make articulate speech issue from the larynx without involving the higher brain centres at all." This was conveyed in the word "duckspeak," meaning "to quack like a duck."[31] The entelechy of the great lingistic reform is to change humanity into a society of quacking ducks.

Orwell's novel is a most horrifying fantasy of an earthly inferno designed for the modern age. Serving the crude quest of power for the sake of power of the few, the state resorts to crude power, psychological means, logic twisting and linguistic destruction to secure its objectives. In a coordinated, systematic, and rational manner — which can well be called scientific — the most sinister aims are pursued. In the process, humanity, or what we recognize as humanity, is being changed, twisted, dehumanized.

Is such a scientific, devilish scheme feasible? Can humanity be degraded to such an extent? The answer is not easy. The attempts in this vein by totalitarian regimes, though quite successful for a time, did not last long enough to prove the case. Even during their rule, there were cases of isolated individuals who retained their full humanity, even if they almost always had to remain in hiding. Thus, it is difficult to assess the possibilities in this respect. What is crystal clear is the warning: the capacity to use scientific and organizational techniques for social and mind control is enormous, and humanity, or the part of humanity which retains and cherishes independent thinking and judgment, must be on its guard.

It must be borne in mind that, beside the dangers of some kind of a *1984* in the first half of the twenty-first century, there loom less horrifying but still menacing situations even in democratic societies. There may be no sinister, power-hungry sadists who wish to control society, but there are forces of advertising, of people responding to and enhancing crowd mentality, there are trends toward uniformity of ideas and thinking, as well as non-thinking, which exert an enormous impact on public opinion and mentality. Big Brother may not be watching us, but we are watching ubiquitous television screens, with their messages, opinions, stereotypes, telespeak, telethink, and non-think.

Soul Purging

While Orwell's book dwells at length on the psychological techniques for controlling the minds of the people by a vicious regime, the issue is picked up in a more detached manner, and not in the context of political issues, by Bertrand Russell. Indeed, Russell focuses on the problem of psychological techniques and control, as it contrasts with and confronts the individual choice of action and way of life. If the psychologist have their way, they will deprive individuals of an autonomous life, of sovereignty over their own existence. The psychologists may have the highest motivation, and possibly steer their patients or clients away from vile action, though also from a noble commitment. Yet, whatever the course of action of the psychologists, the individuals will be purged of their own individuality, of their souls — whether good or evil. Such an intrusion of the scientific psychology poses a central problem for our notion of individual sovereignty, for our fundamental perception of humanity.

Bertrand Russell, the philosopher and mathematician, is not known for his fiction writing. Yet, at a relatively old age, he seemed to have entertained himself and his readers by writing a series of short stories with a clear moral intent. We shall adduce two of them which are related to our issue.

One is called "The Psychoanalyst's Nightmare." It presents one of the members of the profession "who, though orthodox in his waking hours, was afflicted during sleep by the following nightmare."[32] In the dream, a committee of six, presided over by the statue of Shakespeare, was holding its annual meeting in the Limbo Rotary Club. The six members were Hamlet, Lear, Macbeth, Othello, Antony and Romeo. All of them, while alive, had been psychoanalyzed by Macbeth's doctor, Bombasticus. The latter took care of Macbeth's diseased mind, cured him of his fancies of homicide, and he and Lady Macbeth spent their days in good works. In a similar way Lear was cured of his phobias.

Othello, having undergone psychoanalysis, realized that he suffered from inferiority complex, because of the color of his skin, and so he switched Desdemona for a black woman, had a large family, and devoted his life to trade. Did he love his black wife as much as Desdemona? Othello says: "Oh, well, it's a different kind of thing... It's an altogether more adult relation... There is nothing unduly wild about it."[33]

Antony, under the treatment of Dr. Bombasticus, got cured of his fantasy passion for Cleopatra, who had been a mother figure to him because of her liaison with Caesar, his father figure. Expurgated from this misplaced infatuation, Antony returned to his lawful wife, the sister of Octavius, and patched up his quarrel with the latter. This set him on a respectable course and enabled him to put Cleopatra to death — an unpleasant duty, but required from a well-adjusted citizen acting for the public good. Romeo was also cured of his adolescent romance with Juliet and embarked on a socially approved life.

Hamlet, too, owed his cure to Dr. Bombasticus. In the prince's own words: "He made me aware of my incestuous feelings towards my mother, of my unconscious hatred of my father, and of the transference of this feeling to my uncle."[34] Consequently, Hamlet's life proceeded along lines suitable for a prince, and eventually a king. Yet, this last portrait of a reformed Shakespearean hero suddenly collapses, as Hamlet revolts and assumes his dramatic character. He exclaims: "To Hell with Dr. Bombasticus! To Hell with adjustment! To Hell with prudence and the praise of fools!"[35]

At this juncture there is an anguished response from the psychoanalyst. "I am Dr. Bombasticus! I am in Hell! I repent! I killed your souls... I have lived in Hell for preferring subservience to glory: for thinking better of servility than of splendor: for seeking smoothness rather than the lightning-flash: for fearing thunder so much that I preferred a damp, unending drizzle."[36] The nightmare ends leaving five or six characters in limbo, and Dr. Bombasticus in hell, while Hamlet is wafted above by angels.

In Russell's story psychoanalysis is presented as a curative science or technique. Individuals, whose life has taken a tragic turn in Shakespeare's dramas, are cured of their psychological afflictions, and thus enabled to lead a normal, socially acceptable, well-adjusted existence. We witness the victory of the psychological science over human conflict and the consequent misery. Yet, in the process of the cure something is lost. This is expressed in the soliloquy of the repentant Dr. Bombasticus. Human souls are killed by psychoanalysis. Glory, splendor, drama, as part of human existence, are replaced by subservience, servility, and uneventful life. If humanity were to be successfully psychoanalyzed, it would become totally pedestrian, dull, predictable, uniform. That is a price Russell is not ready to pay for the well-intended scientific cure.

This does not mean, of course, that Russell is happy with the deeds of Macbeth and Othello, or the lot of Romeo and Hamlet. As is clear from his other writings, Russell is a rationalist concerned about human well-being and happiness, and certainly would approve any reasonable means for reducing human misery. Yet he is concerned about humanity being deprived of the sense of adventure, glory, reaching beyond the pedestrian, predictable, uniform behavior. He is afraid of attaining a conflict-free life at the expense of the search of the soul, even if often a painful and tormenting search.

The point is vigorously conveyed through the confession of Hamlet, before his rebellious volte-face. Thus speaks the well-adjusted prince: "Oh, well, there are times when I feel a certain regret for the old fire, for the golden words that flowed from my mouth, and for the sharp insight that was at once my torment and my joy." Admitting that the old mad world had a certain merit, he

> ... chose to live in the sane world, the world of earnest men who perform recognized duties without doubt and without question, who never look beneath the surface for fear of what they might see, who honour their father and their mother and repeat the crimes by which their father and their mother flourished, who uphold the state without asking whether it deserves to be upheld, and piously worship a God whom they have made in their own image, and who subscribe to no lie unless it furthers the interests of the strong.[37]

Thus, it is not only the sense of freedom and elation that the individual may experience, and of which he is deprived by a psychological treatment, that lies at the heart of Russell's criticism. He is also concerned about society and civilization. A society of well-adjusted people, who never question established ways — some of which are based on hypocrisy and outright evil — cannot morally advance. Society needs individuals who will probe accepted views, who will expose perfidy, who will question what passes as normal conduct.

It is the scientific cure of such individuals, and their reduction to the stereotypical good citizens, that threatens the criticism of social institutions and accepted beliefs, and thus stifles attempts toward moral progress. Clearly humans have to be assured a sense of initiative, a corner of free will, an element of sovereignty, which will be safe from invasion by applied psychology, by a scientific technique designed to purge out of them all the vestiges of sparkling individuality. In the last resort, it is the primacy of individuality over the pressures of society exercised by psychological means, that offers the promise of the moral advancement of that society. The soul of the individual must be saved from the professional adjusters.

Another story by Russell, "Dr. Southport Vulpes's Nightmare," does not deal with psychology and its possible impact on our civilization, but with mechanical ingenuity and its social consequences. In some ways, the story is reminiscent of Čapek's *R.U.R.*, for robots fulfill all conceivable functions in Dr. Vulpes's dream. Only the robots here do not run amok, but remain subordinate to their human masters.

Dr. Vulpes, an official at the Ministry of Mechanical Production (apparently in the Western bloc) and an enthusiast for robotic replacement of human labor, had the following wishful dream, which depicted the entelechy of a mechanized, automated world. The scene is World War III in its tenth year, with the results inconclusive. The enormous casualties on both sides create a pressure for peace, but the rival governments of East and West are saved from this menace by the technological ingenuity of Dr. Vulpes and his communist counterpart. Having manufactured robots to set the workers free for military service, they now manufacture military robots, including all but the commanding officers.

The engineering enthusiasm of the two scientists knows no bounds. Fearing that politicians will put an end to the long war, they develop plans to get rid of governments. Concerned about the supply of raw material for warfare, they invent robots which can do the work of miners. Through all these inventive enterprises the two scientists develop a deep friendship. Though ostensibly serving opposing nations, ideologies, and governments, they secretly meet to discuss their true common objective: the advancement of their technology through the continuation of war. They finally meet in a tunnel cut through the Caucasus Mountains, where they had all the provisions required for their needs, and wait there for the extinction of the human race, happy in the knowledge that, while the planet lasts, the war would go on, without any human disturbance. Fortunately for the world, but not for Dr. Vulpes, as he wakes up he exclaims "War forever!," which lands him in a jail.

This short story, which combines far-fetched fantasy with a sarcastic satire, is conveniently presented as a dream. Otherwise, it would have been difficult to accept the monomaniacal obsession of Dr. Vulpes as anything but madness, and thus not take it seriously. Of course, the dream remains mad too, but as dreams do not exactly follow the logic of the waking life, and allowance is made for their bizarre nature, their contents can be seriously subjected to interpretation and comment. An insane person will not be listened to; the bizarre dream of a sane person may command attention.

Dr. Vulpes and his Russian friend are intended to represent the ultimate stage of the human penchant for mechanical devices — robots, which would perform all human tasks. This trend to automation was on the ascent at the time Russell wrote the story and in the following decades. Indeed, it could be regarded as a characteristic of our age. The idea of an automatically waged war cannot be dismissed in an age when rockets with nuclear warheads can be fired across the globe at enemy targets, in a virtually effortless manner. Of course, the protagonist's monomaniacal commitment to an all-automated world, and total disregard for humanity, is not merely an exaggeration, but an engineering enthusiasm gone mad, but this is exactly necessary in order to enable Russell to point to the moral of the tale.

For the tale points to the danger of a human system in which technology, in its ever-increasing success, overrides and overrules any other human concern: politics, nationalism, ideology, and simple humanity. Russell does not regard all these concerns with approval. He pokes fun at the ideological underpinnings of the war between the two powers, which correspond to the slogans of the Cold War. "Can we forgo that immortal heritage of freedom for which our ancestors fought?" proclaims the western statesman. "Are you prepared to deny the great destiny which Dialectical Materialism has prepared for those who are emancipated from the chains imposed by base exploiters?" is the corresponding call of the leader of the other side.[38]

Yet the customary notions and perceptions — whether more or less empty slogans, or genuine concerns for peace, which the politicians entertain at one stage — become irrelevant and obsolete under the impact of the new aggressive technology. Russell looks askance at the political world and its ideologies. Yet, in foreseeing the ascendancy of technology, which makes the older divisions obsolete, he does not see it as a solution to the old problem, but as the emergence of another menace — possibly even greater than the former one. This is in line with his thinking that the *technology* of the nuclear weapons makes the political conflict between East and West a comparatively minor issue. The new menace, which is sui generis, has to be addressed independently of political philosophy.[39]

This danger inherent in the ever-growing automation is due to the advantages of the new technology. The robots of Dr. Vulpes and his counterpart are far more efficient than human beings, and altogether superior to them. In the words of the story's protagonists: "Man was liable to sin; robots are not. Man was often foolish; robots never are." Hence the general conclusion: "The behavior of our robots is in all respects better than that of the accidental biological product which has hitherto puffed itself up with foolish pride. How ingenious are their devices! How masterly their strategy! How bold their tactics, and how intrepid their conduct in battle!"[40] Robots are better than humans. Engineering is more perfect than biology. Of course, the speech of the protagonists is presented tongue in cheek. Implicitly Russell points here to the sin of hubris of the new engineers, and deplores it and warns about the dangers. He may not like human pride in its various historical manifestations; he warns us even more against the boundless pride of the new scientists.

Russell's story has a subtitle: "The Victory of Mind Over Matter." In a way, the mental design of the engineers becomes the new power, absolute power. Unlike in Čapek's *R.U.R.*, to be discussed further on, the robots here do not revolt. They remain machines, faithfully and efficiently fulfilling their functions. Yet, in a way, one could suggest an opposite subtitle: "The Victory of Matter Over Mind." For the world of Dr. Vulpes is one in which all things mental, save the minds of the planning engineers, are eradicated. There is neither democracy nor communism. There is neither human memory, nor human aspiration. Presumably, art, music, literature, and philosophy are gone too. What remains is armies of machines, inanimate mechanical devices, programmed by ingenious and sophisticated engineers — virtually as their toy soldiers and toy workers — to satisfy the monomaniacal penchant for technological perfection. What is left of humanity under such a scenario are a few engineering geniuses, commanding an inanimate mechanical world, which might continue after the demise of humanity.

The moral of the tale could well be expanded beyond its literal meaning. Conceivably, the robots are not actually machines, but represent human beings who are virtually as unreflective and as predictable as robots, human beings who are programmed to obey orders as efficiently and as readily as machines. Such a robot-like world would also be the result of the victory of matter over mind, the assertion of control of the few over the behavior of the many — the latter deprived of control over their mind, the former limiting their mind to an obsession with efficiency. That would be tantamount to soul-purging, the dehumanization of humanity — even worse than the combination of wisdom and folly, nobility and baseness, good and evil, which have characterized humankind so far. It would be a Pyrrhic victory of science, if there ever was one.

9

The Menace of the Machine

The threat of mind control and even personality distortion through the application of scientific psychology is one kind of threat about which some writers were concerned. Another menace which has figured in the imagination of creative writers is that of the machine — the essentially unanimated mechanical device, which has been the pride of the Industrial Revolution and the hope for the future of humanity.

The ascendancy of the machine, as a means for relieving the burden of hard work and assuring greater wealth and abundance for all, is an integral part of the history of the nineteenth and twentieth centuries. We have seen the praises lavished on technology in the works of Jules Verne, though we have noted some of his forebodings and misgivings. Recent decades dwarfed his optimistic picture, as technology surpassed many of his visions which had been deemed fantastic in his own time. They also revealed that the concerns remained relevant. Still, such concerns were not overwhelming. For Verne's overall picture of the future role of science and technology in human affairs remained balanced, as, indeed, the real situation at the close of the twentieth century seems to be.

However the menace posed by the machine — machinery in diverse modes of perfection and sophistication — has been explored with more involvement and greater depth by a variety of other writers, who shed more light and different perspectives on this problem. In a general sense, following in the steps of the old legend of the Golem, these writers bring to the problem a sense of urgency which the old legend fails to evoke in its simplistic symbolism. For their fables or stories are conceived in modern idiom, and even if their scenarios of disaster remain fantastic, they are embedded in or linked to technology which to a great extent has become or was to become a part of the human experience. The new Golem is no more a clumsy monster, but a familiar part of human experience. Nor is he anymore linked to religious beliefs and moral principles. He is a machine, dependent on human ingenuity, and yet threatening to become independent, and thereby dangerous. Moreover, this threat of independence cannot be countered by the wisdom and moral concern of a well-meaning rabbi. The machine's threat is essentially material, technological, scientific. The issue has been transposed to an altogether different plane, where prayer and virtue are irrelevant.

In a way, we face here a paradox. As the machine is founded on scientific principles and these principles are the product of human thinking, one would expect a built-in harmony between machinery and humankind. Yet the machine is material, whereas man is not purely material, which creates the possibility of disharmony. As the power of the machine can by far exceed the power of humans who, as living beings, are vulnerable, the encounter between the two may constitute a threat to the ingenious but fragile *Homo sapiens*. In the Golem myth there is a recourse to God to resolve such a threat. From the modern perspective, the machine and man face each other, without a possibility of resorting to a higher power. There is no judge or arbitration when machine and man collide. This, of course, only augments human concern and misgivings.

The examples chosen here vary in literary genre, in style, in the country of origin of the writers. This allows for a diversity of perspectives and sensibilities. It also points to the transnational and transcultural nature of the concern.

The Revolt of the Robots

Karel Čapek, the Czech writer, introduced the word "robot" into the vocabulary of English, as well as other European languages.

The receptiveness of these languages to this foreign word is an indication of the significance of the concept invented by Čapek, which has been growing ever since its birth. Today "robot" is any automaton which performs functions assigned to it by its makers, and such functions have become increasingly complex and sophisticated over the twentieth century. Čapek's original robots achieve a varied degree of functional capacity, according to the design of their makers, and they represent a highly accomplished stage of development, which, bearing in mind the time of their introduction into literature, cannot but be seen as a prophecy. Yet, this does not mean that the fable composed by Čapek, as a whole, has to be seen in the same light. For his Robots undergo a transformation that reaches beyond the mechanical accomplishments of robots in the current sense of the term.

9—The Menace of the Machine

The work in which robots make their first appearance is a play called *R.U.R.* (Rossum's Universal Robots), 1923. The play was translated into English and many other languages, and performed in various places. Significantly, it is set in the future, and thus entails a vision of a situation which, at the time of the composition of the drama, could be regarded as farfetched. The place of the drama is in some unidentified island—another utopian characteristic of the play. Yet, if the author is deliberately vague about the time and place of his drama, this does not diminish from the sense of concern and deep human involvement which the author displays in the plot as it evolves.

In Act I we are introduced to a huge industrial enterprise which manufactures robots by the thousands, which are shipped to various countries. It is a thriving business, run by Harry Domin, the general manager of the establishment. He is served by robots that are indistinguishable in appearance from human beings. They move, function, respond and talk like humans. Helena Glory, the daughter of the president of some country, comes on a visit to the island, on behalf of the Humanity League, whose concern is to protect the robots and ensure their good treatment. The idea is dismissed by Domin and his associates, who point out that, despite their human appearance, the robots are merely mechanical devices. They are also a great economic asset: cheap, efficient, reliable, they assure abundant production and well-being for all. While they are not human, save for their appearance, Dr. Gall, the head of the Physiological and Experimental Department of R.U.R., plans to introduce pain into their system. This for industrial reasons: a sense of pain will prevent them from being injured in their operations, and thus reduce the damage to the machine. As the act ends, we witness that Domin, infatuated with Helena, is going to marry her.

Act II opens ten years later. The seemingly well-working system based on the employment of robots reveals serious strains. In America, when workers rioted against a robot-based economy, the government armed the robots against the rebels. Then robots were put to use as soldiers in wars. They proved most efficient in killing hundreds of thousands of people. Apparently aware of their power, the robots organized, and issued a world manifesto (reminiscent of workers' world manifestoes). On another plane, the world experienced a reduction, or even stoppage, of human births. Apparently, without the need for workers, there appeared a biological reflex of sterility. The demand to restrict the production of robots falls on the deaf ears of the business people interested in making profit. Finally, we witness the revolt of the

Robots. They proclaim superiority over humans and call for the annihilation of humanity.

Act III describes the final catastrophe. The robots, headed by one called Radius, are about to kill all the human personnel of the great factory. Ironically, it was the fact that the robots, or some of them, were given some human traits, that was responsible for their revolt. Being in some ways human, they developed hatred for humanity. The change from mere mechanical devices to quasi-human beings was secretly achieved by Dr. Gall, who claims to have done it out of curiosity. Helena alleges that he did it to please her, because she wanted the robots to be endowed with souls. Thus, the calamity was due either to scientific curiosity, or human compassion. All these recriminations and reflections do not save the lives of the human characters of our drama. Only one, Alquist the architect, who works with his hands like the robots, is spared.

There is an epilogue to the three acts. With humanity gone, and the life of the robots lasting only twenty years, the world anticipates the total extinction of life — natural or artificial. Radius, joined by other robots, ask Alquist to instruct them how to manufacture new robots. Alquist has no inkling how to do it. The formula had been written down at one time, but was destroyed by Helena, indignant about the sterility of the world because of the robots. In this situation of cosmic despair, Alquist encounters two robots, Primus and Helena, who display genuine manifestations of mutual devotion and love, and pronounces them to be Adam and Eve. This suggestion of a new beginning offers a symbolical, if tiny, happy ending to the drama.

The play of Čapek presents a somewhat inconsistent picture of the robots. On the one hand, they are purely mechanical devices, mere machines. On the other hand, some of them acquire some human traits, which make them ruthless and cruel, in a way reminiscent of Frankenstein's monster, or Mr. Hyde, or perhaps the Golem. Yet, the conclusion of the play points to a human transformation in the positive sense of the word, as the new Adam and Eve reveal selfless love and mutual devotion. These metamorphoses of the robots may well be necessary for the dramatic plot, even if they somewhat obscure what is the central message of the play.

Or, perhaps, there is no one message here, but several: the danger of mechanical efficiency, the risk of biological engineering, the futility of human effort to improve human life, the failure of charity and compassion, the redeeming power of love. Our concern here is with the scientific and technological factors and their impact on humanity, and we shall highlight these elements.

Having pointed out the various facets of the play, perhaps it may still be asserted that a major, even the central, message of the work points to the threat of overmechanization to human well-being and civilization. The industrialization of the western world, as it was witnessed in the early part of the twentieth century and after World War I, is brought to its logical conclusion in *R.U.R.* The perceived threat, to put it in simple terms, was that in one way or another the machines would escape their designers' control and take over. Thus the human creator would turn into the victim of the creation. Such general sense of eventual reversal or collapse of human-designed order cannot be dismissed as a mere fantasy or idle speculation in the nuclear age, or, for that matter, in an increasingly automated and computerized civilization of the beginning of the twenty-first century.

Čapek's play convincingly points to the advantages and benefits of the mechanical man, the ultimate in mechanical perfection. There is an insistence, at least in the opening of the play, that the robots are not created on physiological principles, as old Rossum intended, but on mechanical principles, as young Rossum, an engineer, decided. The latter was also guided by economic considerations, in a way typical of modern industrial economy. The robots had to be working machines, the way gasoline-run motors are machines. And the design had to be cost-effective, as we would put it today. Therefore, says Domin, "the Robots are not people. Mechanically they are more perfect than we are, but they have no soul."[1]

Some compelling reasons for creating the robots, or substituting them for human workers, are further adduced. "One Robot can replace two and a half workmen." The human "machine" was not effective. "It no longer answers the requirements of modern engineering. Nature has no idea of keeping pace with modern labor.... From a technical point of view, the whole of childhood is a sheer absurdity. So much time lost."[2] The slow rhythm of nature differs from the fast pace of mechanical production. The imperatives of efficiency and business dictate the choices of modern industry.

Yet there is another side to the coin of mechanical efficiency. This heightened capacity can be useful not only for production, but also for sinister aims, such as suppression of revolt with great ruthlessness and cruelty. The robots, the machines, are not endowed with the quality of mercy. Then there is the revolt of the robots and its ultimate success. While Čapek's revolting robots are led by robots that are not mere machines, but have some distinct human characteristics, the revolt can also be interpreted as symbolizing the machine overcoming humanity. It may be seen as mechanical devices running amok and destroying human life itself. The human sterility due to the robots may corroborate this symbolical interpretation. Humankind by creating robots overreached itself, and created its own destruction. It is this scenario which strikes a resonant chord in our own times.

While Čapek vividly depicts the machine as the nemesis of its inventor, he also elaborates on the roots of humans' inventive endeavor and on human responsibility for creating the armies of robots. Alquist, the architect, puts the blame on all the designers and entrepreneurs of the new mechanical systems. It is not the robots who are to blame, but the people who manufactured them. "For our own selfish ends, for profit, for progress, we have destroyed mankind. Now we'll burst with all our greatness."[3] Here is an accusation against the human motivation for technological and industrial development, or for material progress.

This narrow-minded trend in modern civilization is derided by pointing to the reaction of the enterprising Domin, on learning about the revolt of the Universal Robots. Now, he proclaims, robot factories will be established in every country, the robots speaking diverse languages and being strange to each other. The national robots will hate each other, and fight each other.[4] Technology, put at the service of international and racial divisions, and the consequent business generated, will thrive, and who cares about the consequences. *Pereat mundus, fiat negotium.* (May the world perish, but business thrive.)

There is another component to the human involvement in industrial-technological progress, namely, modern man's orderly, scientific penchant. This is sarcastically symbolized by the glorification of the timetable. "The time-table is more significant than the gospel; more than Homer, more than the whole of Kant. The time-table is the most perfect product of the human mind."[5] Humans approach here the soulless robots. They are guided by considerations of precision and efficiency — invaluable in technology and industrial organization; but neglect what constitutes their spiritual identity. When people and robots come to resemble each other, the eclipse of civilization is imminent.

It is in line with this critical attitude towards the modern trends, that Čapek makes Alquist, the man who works with his hands, pronounce: "I'm afraid of all this progress, and these new-fangled ideas." He even wishes there was a prayer against progress, and formulates one himself: "Oh, Lord, I thank thee for having given me toil. Enlighten Domin and all those who are astray; destroy their work, and aid mankind to return to their labors; let them not suffer harm in soul or body; deliver us from the Robots...."[6] Here is a full-scale retreat from technology, enterprise, efficiency.

While the creation of robots seems to stem mainly from business drive and expectation of profit — reasons looked askance at — Čapek also suggests unselfish motivation for the creation of robots and what they represent. Thus Domin expects that in ten years the robots "will produce so much corn, so much cloth, so much everything, that things will be practically without price. There will be no poverty. All work will be done by living machines. Everybody will be free from worry and liberated from the degradation of labor. Everybody will live only to perfect himself... But then the servitude of man to man and the enslavement of man to matter will cease."[7] The world of automation will be a world of plenty, and human toil will be reduced to nothing. People will be free and equal, and dedicate their lives to self-perfection, to a spiritual ideal.

This rosy utopian picture of the future is reminiscent of the Marxian image of society after the communist revolution. Equality, freedom and a new phase of humanity with new vistas of self-fulfillment projected by Marx and Engels, are reiterated by Čapek's character. The most notable difference, however, is that in distinction from Marxism the future bliss is not the consequence of a social revolution, but of a technological change. The novel technology holds out the promise of a blissful existence for humanity.

Alas, this promise is not fulfilled. And apparently Čapek has doubts about the feasibility of a technological salvation. Traditional human civilization, combining toil with spiritual aspirations, seems to be Čapek's notion of the right way. Indeed, he seems to point to the danger of attempting the salvation of humankind by technological means, even if the intent is sincere. The genuine commitment of the reformer or the revolutionary is in no way a guarantee of the success of the endeavor. It may lead to its very opposite. The total embrace of technology as the main road to the summum bonum — whether it be financial boon or human emancipation — leads to disaster. Both selfishness and altruism fail if they choose the wrong way of action — the narrow techno-economic pursuit.

For there are other dimensions to life. There is music, there is beauty. "What a lot of lovely things there are!"[8] The self-confinement to material objectives — attainable through mechanical ingenuity and efficient organization — deprives humanity of the splendor of full existence. The modern world stands accused of forcing itself into the straitjacket of material success and progress, and neglecting the finer things of life. That way calamity lies.

The Machine as God

Edward Morgan Forster was one of the prominent English writers of the twentieth century. His place in this study is almost accidental, for his sphere of interest lies mostly outside matters of science and technology. Yet, one of his stories falls very clearly into our domain. It is called "The Machine Stops" and it was published before World War I, in 1909.

Chronologically it preceded Čapek's play and ought to have been discussed before it. Yet there is a reason for the reversal of order. Čapek's robots had originally been pure machines, and for the most part remained such, but later some acquired human sensibilities. Therefore their conflict with humanity, or their menace to human existence, is not purely of a technological nature, is not clearly and absolutely mechanical. In Forster's story this is not the case: it is the machine, the technology, which in quintessential nature treats humanity and human civilization one way or another. Thus, Forster's story is a step further in the development of the idea of mechanical dangers. In place of a humanoid machine, not dissociated from Frankenstein's monster and some such quasi-mythical stories, we have an inanimate creation exerting unforeseen threats to its human creator.

Forster wrote his story as a reaction or a rebuttal to the work of H.G. Wells in the latter's sanguine phase, when he believed in science and progress and their fruitful and beneficial symbiosis. As E. M. Forster put it: "'*The Machine Stops*' is a counterblast to one of the heavens of H.G. Wells."[9] Conceivably, it could have been the blissful world of *A Modern Utopia*, discussed above.

Wells and Forster, though contemporaries, are worlds apart in their writing. Wells is essentially a believer in science, even if he warns against some of its potential excesses. He is fundamentally a rationalist who, even if at one time despairing of human progress and salvation, cannot imagine them as resulting from any other source than reason, knowledge, science. Forster is a lyrical writer, looking for the elusive poetic strings in the human soul. He does not tread along the solid roads of reason, but seeks the mysterious realms of beauty and sentiment. It is virtually impossible to visualize him as an enthusiast of science. He will listen to the nightingale in admiration, but will not give a hoot as to how evolution made the bird a singer.

"The Machine Stops" is set in some distant future. The world appears to be unified and uniform. All the people live in the same manner and each individual occupies a similar room, with the same furnishings and devices.

Each room is hexagonal, "like the cell of a bee." A room has neither windows nor lamps, "yet it is filled with a soft radiance." There appears to be no aperture, "yet the air is fresh." There is music without instruments. The furniture consists of an arm-chair and a reading desk. This description of the room, with which the story opens, concludes with the indication of its occupant, a woman — "a swaddled lump of flesh ... with a face as white as a fungus."[10]

The opening sets the tone for the story. The new world is technically perfect. It benefits from some mysterious technological achievements: artificial or artificially modified fresh air, soft radiance instead of blinding light, music from a hidden source. The furnishing is minimal and the space limited — apparently because no more is needed. Yet the woman has a face as white as a fungus. Her sickly appearance is somehow linked to the technological perfection and the absence of contact with real sun and air and other human beings. The new technological culture contradicts some basic human needs. Of course, being the product of this culture, the woman is not aware of it.

Though physically isolated, Vashti — as is the name of the woman — knows several thousand people, through means of communication which are at everybody's disposal. These include instant telephonic contact, enhanced by "cinemataphones," which enable the talkers to see the images of one another. Thus Vashti can contact her son on the other side of the globe and see him while they are talking. She can also give a lecture to and be seen by a large audience, not assembled in a hall, but dispersed in individual rooms like her own.

The room, being not only the place of work but also the residence, has all the amenities necessary for convenient life. At the activation of a button or a switch, she can summon a bed, a bath, emerging from the floor. Similarly, she can get food and communicate with her friends. Indeed, there is even automatic medical emergency treatment. "The room, though it contained nothing, was in touch with all that she cared for in the world."[11] Self-sufficiency! Splendid isolation!

An exception to the automatic, push-button system was one book, *The Book of the Machine*, "a survival from the ages of the litter."[12] This book, cherished in an almost religious way, provided the technical information how to use the various buttons, and contained the timetable of the airships traveling over the world. The book was cherished because of the essential information it contained, and because it symbolized the entire system, attributed to the Machine. The Machine — a central inanimate character in the story, and appearing in its title — represents both the totality of the mechanical system and the basic idea of a mechanical civilization. That *The Book of the Machine* is the only survival of the age of books is, of course, an ironic comment on the transformation of civilization from a world of books into a world of machines.

Yet the transformation is even more radical. It involved the abandonment of the surface of the earth and turning the depths of the earth into human habitation. It eradicated the notion of getting people to specific beautiful locations. The surface of the earth was a wasteland, and the inner rooms were provided with access to one's heart's desire. Instead of "bringing people to things," as in the old days, things were brought to people.[13] One could say that communication succeeded transportation. Still, global transportation was still maintained for occasional travelers. Thus, Vashti could leave her room — though she did it reluctantly — and get to an airship which took her from what used to be New Zealand to one-time England, where her son Kuno had an identical living space.

Vashti had some emotional ties to her son, even though procreation was controlled by the authorities and children were brought up outside any family circle. As a matter of fact, there were no families — only isolated individuals, enjoying their contact with chosen friends through the medium of mechanical communication. Still, as Kuno insists on seeing her, she undertakes the trip to what used to be England.

If Vashti is a satisfied and complacent citizen of the new world, Kuno is not. He is denied a request to become a father, because the Committee (representing the Authority) does not consider him the right type. He has curiosity and a sense of yearning for the other world, which has become obsolete and derelict. Thus he undertakes a trip to the surface of the earth and does so without an egression permit from the Committee. There he admires the hills and the vegetation. His yearning for the organic, for nature, for past humanity ripens. The Mending Apparatus, another tentacle of the Machine, both rescues him from injury and brings him back to civilization. Yet his transgression is serious and may involve the death penalty. Actually, he survives.

The civilization, over some years, shows some changes and developments. The respirators, necessary for trips to the surface of the earth — for the underground inhabitants cannot breathe natural air — are abolished. Contact with the arid surface is useless and so visiting it is deemed superfluous. Then religion is reestablished, focusing on the adoration of the Machine, expressed in diverse forms. It also marks the decline of human knowledge, and the reliance on the Machine. We face decadence of humanity and progress of technology.

And then starts a dramatic reversal. It is indicated by a call from Kuno to his mother, stating that the Machine stops. At first this is taken as an absurd idea. Yet some concrete manifestations follow. First the transmission of music deteriorates. Then the sleeping apparatus fails. The Mending Apparatus which should take care of such mishaps requires mending itself. Then the lighting fails. Subsequently the entire communication system breaks down. Silence, total silence ensues. This is the death of civilization. Chaotic scenes of crowds looking for rescue follow, people are dying. This is the demise of humanity, which cannot endure, having lost all the technological support on which it had relied.

In the concluding scene, Kuno faces his mother and touches her — contrary to the rules of conduct of the collapsing civilization. She, too, realizes the mistakes of the Machine age. As they both are dying, their solace is that, according to Kuno, some former human beings have survived on the surface, and so humanity will not perish. Vashti, in the depth of her anguish, fears that they will start the Machine again. Kuno reassures her that they will not, as "humanity has learnt its lesson."[14]

While the summary of Forster's story reflects much of his attitude to science and technology, certain cardinal points ought to be highlighted, even at the risk of some repetition. One startling feature of the story is the uncanny capacity of Forster to foresee at the beginning of the century certain technological developments, which came to be realized decades later, and in some respects only towards its end. The network of communication which is at the command of Vashti and her contemporaries combines the features of global telephone and in some ways television connections, as well as e-mail. The purification of the air, the self-sufficiency in the underground room, the ease of transportation, all sound modern and attained or attainable. This predictive capacity is so much more amazing, as Forster had none of the enthusiastic attitude to science and technology of a Jules Verne or H.G. Wells, and his literary interests lay on an altogether different plane.

What is perhaps even more startling, and certainly more important, is the sense of an automated civilization which Forster's story conveyed. At the beginning of the twenty-first century humanity is not there — yet. However, we can easily envisage a way of life in which automatic, or near-automatic, machines and systems provide us with our daily needs, and human contact is reduced to a minimum.

The octagonal room in a human beehive is not such a distant idea in an age when people sit in an armchair watching television, listening to radio, looking for information on the Internet, or interacting through electronic devices, while enjoying thermostatically controlled environments, and having supplies of food in refrigerators and freezers, and so forth. The image of automated living conditions, created by Forster at the beginning of the century, reveals a prophetic perception of a Zeitgeist which was far from the reality of his world.

As already indicated, the broad perception of the new era was expressed in the term "Machine," which symbolized and represented the essence of the new civilization. Today we would have chosen another term, such as "Automation" or "Computer," or "Electronic Control." Yet, "Machine" is quite adequate, in that it points to the mechanical origin of the trend toward present-day technology that continues to progress. Forster could not think a hundred years ago of concepts and technologies yet unborn. Still, he clearly conveyed the general sense of their functional capacity.

With all his foresight of the role of technology in future civilization, Forster is firmly opposed to the ascendancy of technology. This, indeed, is the gist of this story. He opposes the Machine, because it puts a distance between humans and nature, which Forster sees as an essential ingredient for a sense of human well-being. He conveys his attitude by a satirical presentation of the opposite notions of the Machine civilization.

Thus, when Vashti notices sunlight penetrating through the window of the airship, she is annoyed. When the ship flies over the fantastic mountain shapes of the Caucasus, she murmurs "No ideas here," and hides "the Caucasus behind a metal blind." Flying over a golden sea in which lay "many small islands and one peninsula," she repeats "No ideas here," and hides "Greece behind a metal blind."[15] Nature does not exist for her, and even geographical regions of spectacular past culture, such as Greece, remain meaningless. No contact with nature, no contact with the past. Ideas, as well as sentiments and emotions (if left at all), flow through the technical lines of communication and are void of the traditional sources of inspiration.

Not only nature and human history are thrown overboard by the scientific, technological society; so is the contact with other human beings—at least any physical contact. Vashti is most reluctant to visit her son, though she is emotionally not indifferent to him, because she can talk with him and see him on her apparatus. Technology makes actual meeting superfluous, or so it seems.

Consequently a notion develops that to touch a person is improper. When the flight attendant touches her to prevent a fall, Vashti is quite annoyed. Even when Kuno, "flesh of her flesh," stood beside her, "she was too well-bred to shake him by the hand."[16] The perfection of technology undermines certain fundamental, instinctive urges and yearnings in people, and transforms them into some kind of artificial beings. The point is stressed by contrasting the artificial and dehumanized Vashti with her human, organic, natural son.

Though the Machine was created to serve and help people, it is essentially alien to the finer aspects of humanity, and, because of its power, undermines and destroys these essential traits of humanity. It is an invention which, in its efficiency and success, becomes counterproductive and even destructive. The point is eloquently conveyed by Kuno, as he addresses his mother. "Cannot you see ... that it is we who are dying, and that down here the only thing that really lives is the Machine? We created the Machine, to do our will.... It has robbed us of the sense of space and of the sense of touch, it has blurred every human relation and narrowed down love to a carnal act.... The Machine proceeds — but not to our goals."[17] In other words, the fact that the Machine is a mechanical device precludes a true symbiotic relationship, precludes a true harmony between people and their invention. And once the invention is so efficient and powerful, the inventors become the victim of their artifact.

Still this inherent opposition of man and machine need not lead to a catastrophe — even if it results in an emotionally and socially anemic humanity. Yet a comprehensive disaster — and not merely the justified discontent of Kuno, the spokesman for Forster — is to follow. For the Machine and the civilization which is founded on it carry the seeds of their own downfall. It is not only the fall of man, bewailed by Kuno, which results from the rule of the Machine; ultimately it is the fall of the Machine, which engulfs the physical existence of humanity, that is the consequence of the Machine civilization. There is an inherent logic, a virtually inevitable dialectic, that brings the decline about.

The Machine was invented to help people and make them happy. As it succeeded in fulfilling its manifest functions, it increased human reliance on it, and even reverence for it. "The Machine feeds us and clothes us and houses us; through it we speak to one another, through it we see one another, in it we have our being.... The Machine is omnipotent, eternal; blessed is the Machine."[18] The Machine becomes god. Yet such religious and practical trust in it made people neglect the way it worked. The master brains perished, and no one took care to cultivate and sustain the scientific knowledge required for understanding, and, if need be, repairing the system. So when the Machine started breaking down, there was no one competent to repair it, and the whole system collapsed.

Thus, in the last resort, however perfect the Machine might have been, it remained dependent on human intelligence. If people forgot this dependence — perhaps because of its excellence they ran into grave dangers, or even faced a catastrophe. Though Forster may not have been an enthusiast of science, he realized that it remained the foundation of technology, and knew that reliance on the latter, without the support of the former, was very risky. The working of the machine must be understood to secure its benefits and efficacy.

Humanity as it stands today has not come to the brink of disaster because of its technological advancement. There are still people who understand the various advanced systems and can repair or reproduce them. At the same time, we have often encountered intimations of human failure in the face of technological mishaps, and of human incompetency due to reliance on technological devices. This can be illustrated in matters minor and cardinal.

How many times we cannot get financial information because "the computers are down"? How many school children retain the knowledge of multiplication and division, finding square root and the like, in an age when the pocket calculator provides a fast and easy answer? Have we not faced electrical "brownout" over vast regions, which could not be easily repaired? Last, but not least, have we not experienced a meltdown of nuclear energy plants, with disastrous consequences? The support of knowledge for technological inventions and installations remains indispensable. Forster's warning, though clearly exaggerated, as any literary caution is likely to be, is more relevant today than it was in the time of his writing.

The Failure of Science

The work to be dealt with in this section transcends the issue of the conflict between humans and machines, in that it broadens the technological achievements and capacity into the even wider complex of science and scientific approach. To be sure, in doing so, it does not in any way belittle the role of technology as it affects, or may affect, the human condition. Indeed, the theme of the work is even wider than scrutinizing the role of science in modern life, for it brings to judgment what we usually refer to as Western Civilization. That this is done by a writer conspicuous for the range of his cultural horizons and the sophistication of his intellectual discernment, makes his indictment so much more poignant.

Aldous Huxley, the English man of letters known most widely for his *Brave New World* (to be discussed in another chapter), counts among his diverse books a rather slim volume, entitled *Ape and Essence*, published in 1948. Though classified as a novel, it is, for the most part, presented as a film script, which facilitates the presentation of the narrative in a somewhat sketchy and fragmentary way. This, however, does not detract from the forceful exposition of the author's ideas, or the conveyance of his moral. For the story, and the direct argument intertwined with it, is deliberately didactic—which is not meant here as a criticism.

Indeed, as the publication date indicates, the book was written in the shadow of World War II and its unspeakable horrors, and at the onset of the nuclear age and its menace for the future of humankind. There could hardly be a more somber moment of human history for reflection on human destiny. Yet, while affected by the peculiar junction in the history of humanity, Huxley does not limit his vision to the years, or decades, of his personal experience. He comments on issues of earlier times, and ventures into forebodings about the far future of humankind. Only that the present may well have tinted that past and that future with its dark colors.

The story opens in the first person account of a man connected to the Hollywood film world, joined by a colleague, a man of little character, with a penchant for posturing. As the two are walking through Hollywood, a few scripts fall off a truck, loaded with material, used or discarded, destined for the incinerator. One of the scripts, by one William Tallis of Murcia, California, entitled "Ape and Essence," marked as rejected, holds the attention of the narrator. The following Sunday the two colleagues make their way to a desolate house, only to find that Tallis, an apparently lonely man of sixty-six, had died six weeks earlier. The narrator concludes: "I print the text of 'Ape and Essence' as I found it."[19]

Setting the book, script, message, and ideas in the framework of Hollywood seems to serve a purpose. The triviality, superficiality, commercialism, and phoniness of the Hollywood film-production world offers a sharp contrast to the sincerity, deep concern and clear vision conveyed in the discarded script. This may well symbolize the contrast between normalcy and reality on the one hand, and the vision of truth, the illumination of an idea, on the other hand. That the worthwhile script was doomed to oblivion, while some other, intrinsically worthless films made big money, is part of the abysmal failure of modern civilization.

The script opens with the presentation of an audience of baboons entertained by a female baboon, in a manner which clearly parallels a human situation. This is a fragment of the baboon civilization, which uses human beings, such as Michael Faraday and Albert Einstein, as domesticated animals and objects of sadistic torment. The society of baboons has its army and faces another baboon society with its army. They too have an identical Einstein, and both scientists are forced to participate in the war between the baboon nations, as experts in mass destruction. The macabre picture is followed by the music of "Land of Hope and Glory" and "Onward, Christian Soldiers," followed by a benediction of the Right Reverend Baboon-Bishop.

Clearly, the picture is a savage satire of humanity, in which the mediocre, unthinking masses repress, use, and abuse the men of genius. Pasteur joins others of comparable stature as a mascot led on a chain. The human institutions of state and church, and, above all, of the army, errant in their endeavors, characterize the two opposing societies. Their empty slogans, anticommunist or anticapitalist, underscore the stupidity and viciousness of the baboons, pretending to be human, or of the humans who really are dressed-up baboons.

Then the narration switches to another scene. It is the year 2108, as a scientific expedition from New Zealand approaches the coast of California. New Zealand, along with Equatorial Africa, were spared in the Third World War, which took place over a century earlier. Only now could they venture on such an expedition, because of the radioactive contamination outside their regions. While the Africans crossed the Mediterranean and perform their tribal dances in the Westminster Palace and their tribal rites at the Vatican — Huxley seems deliberately to choose the seat of democracy and the center of Christianity for the display of reversal to barbarism — the New Zealand party aims at the Americas.

As a group of scientists from the expedition lands in the vicinity of what used to be Hollywood, one of them, Dr. Poole, the chief botanist of the expedition, is kidnapped by the natives of the place. The eventual attempts to find him are abruptly ended when the searching party is attacked with bows and arrows, and some of them become casualties. Thus Dr. Poole is left alone and has to fend for himself in the new civilization which has emerged from the nuclear catastrophe.

9—The Menace of the Machine

His first encounter is with a group that digs up ancient graves to obtain valuables, such as jewelry or even the fancy clothes of dead Hollywood personalities. At one point they consider burying Dr. Poole alive — just as a means of entertainment. He is rescued, however, when the workers' supervisor realizes that Poole may have some useful know-how of times past, which has been lost by the local civilization.

After this grim introduction, what follows is an insight into the new civilization, which only amplifies and widens the horrific picture. The society suffers from an abundance of people with congenital malformations, due to ionic radiation lasting for a long time after the war. Those with tolerable malformations live, those with excessive ones are killed when still babies, in a public display celebrated once a year. It is a practical measure aiming at the reduction of affliction, and it serves as a means of discouraging reproduction. The killing is celebrated as a sacrifice to deity who is no other than Belial, Beelzebub, Azazel, Lucifer. The priests are adorned with horns, and people make the sign of the horn — all consistent with this anti-religion religion. As an eminent prelate explains it to the religious Dr. Poole, the history of humankind and the lot of humanity make the belief in the devil much more plausible than the belief in a benevolent God.

The concern about genetic malformation seems to underlie the perceptions and practices of the society concerning the relations between man and woman. The latter are referred to in derogatory terms, emotional attachment and marriage are forbidden, and so are sexual relations during most of the time. Only two weeks in a year all the taboos are canceled, and, following the slaughter of the malformed babies, an orgy of free public sex ensues. The reproductive consequences are subject to the rules of priestly selection: the whole to live, the malformed to die. The priests themselves are castrated, so as not to succumb to temptation.

The material conditions of life are quite miserable, which makes Dr. Poole, a botanist who may find a way for increasing the production of food, a valuable asset. While he is working on his scientific projects, he falls in love with a girl who returns his emotions. Because of his knowledge and helpful involvement, he is encouraged to join the priesthood and threatened with the prerequisite castration. So he makes his escape with the girl, and they head to a place where people live normal lives, and where they could marry. The endeavor is risky, for, if caught, both would be buried alive. Yet, as the script comes to its conclusion, they seem to be on the point of succeeding.

The conclusion, even if technically a happy ending, and perhaps intended to offer a glimmer of hope to humanity, cannot relieve the sense of despair and horror which animates the story. Indeed, some of the images conveyed in the script are almost too horrific to take in. The overall indictment of what we proudly call advanced, superior, modern civilization, could hardly be harsher. The despair of human progress could not be deeper. It is within this general framework that I will try to point out Huxley's attitude to science and technology, and the role they play in the scenario of the final collapse of civilization, as well as in its period of alleged bloom.

One accusation, rather common in our times, points to the menace of a catastrophic nuclear war. The modern, sophisticated, scientific technology, which has proved its efficacy in Hiroshima and Nagasaki, poses a threat to vast numbers of humanity and to civilization as we know it. Huxley conveys the idea by projecting a Third World War, with the dangerous radioactive conditions continuing after its conclusion. The great technological achievement has turned, with vengeance, against its human creators.

Yet the author reaches beyond this virtually self-evident — and in subsequent years much belabored — point. He poses, in a broad and abstract way, the question as to how ends and means are determined by humanity. Means obviously include technological and scientific measures, while ends seem to depend on some willful determination of unclear origin. The answer he offers is startling in its fundamental absurdity, and sends chill down the spine: "Ends are ape-chosen; only the means are man's." If we remember that apes represent the crude, vulgar, unthinking humanity, and "man" stands here for *Homo sapiens*, the creature of reason — the scientist, the mathematician, the philosopher — the tragic absurdity becomes clear.

The script elaborates: "Reason comes running" to gratify the wishes of the ape-man, Hegel's *Philosophy of History* serves the state of Prussia, medicine administers the Ape-King's aphrodisiac, calculus is used to aim rockets accurately "at the orphanage across the ocean."[20] Reason and knowledgeable people serve those who command power, however senseless and cruel their demands and needs may be. Reason is overwhelmed and actually ruled by unreason. The intrinsically superior serves the clearly inferior. The rational element in humanity is subservient to the irrational. The desirable relationship is subverted.

This situation is summed up, or rephrased, in another way. As the narrator in the script puts it: "Knowledge is merely another form of ignorance — highly organized, of course, and eminently scientific, but for that very reason all the more complete, all the more productive of angry apes."[21] Knowledge testifies to, or results in, a more complete ignorance, because the consequence of combining science with brute senselessness will only increase the disastrous results in an immensurable manner. Intelligence used by brutal force leads to consequences which are more faulty and catastrophic than those resulting from simple ignorance. The point is reminiscent of Swift's comment in *Gulliver's Travels* that the corruption of reason "might be worse than brutality itself."[22]

There is also a more evenhanded and somewhat milder reflection on the place of science and technology in human affairs, even if the conclusion remains pessimistic. There is an admission of some of the good sides, beside exposition of the detriments, even if the latter seem to tip the balance and justify fear as the prevailing emotion. "Fear of the much touted technology which, while it raises our standard of living, increases the probability of our violently dying. Fear of science which takes away with one hand even more than what it so profusely gives with the other." Huxley adds the fear of the failing institutions, such as the state, and the fear of the people in power, manifestations which, though beyond our focal concern about science and technology, fit into the general issue of human failure to separate the beneficial from the harmful and to assure the benefits without overpaying for them with suffering. The case of war, unwanted yet occurring, brings the argument to its culminating point.[23]

While one may dispute the somewhat sweeping allegations of the negative balance sheet of the findings of science and technology suggested here — an evaluation of the pros and cons in this regard would have to be much more detailed and specific — it is still an uncontestable conclusion that science and technology are not an unqualified boon for humanity.

Whatever the balance of benefits and detriments of science, the narrator in the script puts the blame on the failing of science to do unequivocal good for humanity by adducing a famous French scientist and philosopher. "Pascal explained it all more than three hundred years ago. 'We make an idol of truth; for truth without charity is not God, but his image and idol, which we must neither love nor worship.' You lived for the worship of an idol. But, in the last analysis, the name of every idol is Moloch."[24] The scientist, however genuinely committed to the pursuit of knowledge, of truth, actually worships Moloch, unless his search and work is informed by, bound with, overridden by charity. "Love thy neighbor" must be linked to the pursuit of truth, in order to prevent the abuse of truth and knowledge, of science and technology, by erring or wicked institutions and people.

As this linkage of knowledge to charity has been missing, humanity has faced horrid, catastrophic consequences, especially in modern times. Huxley refers to it as "the death, by suicide, of twentieth-century science."[25] For he depicts, in the present book, the demise of science itself due to its inherent advancement and perfection. For a world with nuclear weapons, and chemical and biological means of destruction at its disposal, may well destroy even the scientific edifice which created such advanced weapons, and the scientists who dedicated their lives to such magnificent achievements. They will be replaced by malformed, degenerate specimens of humanity. "A characteristic product of progressive technology" will be "a harelipped, Mongolian idiot."[26]

Huxley does not reserve his criticism of science to twentieth-century nuclear technology and the like. He sees the root of the problem in the sudden breakthrough and the eventual invasive application of science from the seventeenth century on. He conveys the argument through the mouth of the Arch-Vicar of St. Azazel. The human ego started to make headway against "the Order of Things," what we might call "the order of nature." This upset the balance. The lightening of burden, due to the machines, led to the subordination of flesh to iron and the mind becoming "the slave of wheels." As the machine became foolproof, it would also make people inspirationproof. Thus, genius and individuality — indeed, independent thinking — were being undermined by the machine. The tool was turning into the master. Abundance of food and its transportation from the New World, another consequence of the technological progress, resulted in increase of population, with its own voracious appetite and its "New Hunger," which led to total wars. The balance which underlay human civilization was upset, and the consequence must have been catastrophic, one way or another.[27]

Some of this argument may be questioned — it is by no means clear, for example, whether economic factors are chiefly responsible for modern wars — and perhaps Huxley puts it in the mouth of his *advocatus diaboli* to indicate an extreme partisan point of view. Yet there is little doubt that the author accepts the gist of it. This is well conveyed in the following statement, still coming from the lips of the cynical Arch-Vicar, referring to Belial, the diabolical deity. "He foresaw that men would be made so overwhelmingly bumptious by the miracles of their own technology that they would soon lose all sense of reality. And that's precisely what happened. These wretched slaves of wheels and ledgers began to congratulate themselves on being the Conquerors of Nature." The technological success led to human hubris and this had no limits. The claim of the conquest of nature is derided by pointing to ecological abuse: fouling the rivers, destroying the forests, squandering the minerals—"an orgy of criminal imbecility." Technological progress coupled with ecological ignorance and neglect was a way to disaster, even without a nuclear collision.[28]

The answer to the problem of the errant human is directly opposite to the historical development—notably in the scientific technological era. Those can enjoy existence, fill their life with joy, only who live in accord "with the given Order of the world." Those who want to improve upon that order, to rebel against it, become estranged from the joy of life. "Love, Joy and Peace ... are the fruits of the spirit" that is the essence of humanity "and the essence of the world. But the fruits of the ape-mind, the fruits of the monkey's presumption and revolt, are hate and unceasing restlessness and a chronic misery."[29] Thus it is important not only to link knowledge with charity, but also to pursue it in harmony with the fundamentally peaceful and congenial nature of the world. The attempt of humans to confront nature, to master or to trick it, is an endeavor of the ape in humanity, of the sinister and restless and fundamentally unhappy element in humanity, to disregard the essence of things. This seems to be the conclusion and the advice of Huxley, epigrammatically conveyed in the title "Ape and Essence."

Does Huxley resolve the problem which he so aptly poses? Can people find a harmonious coexistence with nature by being true to their essence? The answer seems to us to be more complicated. For one thing, the order of the world is not all expression of love, joy and peace. We do not witness these in the animal kingdom, we do not trace these in natural selection and evolution. As to humanity, much of its endeavor to improve on nature—at least as far as its own condition is concerned—may well run counter to the alleged harmony, as Huxley points out. The material human civilization does not necessarily express the natural order. The expansion of human habitat and the improvement in the material quality of life owe their achievements to science and technology, possibly driven by human restlessness. The quiet, placid disposition does not go along with innovation. Yet this need not be disastrous. For humans are a part of nature, and yet stand apart from nature.

This is our ambiguous position; this is *our* nature.

Having said that, it is clear that Huxley's warning against the menace of modern technology in its crude manifestations in nuclear weapons cannot be overemphasized. The ethical neutrality of scientists is certainly justly criticized. The implicit trust in any technical project, without regard to ecological limitations, is outright foolish, just another manifestation of a blind and narrow belief in science and technology. The threat that technological progress and the consequent cushioned life may undermine the very ingenuity and knowledge that made this progress possible, is another feat of the crafty menace of the machine. These dangers may not be irreversible, but they loom large, and the warnings are as timely today, as they were prophetic when articulated by Aldous Huxley. It is doubtful whether humanity can return to its supposed symbiotic relationship with nature. It has, however, to find a *modus vivendi* which will enable it to exist, and this cannot be achieved without the understanding of nature and some sense of humility towards its surroundings.

10

The Threat of Paradise

Humans, whose lives are short and full of suffering, whether personal or communal, have been looking for an improvement in their condition and for a way to overcome their afflictions. Such efforts have been one of the major aspects of civilization. Such endeavors have been evident not only in various concrete efforts of a technological kind or of an organizational nature, but also in myths and ideologies. The myths of the "golden age" and of paradise have found their continuation or counterparts in speculative plans of philosophers and in utopian visions of the future. Such visions have occasionally been linked to technological projections and even more typically to the overall rule of reason and rational judgment and principles. This should not be surprising, as much social malaise seems to be rooted in irrational human propensities manifest in individual and public life.

Yet, the belief that pure reason offers a solution to all human ills has not remained unchallenged. To equate reason with good, and all the irrational human elements — including fantasy, dreams, yearning, emotions — with misery or evil, is a gross simplification of human nature. The situation is much more complex. Yet the temptation to offer solutions and facile answers has not been resisted by thinkers ancient and modern.

The problem has implications beyond the intellectual or theoretical exercise. For the designers of social perfection have often recommended the employment of force and coercion to implement their notions of the good society, which has occasionally led to disastrous results. Aldous Huxley conveys the problem succinctly, when he refers to "a specious logic" that "leads to tyranny which, in the *Republic*, is held up as the ideal form of government." The application of alleged logic and the scientific approach typifies not only Plato in antiquity, but also Marxists and fascists in our times. "They simplify, they abstract, they eliminate all that, for their purposes, is irrelevant and ignore whatever they choose to regard as inessential; they impose a style, they compel the facts to verify a favorite hypothesis" The consequence of all this is that "the prisons are full, political heretics are worked to death as slaves, the rights and preferences of mere individuals are ignored."[1]

It could well be added that the penchant for following a formula for perfection need not be restricted to communist and fascist regimes, which have proved to serve sinister interests, beside claiming their noble intents. The trust in reason and science may prove faulty and dangerous even when no ulterior motive is present and even when it is not confined to a single overriding ideology. Even in democratic and liberal societies people may trust the findings and pronouncements of physiologists, psychologists and sociologists, failing to realize that the human soul has not been exhaustively explored and mapped by all the advanced sciences. Even the complex findings of the so-called behavioral sciences may fall short of understanding the mysteries of the human mind and soul. Overconfidence in science may ignore and endanger some elusive yet vital elements of the human mind.

If Zamiatin's *We* exposes the danger to humanity resulting from the allegedly rational system of a self-confident but ruthless regime, like the communist state, Huxley's *Brave New World* points to the dangers inherent in the benign and seemingly humane treatment of a kind and philanthropic utopian system. In both instances human well-being and happiness is the ostensible and declared objective of the system. In both cases the systems fail, because they ignore certain imponderable elements in human soul, which not only have not been scientifically explained, but appear to elude and resist rational analysis and prediction — that is to say, remain beyond the long arm of science.

Thus, the offer of paradise, the promise of utopian bliss, turns into some kind of a faulty design. The fault is not self-evident, and may be difficult to pinpoint. Yet, for one reason or another, or perhaps for no clear reason, some people are not ready for the bliss which they have been seeking for ages. As paradise comes imperceptibly closer it turns into a threat to humanity, as it is perceived and felt by the more reflective and sensitive specimens of the species.

Happiness and Freedom

We, a novel by the Russian writer Eugene Zamiatin, was composed in 1920, and published in English translation in 1924 — significantly, some years before its publication in the original Russian. The reason for this peculiar sequence, as well as for the fact that the Russian text was published outside the Soviet Union, was the political nature of the novel, linked to and addressed to the new communist regime.

Curiously, Zamiatin had been an ardent revolutionary, suffering imprisonment and banishment at the hands of the czarist regime, but his enthusiasm for the new Soviet Union waned fast. The disillusionment could not be more vigorously expressed than in the bitter and merciless satire of *We*. The dogmatism, the arrogance, the disregard of individuality, the insistence on conformity, the pedestrian culture, the police control, the ruthlessness and cruelty of the new revolutionary system are exposed, as is its self-righteous belief that it assures the happiness of the people.

Yet, as even this summary indicates, the criticism is addressed not merely at the Soviet Union's communism, which is not mentioned by name at all, but at a larger menace — the belief in administering happiness to humanity by imposing on it a rational and scientific system and excluding any deviation claimed in the name of personal freedom. It is not merely the self-confident arrogance of dialectical materialism in its social application that is exposed and condemned, but the hubris of reason which claims to comprehend human needs, and in order to gratify these excludes and banishes all dreams, desires, and emotions, which do not fit into the rational and scientific scheme or design of the benevolent, yet merciless, authority.

Thus, the novel is profoundly linked to the issue of the role of science and rationality in the utopian society and the need for imposing limitations on this role. That the world depicted by Zamiatin is also replete with advanced technological achievements and applications only amplifies the panorama of the overall scientific design, expressed on various levels of individual and social existence. There is a grand design, a comprehensive and coherent philosophy, which is translated into reality by rational laws and institutions and by architectural and technological inventions. They all combine into a consistent whole, which benefits all its parts. Yet, this seemingly perfect system has a fundamental flaw in that it ignores the unpredictable, irrational, free element in people.

The story itself, written in the form of a diary, presents the "United State" controlling the entire world, having been established one thousand years ago. In other words, the story takes us into the end of the third millennium A.D., and the entelechy of the rational development of human society, as seen by the rulers of that society. Having reached such perfection and maturity, the United State plans to send a spaceship, called the Integral, into the universe, to spread its gospel of the perfect rational civilization to the beings of other planets for their own good — whether they want it or not. Thus the zeal to spread the benefits of the rational way of life is proclaimed. (Conceivably, the writer here mocks the communist zeal to spread the creed throughout the world.) The citizens of the United State are not referred to as "people," but as "Numbers." They have no private or family names, but each individual is marked by a letter and number. Instead of men and women, there are he–Numbers and she–Numbers. Both sexes have standard unifs (uniforms); each individual occupies an identical apartment, similarly furnished; the houses are of one pattern; and the walls made of transparent glass, so that people can watch each other. At certain prescribed hours one is allowed to draw the curtains, to allow for sexual intercourse.

These relations also follow a prescribed code. Anyone can ask for a sexual relationship with anyone else and is issued a permit. Within this regulated promiscuity some emotional attachments may form, but they do not override the system and they do not lead to the formation of family. Procreation is strictly controlled by the state, which decides who may produce children, according to certain established norms, and the babies are taken away from the parents and brought up by the state without any natural link being allowed. Numbers live in a city and do not travel to other places, because roads were destroyed during the Two Hundred Years' War, and because traveling is meaningless, with all cities evidently built in a similar pattern. Thus, sedentary life is the established way, though this does not preclude local travel by "aeros" (a kind of a flying automobile) and regular walks (always a collective exercise, four abreast) at prescribed hours. Indeed, the personal life of all the Numbers follows the "Tables," which also determine the time to eat, to sleep, the personal hours and so on.

The Tables, whose primitive precursor was "that greatest of all monuments of ancient literature, the Official Railroad Guide," assure uniformity. "Every morning..., at the same hour, at the same minute, we wake up, millions of us at once. At the very same hour ... we begin our work, and ... we finish it. United into a single body..., at the very same second, designated by the Tables, we carry the spoons to our mouths; at the same second we all go out to walk, ... and then to bed."[2] This stress on the collective uniformity and the complementary reduction — virtually abolition — of individuality is symbolized by the book's, and diary's, title: *We*. Though an individual protagonist writes it, he intends to express the collective consciousness. He is, at least at the outset of the story, the perfect product of the United State.

10—The Threat of Paradise

The Two Hundred Years' War was between the city and the land. In the end the city won and became independent of land by developing petroleum food. Once rid of hunger, the state proceeded to get rid of the affection of love and the concomitant passion of jealousy. Thus sex turned into a function like eating or sleeping, without any attendant suffering. Another impediment to happiness was removed.

The city is separated from the surrounding land by the Green Wall, a division between civilization and nature. Nature is considered imperfect, faulty, and dangerous, and is out of bounds for Numbers. Indeed, even sunlight and weather in the city seem to be controlled to accord with the convenience of civilization. Science, reason, and logic rule supreme.

The political authority of the United State is in the hands of the Well-Doer, annually reelected to office on the Day of Unanimity, by the open vote of the public assembly. The enforcement of the law is entrusted to the Guardians. They are the ubiquitous spies making sure that nobody deviates from the rules prescribed by the Tables. Cases of transgressions lead to investigation by sophisticated scientific torture, which may be followed by public execution enacted by the Well-Doer through the Machine, which turn the culprit into nothing. Such occasions are not unlike a religious ceremony, accompanied by the ecstasy of the onlookers.

The protagonist of the story is D-503, a mathematician and the builder of the Integral, to be finished in one hundred and twenty days. His diary, intended for future generations, conveys the story from his personal perspective, which is in no way constant. Indeed, it oscillates between expressing the orthodox stand of the United State, and some disturbing emotions which are in conflict with the official philosophy. This conflict is the leitmotif of the account, though it is intertwined with other persons and with occurrences which are combined into the plot of the developing drama.

D-503 has a fairly steady relationship with O-90, who is even more strongly attached to him. This does not interfere with her relationship to another he–Number, a poet. While D-503 complies with this situation, in accordance with the system, he encounters I-330, a she–Number of a different kind. In contrast to O-90's dependent, feminine, maternal nature, I-330 is a defiant, dominant and self-assured personality, with ideas and aims transcending her personal well-being. She exerts an irresistible charm on D-503, who falls in love with her — love in the atavistic sense, accompanied by exclusiveness and jealousy. I-330 responds, though it is not quite clear whether she does it out of a genuine feeling, or because of her political designs.

For I-330 is in conspiracy with some others who aim at no less a goal than overturning the present regime and returning to some form of an earlier civilization. The meeting place of the protagonist and his lover occasionally takes place in the Ancient Home, an official museum which displays the primitive way of life of earlier generations — opaque walls, strange furniture, various non-functional embellishments. At one point I-330 takes D-503 behind the Green Wall, where he touches natural ground, sees red sky, and encounters naked savages, the residue of humanity outside the civilized world.

The meetings with I-330 involve some transgressions of the regulations and the prescribed time-table, but I-330 has the right connections which supply D-503 with medical excuses for the irregularities. As the protagonist's passion for I-330 develops, he is ready to do whatever she asks — even to make the Integral land on the wrong side of the Green Wall during its first experimental flight. Alas, this fails due to the interference of the Guardians.

On the personal level, O-90 has convinced D-503 to make her pregnant, despite the realization that this will lead to her execution (for she is ten centimeters too short to qualify for maternity). Her maternal instincts combined with her love for D-503 urge her to take this desperate step. When D-503 tries to save her with the help of I-330, she refuses — obviously because of jealousy. Yet, eventually she accepts the offer and is taken by I-330 beyond the Green Wall, assuring her and her baby's survival.

On the public level, the forces of revolt make their presence known by voting in great numbers against the reelection of the Well-Doer. While this outrage is officially explained as a sick aberration and, contravening the facts, the unanimity of the "yes" vote is proclaimed, the social order shows cracks in various ways. The daily marches are disturbed, he–Numbers and she–Numbers embrace in public, and the Green Wall is blown up. The government, however, takes strict measures. It commands, on the penalty of death, that everybody undergo a newly invented brain surgery, which eradicates fancy and turns people into virtual automatons. This, of course, will assure absolute compliance with the system.

The protagonist, seemingly committed to join the revolution, is persistently beset by doubts. Are his emotions a sickness, or a new dimension of life? Is his sense of having a soul of intrinsic worth, or an abnormal symptom? Is the revolt justified, or is it a crime? His overriding passion for I-330 tips the balance. When, however, he is summoned to the Well-Doer, the latter suggests that he, D-503, has been used by the rebels, and this changes his attitude at once. Evidently feeling betrayed by I-330, he reports on his own conduct to the Guardians, undergoes the surgery which cures him of his soul, and betrays I-330. Then he watches, indifferently, the torture of I-330, who remains silent and does not betray her fellow conspirators. The revolt is going to be overcome, to the protagonist's satisfaction.

While the outline of the story touches on the elements of science and technology, which are linked to and intertwined with the fantastic world and the dramatic events depicted in the novel, these aspects have to be highlighted and analyzed in a more focused way. Needless to say, whatever may be said in praise of science by the protagonist — though he all too often vacillates in his opinion — is exactly the opposite of Zamiatin's stand.

Zamiatin chose for his protagonist a mathematician in charge of a grand technological project, which makes him, to some extent, an applied mathematician. Indeed, D-503 thinks in mathematical symbols, even when he deals with a subject matter which is quite remote from mathematics, such as the recesses of human mind. The Integral, a mathematical concept, symbolizes the peak of aspiration and the apex of self-confidence of the scientific society, and its solid mathematical foundation. Not that all science and all the rational regulations can be reduced to mathematical formulas, but mathematics is the anchor and the symbol of the civilization depicted by the protagonist.

D-503 speaks about mathematics like a religious mystic. "To integrate the colossal, universal equation! To unbend the wild curve, to straighten it out to a tangent — to a straight line! For the United State is a straight line, a great, divine, precise, wise line, the wisest of lines!"[3]

Such language may, perhaps, be made more palatable, if we compare it with the Platonic trust in logically perceived eternal ideas as the abstract patterns which ought to be emulated in human experience. The straight line, realized by the United State, may parallel the idea of good which guides Platonic recommendations for humans and society. The straight line may well symbolize reason, the only authority to be entrusted with the control and rule of the chaotic universe, whether of nature or of humanity, symbolized by the curve. That people become Numbers may appear like the hallucinations of a mathematician gone mad, but is consistent with this mathematical orientation. Numbers can be ordered, organized, manipulated in an easy way, while human beings, each with his or her own individuality, defy the simplicity and clarity of mathematically inspired control.

Mathematics has its applications in technology, or technology is constructed and run on principles closely linked to mathematical formulas and calculations. Consequently, the protagonist and his fellow Numbers display admiration for the mathematically and scientifically controlled technology and the civilization enjoying it, and an aversion to nature, which is at the mercy of erratic and unpredictable forces. Thus D-503 dislikes spring, because it brings pollen of flowers from behind the Green Wall which sweetens the lips. "This somewhat disturbs my logical thinking." He likes the blue sky not marred by a cloud, and ridicules the primitive taste of the ancient poets, who were "inspired by these senseless, formless, stupidly rushing accumulations of vapor! I love ... only such a sky — a sterile, faultless sky. On such days the whole universe seems to be moulded of the same eternal glass, like the Green Wall, and like all our buildings."[4]

No wonder that D-503 distrusts the vagaries of nature, of things out of reliable human control, just as he fears the unknown future. As he puts it: "It is unnatural for a thinking and seeing human being to live among irregularities, unknowns, X's."[5] Any threat to the status quo entails such dangers. For mathematically formulated science is essentially static and excludes or avoids irregular developments.

The pervasive scientific orientation has an overwhelming impact on the social order. Social order must be adapted to the postulates and requirements of a strictly scientific approach. Science cannot possibly encompass the idiosyncrasy and consequent diversity of individual personalities. Therefore uniformity must be imposed on human behavior, aiming at the uniformity of humanity. This is the reason why the Tables, prescribing uniform conduct, are so cherished. Human beings may not yet be perfectly uniform, but the scientific forces propel them in this direction.

Uniformity facilitates scientific generalizations and predictability, and thereby precludes freedom. Freedom is the enemy of science and logic. It also contradicts art. Dance is beautiful, "because it is an *unfree* movement... Because the deep meaning of the dance is contained in its absolute, ecstatic submission, in the ideal *non-freedom*."[6] Then, of course, freedom is the condition which makes crime possible. Zero freedom means no crime! Consequently, freedom is the antithesis of civilized life. Thus the protagonist, during his pietistic, rational phase, makes the following comment about the way of life of the ancients: "Yet how could they have State logic, since they lived in a condition of freedom like beasts, like apes, like herds?"[7] Civilization must be based on a finite closed system, regulated by logic and controlled by scientific techniques.

Such a systematic scheme of civilization facilitates the assurance of happiness as well. Freedom may lead to erratic actions and consequent dire results.

10—The Threat of Paradise

Absolute control by science and scientific order enables the rulers of the society to ensure the benefits which are recognized as such by scientific inquiry, and thus to secure overall happiness. Our protagonist waxes enthusiastic about the happiness expressed and symbolized by the multiplication table. In the words of a poet:

> Two times two — eternal lovers;
> Inseparable in passion four....[8]

As D-503 watches the lowered curtains in the glass homes at the appointed sex hour, he muses about the "Taylorized happiness," referring to one of the regulations established by a benefactor of humanity of that name. Happiness in a rationally controlled society — and there can be no happiness otherwise — must be uniform, predictable, systematically apportioned.

Of course, human beings can err. The power of logic may not be a sufficient force to assure that everybody will abide by the rules all the time and thus walk on the path of happiness. Therefore supervision and, if need be, coercion are needed to assure the rule of science. The Guardians — spies, in common language — are there to watch over people. D-503 is extremely grateful for this arrangement, and as he is spied on while reading poetry, he cannot but see in the system "the materialization of the dream of the ancients about a Guardian Angel." With biting irony, Zamiatin puts into his mouth the following words: "It is pleasant to feel that somebody's penetrating eye is watching you from behind your shoulder, lovingly guarding you from making the most minute mistake, from the most minute incorrect step."[9] In a world where mathematical precision rules, the benevolent attention of the teacher assures the correctness of the calculation and the right solutions. Yet, if despite all this, some Numbers err and deviate from the prescribed conduct, the state employs coercive measures to set things right. A cardinal means to investigate the deviants is the Gas Bell, based on the science of physics, using scientific techniques to achieve the investigator's aim. It must not be likened to the Inquisition, even if it may be similarly "unpleasant," for its purpose is "to guard the security of the United State — in other words, the happiness of millions."[10]

If happiness is the product of a scientifically controlled humanity, what is to be done about the irrational human elements, elements whose existence cannot be denied? They can be repressed and suppressed, but they seem to make their presence known in various forms, whether in what the United State regards as personal aberrations or in an outright political dissent. Such irregularities have to be defined in scientific terms of course, as long as science is accepted as the ultimate and absolute arbiter of what is true and what is desirable.

One kind of aberration is dreaming, and it is viewed as sickness. This is how D-503 reacts to the experience of a dream. "I am sick, it is clear; I never saw dreams before. They say that to see dreams was a common normal thing with the ancients.... But we, people of today, we know all too well that dreaming is a serious mental disease." Claiming that his brain is a "precise, clean, glittering mechanism," he cannot but see a dream as a foreign element.[11]

Whether it is dreaming only in the literal sense, or also in a wider meaning, is not indicated, but it is safe to assume that both such not strictly rational activities of the mind fall under the category of sickness. For if it could be suggested that daydreaming may often serve as the source of inspiration, which may evolve into artistic creativity, such inspiration is also dismissed as a manifestation of sickness — in fact, "an extinct form of epilepsy." In the new civilization, music is the product of a mathematical composition. A recently invented musicometer enables anyone, by merely rotating a handle, "to produce about three sonatas per hour."[12]

Together with dreams and inspiration go emotions and what we might call deeper and nobler feelings. As noted, love is substituted by physiological function, regulated and apportioned like the supply of food. Maternal instincts are ignored and eradicated. When a dozen men are killed in an accident related to the Integral, its builder, D-503, calculates that "a dozen Numbers represent scarcely one hundred millionth part of the United State. Then he comments: "Pity, a result of arithmetical ignorance, was known to the ancients; to us it seems absurd."[13] It is all numbers and calculations, and whatever does not fit into quantification or a mathematical formula, or cannot be mastered by orderly knowledge, is a mere illusion and does not exist. For "the unknown is naturally the enemy of man. And *Homo sapiens* only then becomes man in the complete sense of the word, when his punctuation includes no question marks...."[14]

Yet this picture of perfection has not been attained. Many people fall short of the ideal of rational, controlled, predictable human beings. As noted, D-503 himself increasingly develops symptoms of deviation from the desirable, or even prevalent, norm, due to his infatuation with I-330. His sickness, for it is taken as such, is diagnosed as developing a soul, a sickness which is spreading and feared to assume epidemic proportions. Of course, it is in the nature of such mental sickness that the person afflicted with it does not recognize it as such. D-503 agonizes how to reconcile such alleged sickness with his orderly mathematical way of thinking. There is the irrational number, the square root of minus one, $\sqrt{-1}$, to which there seems to be no corresponding reality and no feasible application. Confident that "mathematics ... never makes mistakes," irrational numbers must have corresponding real existence. And so the square root of minus one may be "nothing else but my 'soul.'"[15]

Needless to say, the authorities of the United State do not digress into such speculations. They stick to their ideal of humanity: predictable, controllable, and devoid of the disturbing element of fancy and dreaming in one form or another. The wording of the *State Journal*, addressing its readers, makes the point crystal clear. "Until today your own creation, engines, were more perfect than you.... The philosophy of the cranes, presses, and pumps is complete and clear like a circle... But have you not become as precise as a pendulum?" The answer to this question is a regretful "No." For "there is one difference: MECHANISMS HAVE NO FANCY." And the *Journal* elaborates: "Did you ever notice a pump cylinder with a wide, distant, sensuously dreaming smile while it was working? ... NO. Yet on your own faces ... the Guardians have more and more frequently seen those smiles, and they have heard your sighs." Still this "is not your fault; you are ill. And the name of your illness is: FANCY." Luckily, this imperfection, which makes people inferior to the machines they produce, has its physiological source and can be dealt with medically. "The latest discovery of our state science is that there is a center for fancy—a miserable little nervous knot in the lower region of the frontal lobe of the brain. A triple treatment of this knot with X-rays will cure you of fancy."[16]

The ideal human is the machine-like human. The source of the human soul is in physiology, and physiology can be treated by medical science, and thus reduce—no, elevate—humans to the level of the machine, and make them fit into the overall scientific order of civilization.

Here are the "encouraging" words, exhorting people to submit to the Great Operation. "There they will cure you; there they will overfeed you with that leavened happiness. Satiated, you will slumber peacefully, organized, keeping time, and snoring sweetly. Is it possible that you do not hear yet that great symphony of snoring? ... Don't you realize that they want to liberate you from these gnawing, worm-like torturing question marks?"[17] The ideal of the uniform, predictable, happy humanity, that symphony of snoring, is contrasted with humanity tormented with unanswerable questions, but retaining its unpredictability, its freedom, its soul. Of course, there is no doubt which of the two Zamiatin opts for.

Zamiatin's presentation of science, and of a scientifically controlled society, is nothing short of a caricature. If the nature of caricature is to exaggerate certain characteristics of the subject of ridicule, this may well be true of Zamiatin's depiction of the United State's scientific approach. Though Zamiatin does not specify in what way this science fails, the failings may be implicit in his story and are worth being identified and explicitly stated. For it is our assumption that Zamiatin did not reject science as such, nor did he advocate to return to the savage society beyond the Green Wall. He presents the "natural" alternative to the United State, but this does not mean that this is the only alternative of humanity to the kind of logical, scientific society which he abhors.

One characteristic of the scientific approach which appears to be criticized and rejected in *We* is its dogmatic nature. The science of the United State is not encumbered by doubts. It is not modeled on experimental science, always ready to check its conclusions, and, if need be, revise them in view of new evidence. It is modeled on mathematics, a deductive discipline, which reaches absolutely true conclusions. Such a dogmatic approach characterizes the theory of dialectical materialism (itself affected by Hegel's deductive metaphysics), the ideological foundation of soviet communism. The social rules, the political institutions, the human ideals of such a system become a matter of unconditional *belief*, though the system pretends to be rational *science*. There is no place here for doubts, for "maybe," for "perhaps." All is absolutely true, and this truth aims at attaining blessedness.

Therefore the mission of the Integral is "to subjugate to the grateful yoke of reason the unknown beings who live on other planets, and who are perhaps still in the primitive state of freedom. If they will not understand that we are bringing them a mathematically faultless happiness, our duty will be to force them to be happy."[18] The phrasing is reminiscent of the assertion of Rousseau that to impose the general will of a society on a dissenting individual is no more than "to compel a man to be free."[19] That enforced happiness may be as questionable as an enforced freedom is a conclusion clearly intended by Zamiatin, and with very good reason. He may also doubt — and the book constantly dwells on this issue — whether happiness is the only, or even the most important, purpose of human existence. This issue, however, is outside the frame of reference of the present study.

Another implicitly criticized characteristic of the science of the United

State is its comprehensive, all-embracing nature. The idea that science may apply to a number of human observations and experiences and that technology may be helpful in a variety of human endeavors, but that there are spheres and domains which elude rational inquiry and systematic comprehension, let alone mechanical control, is entirely alien to the rulers of the United State. Everything is scientized, and whatever escapes the control of science, either does not exist, or is an aberration to be eradicated. Science, and science only, is in charge. Therefore music can be created by a technological device, and psychological problems, or manifestations seen as such, can be treated by medical techniques. Here another aspect of the materialistic philosophy — evidently Marxian — comes to the fore. Needless to say, whether for better or for worse, science does not exercise exclusive authority over the entire domain of human experience and affairs — at least, not yet!

A somewhat less obvious point, which Zamiatin may have overdone, is the equation of science with absolute determinism, and thereby the exclusion of freedom in a world controlled by, or believed to be controlled by, science. The praise for dance — which may come to represent any artistic expression — because of its unfree movement, that is to say, because it is subject to certain rules and limitations (an issue referred to above), reflects the fallacy concerned. Being subject to rules need not mean absence of freedom. The point has been illustrated by a modern philosopher, who points out that the exact rules of the chess game do not preclude an enormous diversity of games, determined by the players.[20] The same may hold true of artistic freedom within certain limitations of forms and aesthetic rules. If this point may be further expanded, the lesson offered here is that science and art, order and freedom, reason and free will, are not incompatible. Zamiatin did not make this point, but presumably he would have agreed with it. It is the arrogance of reason and the totalitarian claim of science which he abhorred — especially when it claimed mastery over all established customs and tradition and over the mystery of human spirit. His message is not "Beware of reason!" Rather: "Beware of arrogant and ruthless reason, especially when it claims to be dedicated to human happiness."

The Siren Song of Bliss

While Zamiatin's *We* portrays a society dedicated to human happiness, this society institutes its designs and practices with the ruthlessness of a dictatorial and totalitarian regime, which reflected the actual experience of such a system and was a precursor to even worse excesses. Consequently it is almost impossible to dissociate the United State of the distant future from the European experience of the first half of the twentieth century. It is the ruthlessness and cruelty of the United State, rather than its alleged beneficial aim, that remains the aftertaste left by the story.

Huxley's *Brave New World*, another presentation of a happy world, portrays a kinder and gentler regime. No crude force and no torture and executions are employed to assure a happy and harmonious society. The means employed are much more sophisticated and therefore much more effective. Yet the resulting humanity in its seductive bliss is not quite humanity as we know it, or as Huxley would wish it to be. Thus we are facing another satire — less obvious and less explicit, but no less pungent and powerful, once the impact of the novel is allowed to settle.

Aldous Huxley first published the novel in 1932. Since then it has been reprinted many times and remained a widely-known classic in its genre of utopian, or rather anti-utopian, literature. Despite the passage of time which may have made the work dated in some respects, Huxley resisted the temptation of changing the original text, though he did make some comments on it, partially critical, which are of interest to the serious reader of the original work.

Like Zamiatin's *We*, the world Huxley confronts us with is in the distant future, though half as distant as in Zamiatin's book — to be exact, in "A.F." 632. A.F. replaces A.D., and is counted from the first appearance of the Model-T Ford, 1908 A.D. Thus A.F. 632 would correspond to 2540 A.D. That Huxley introduces a new chronological scheme is, of course, quite deliberate. Ford, or the assembly-line of the Ford factory, symbolizes the new kind of civilization in which traditional perceptions and values, including religion, have been replaced by a mechanical world, a world in which human beings themselves are produced by a manufacturing process and behave in an orderly, predictable, controlled manner. Humanity is produced by assembly-line techniques and resembles the products of mechanized manufacturing — with a few exceptions, which are also taken care of by the system.

The world which Huxley describes has abolished family and natural reproduction in favor of a strictly planned increase of population in hatcheries. Ova of voluntary donors, surgically removed from ovaries, are artificially fertilized, and the embryos chemically controlled to produce different varieties of babies — from the lowest "epsilons" to the highest "alphas." Each category is predestined to belong to a specific caste, and each caste is designed to perform social tasks suited to its mental capacity. On top of it, by applying a so-called "Bokanovsky's process," up to ninety-six identical twins can be produced, which is of special advantage for lower castes destined to perform mechanical jobs where coordination is a great advantage.

Babies, from earliest days, are exposed to systematic conditioning, designed to make them like the task they are predestined to perform and to dislike what they will not be able to attain. This will prevent them from being unhappy in their adult lives and from striving to change their role and station in life, thereby causing social instability. Moreover, they are exposed to repetitious slogans — whether during sleep (hypnopedia) or in waking hours — which inculcate in them certain basic values and judgments, which agree with and promote their social roles.

This system produces happy people, for, as the Director of Hatcheries and Conditioning explains, "the secret of happiness and virtue" is "liking what you've *got* to do. All conditioning aims at that: making people like their unescapable social destiny."[21] Any residual dissatisfaction, or temporary moodiness, is taken care of by *soma*, a narcotic which creates pleasant hallucinations, without perceptible side-effects. People are sustained in youthful condition by means of drugs till old age, when they suddenly die. There is no aging and change; only stability and cessation.

This world is characterized by what it has eradicated, not less than by what it has instituted. As noted, there are no marriages and no private families. Viviparous birth is a shocking affair, "mother" and "father" obscene words, while promiscuity, with secure means to prevent pregnancy, is encouraged and generally practiced. Any instinctive urges of a woman for motherhood are treated with medications. While families are banned and romance and personal attachments discouraged, the sense of belonging to the larger community and a sense of social commitment are encouraged and cultivated by repeated slogans and hypnopedia. The exclusiveness of close relations among few people is replaced by social allegiance. In the words of one slogan, "everyone belongs to everyone else."[22] This results in reduction of emotional life, which is only for the better. The less emotions, the less suffering.

The system discourages looking into the past. "History is bunk." And so, "Athens and Rome, Jerusalem and the Middle Kingdom — all were gone."[23] They are all replaced by the new system, dictated by the rational design of society and human life, a system of stability inherently averse to change.

Along with history, books are banned — at least those published before A.F. 150 (2058 A.D.).

Religion and the notion of soul are manifestations of the irrelevant past. The new religion substitutes Ford for God, and the cross is cut to a T, reminiscent of the T-model, and the sign of T is reverently made over the stomach — apparently Huxley's allusion to the materialistic nature of this civilization. *Soma*, mentioned above, is praised as having "all the advantages of Christianity and alcohol: none of their defects."[24] There are also various pseudo-religious observances and ceremonies, including fortnightly Solidarity Services, which start with solemn hymns, continue with ecstasy, and end in an orgy, a final consummation of solidarity.

Yet, if all is new in this civilization and history is obsolete, there is a brief mention of how it all came about, a rudimentary history of the transition from the ancient to the modern and final stage. There is mention of the Nine Years' War, which began in A.F. 141, and which involved massive air-bombing with anthrax, infecting water supplies, and which led to an economic collapse. Humanity faced the choice between world control and destruction. It chose the former and thus a united world government was established. The crude violent suppression of various opposition sectors, clinging to the old culture or to simple life, was superseded by the gentler and more efficient techniques of conditioning and hypnopedia. The new world struck roots and took shape.

Besides the description of the utopia, its institutions and their working, which is perhaps the most fascinating aspect of the novel, Huxley intertwines it with a plot, which starts at a slow pace and then assumes a dramatic quality and eventually is resolved in a tragic way. There are several main characters. One is the already mentioned director of Hatcheries and Conditioning of Central London, an important post, as it involves the creation of life and shaping of the minds and attitudes of the newborn. The Director, as I will refer to him, is a person with a sense of self-importance and an authoritarian disposition. Another man, of even higher status, is Mustapha Mond, who is one of the ten World Controllers, in charge of Western Europe. He is all authority combined with sweet reason.

Bernard Marx of the Psychology Bureau is lower placed, but still an A+ and thus a member of the high caste. He suffers from what are regarded as some flaws. He is shorter than members of his class and his emotions and judgments deviate from the ways inculcated in the members of his caste. Thus, his liking for, even infatuation with, the beautiful Lenina Crowne, a B caste member, is too personal, and he is upset that his acquaintances speak of her as if she was just a bit of meat, as indeed is her own perception of herself. Bernard Marx looks for some emotional depth in his relations with her, and not merely for physiological gratification. He wants some privacy, which contrasts with Lenina's normal love of crowds. He fails to feel a part of a group during a religious-sexual worship session, even though he pretends to be like the others. His peculiarities are noticed and attributed to a mistaken addition of alcohol to the bottle in which he was gestated. While different from and feeling alien in the perfect world, in the great utopia, he displays a rather timid and weak character, and does not assert his opinion and stance, out of concern for his career. Huxley uses this unique and individualistic figure to introduce a counterpoint to the mostly stereotypic characters of the utopian world.

A close friend of Bernard is Helmholtz Watson, also a distinct individual, who looks askance at the perfect world. Yet he does so not in a timid and hesitant manner, but in an unabashed and self-confident way. His uniqueness is due to his exceptional intelligence, not to mention his good looks. He is a lecturer at the College of Emotional Engineering and he composes "feely scenarios" (film scripts), as well as slogans and hypnopedic rhymes. Yet he is dissatisfied with the inherent triviality of his work and phony creation, and yearns to express himself in a genuine way, even if he does not know what it is he wants to say. Two additional important characters will be introduced in the following sketchy presentation of the story.

Bernard Marx takes Lenina for a trip to an Indian reservation in New Mexico, where people live the way they used to from times immemorial. The travelers descend into an ancient world and a particularly primitive variety of it. The material conditions are elementary, while the religious beliefs and cults are of a syncretistic Christian-Indian nature. Before leaving for the trip, the Director tells Bernard that he made such a voyage twenty-five years ago in the company of a girl who vanished during the trip and could not be found.

On the reservation, Bernard and Lenina encounter a young man with a white complexion, visibly different from the Indians. He speaks their language and English, which he learned from his mother, Linda. Linda — neglected, obese, dirty — is no other than the lost companion of the Director; she had been injured and thus lost, and then cut off from civilization. Her son John was fathered by the Director. Linda, who has all those years cultivated her original upbringing and tried to impress her son with the glory of civilized life, has not endeared herself to the natives, particularly because of her promiscuous ways.

Her son suffered as an alien, as well. Therefore, when Bernard — having contacted Mustapha Mond, aroused his curiosity and gotten the required permission — offers to take them to London, they are all too eager to go. John, who has been improving his English by reading Shakespeare — an old copy of the bard's works, long banned in England, got into his hands — is looking forward to the encounter with elevated spirits. "O brave new world that has such people in it," he quotes Miranda in *The Tempest*.[25] His enthusiastic outcry is used by Huxley for the title of the book, lending it an ironic meaning.

Bernard and Lenina, as well as Linda and John, come to London. Bernard is publicly reprimanded by the Director for his generally unorthodox behavior in his private life, and threatened with banishment to an island reserved for maladjusted individuals. However, he plays his trump card by calling in Linda and John. Linda instantly recognizes her lost lover and compromises him in full view of his subordinates. John calls him "Father," which is another compromising obscenity. Consequently, it is the Director who resigns while Bernard triumphs. The appearance of John, or the Savage as he is called, causes a sensation and everybody who is a somebody wants to meet him, through the intervention of Bernard, who basks in the glory of public recognition. Linda, on the other hand, with her revolting appearance, is all but forgotten, and indolently enjoys herself, with radio and television always on, and *soma* within reach.

The Savage does not enjoy his popularity. He soon realizes the discrepancy between his own convictions and emotions and the world around him, which he increasingly despises. He falls in love with Lenina, but when she responds by a direct invitation to sexual intercourse, he gets furious, calls her a strumpet and hits her. The ideal of his romantic and chivalrous love is shattered. The death of his mother further exacerbates his malaise and his spite for the surrounding civilization with its promiscuity, erotic feelies (films) and *soma*, and absence of any deep emotions, yearnings, and ideals. He wants to leave for an island together with Bernard and Helmholtz, who are banished there for their own good and for the good of society, but is not allowed to. Mustapha Mond finds him too interesting an experiment to let him go.

Still, the Savage withdraws to an isolated place in the country, some distance from London, determined to live in isolation, and to subsist on his own garden and on hunting (with bow and arrows). In frustration and remorse he reverts to the practice of penitence and occasionally flagellates himself. This is caught on camera by a hiding reporter and when the news gets out, crowds arrive from London to watch the titillating performance. The Savage threatens them with a whip, and when one woman comes too close, he whips her and then himself, to the frenzied excitement of the onlookers. The sensation increases and a new huge wave of curious spectators arrives. They find him dangling. He has committed suicide — which concludes the story.

The civilization Huxley describes is replete with technological amenities, some of which were not available at the time of his writing, or were at an early stage of development. Some may still not be realized. Yet this aspect of the book is hardly amazing. The trans–Atlantic transportation by a rocket is not startling in an age of supersonic flights. Private helicopters superseding private cars have not been realized — probably due to the problem of air-traffic congestion which would result from such change in transportation. We may not have feelies, but the cinematic techniques have turned the screen into a quite realistic experience.

Yet the most prominent and characteristic feature of the book is the attention it devotes to human sciences, that is to say, to sciences whose object of inquiry, and consequent application and manipulation, is humankind. In the words of Huxley in his foreword: "The theme of *Brave New World* is not the advancement of science as such; it is the advancement of science as it affects human individuals. The triumphs of physics, chemistry and engineering are tacitly taken for granted. The only scientific advances to be specifically described are those involving the application to human beings of the results of future research in biology, physiology and psychology."[26] And, indeed, Huxley applies such future findings to his utopian society with remarkable gusto. All the enthusiasm of the luminaries of the new world is most ingeniously conveyed in the descriptions of the hatcheries, the psychological engineering, and the educational conditioning. The disciplined laboratory workers, the perfectly ordered bottles containing future humanity, the strict and efficient teacher-conditioners, are a nightmare come to life. The applied human sciences shape and control humanity to perfection.

All this is possible not only because of the advancement of science, but also because of the supreme organization in the application of science to chosen objectives. In other words, it is not only knowledge, but also the assembly-line organization, which facilitates the manufacturing of the various categories of humanity. The Fordesque approach is applied to a much more ambitious production. Here is how the system is summarized in the story:

> Every one was busy, everything in ordered motion. Under the microscopes ... spermatozoa were burrowing head first into eggs; and, fertilized, the eggs were

> expanding, dividing.... From the Social Predestination Room the escalators went rumbling down into the basement, and there ... the foetuses grew.... In the Decanting Room, the newly-unbottled babes uttered their first yell of horror and amazement.... On all the eleven floors of Nurseries it was feeding time. From eighteen hundred bottles eighteen hundred carefully labelled infants were simultaneously sucking down their pint of pasteurized external secretion. Above them, in ten successive layers of dormitory, the little boys and girls ... were as busy as anyone else ... listening unconsciously to hypnopaedic lessons in hygiene and sociability, in class-consciousness and the toddler's love-life.[27]

The consequence of the system is a stratified society in which every individual knows his or her role and is happy in fulfilling it. Human beings are adjusted to their designated functions the way parts fit into a machine. They unlearn instinctive urges which are in the way of their future function by psychological conditioning, even to the point of administering electric shocks to babies in a nursery, to discourage them from liking books and flowers.[28] They learn the suitable attitudes by repetitious hypnopedia.

Even when on an unforeseen occasion a crowd of "deltas" becomes riotous, the police takes care of the situation by pumping *soma* vapor into the air and by activating the Synthetic Music Box to produce a soothing speech, the voice of reason and good feeling. "The sound-track roll was unwinding itself in Synthetic Anti-Riot Speech Number Two (Medium Strength)."[29] People could be easily controlled, with the exception of the most intelligent, whose social function required a latitude of independent thinking, not quite compatible with strict conditioning. Therefore some in this category, like Helmholtz, are not happy with their role, and some, like Mustapha Mond, make a conscious choice to be leaders, even if they remain aware of the attraction of creative individualism.

The strict scientific regimentation of society — indeed, the shaping of people according to a predestined model from conception through life — has its cost. It is achieved at the sacrifice of cherished principles. First to go is freedom. For whatever the limitations of naturally procreated human beings, and whatever the social-cultural restrictions in their upbringing and education, these are dwarfed by the systematic control of Huxley's utopia, or anti-utopia. The lack of freedom affects individual emotions, such as love, and personal relations. Indeed, one is not even free to suffer. Religious yearning is superseded by pseudo-religious gratification. Truth itself becomes the product of effective propaganda. In the words of Bernard Marx, "Sixty-two thousand four hundred repetitions make one truth."[30] While this may not be the case of the alpha-plus leadership which determines what is to be truth, it applies to the vast gray masses, including the complacent "betas."

All this is deemed worthy in order to achieve the society's goal — which is not adulation of science and scientific progress, but social stability, or prevention of social unrest and turbulence. This worthwhile goal can be attained, as the logical argument suggests, by making people happy. The only way to assure their happiness is to make them like what they have to do. In the words of Huxley in his foreword, the problem of happiness is tantamount to "the problem of making people love their servitude."[31] The chemically controlled gestation and the conditioning achieve this goal. The psychological outlets, such as promiscuity, *soma* and the feelies, help to make the cup of happiness run over.

Such a logical and rational pursuit of clear goals can itself be regarded as scientific social planning, even if it is not called by this name. The exclusive commitment to this planning makes certain traditional ways superfluous, if not outright harmful. The depth of emotions between loving individuals or between parents and children can be a source of anguish. Individuality may be detrimental to social cohesion and cooperation. "In a properly organized society..., nobody has any opportunities for being noble or heroic."[32] As for religion, "God isn't compatible with machinery and scientific medicine and universal happiness."[33] Thus the foundation of ancient civilization must be completely changed in order to build a brave new world.

Interestingly, the new civilization, though deeply ingrained in science and scientific approach, is not committed to ever-growing scientific and technological progress. Its commitment first and above all is to social stability, to a static society in which all the unsettling factors are overcome, and which consequently has no reason to change. Utopia, or what is perceived by its leaders as the ultimate formula for social stability and happiness, is static, just as a mathematical formula is final and thus static. This attitude is reflected in the technological economic organization. While the Inventions Office has various plans for labor-saving processes which could cut lower-caste working hours to one half of the present norm, they are not put into practice. For such change, having been introduced on an experimental basis, had undesirable consequences: "Unrest and a large increase in the consumption of soma." Indeed, stability could be endangered by new inventions. "Every discovery in pure science is potentially subversive."[34]

To be sure, the restraint on the pursuit of knowledge, as well as on the artistic quest of beauty, was not instituted all at once. At one time, "knowledge was the highest good, truth the supreme value." Then "Our Ford himself did a great deal to shift the emphasis from truth and beauty to comfort and happiness." This was linked to the system of mass-production and to the demand of the masses, who preferred happiness to truth and beauty. We could say, in line with Huxley's argument, that this was the democratic imperative. Yet, if the quest of truth and beauty could still survive and unrestricted scientific research be allowed, a change came with the Nine Years' War. "What's the point of truth or beauty or knowledge when the anthrax bombs are popping all around you? That was when science first began to be controlled."[35] What does the Controller who presents this case mean? That scientific innovators may introduce some unknown, destabilizing factor, and thus endanger the equilibrium of society? Or is this a hint at the dangerous invention, which may lead to catastrophic consequences — such as the mentioned anthrax bombs or the future nuclear weapons? Conceivably he means both, even if the stress is on the military use of scientific inventions.

Still, the Controller's concern about scientific, philosophical speculations and aspirations clearly reaches beyond the actual dangers of applied science and technology when he censors a theoretical paper on "A New Theory of Biology," which introduces the concept of purpose into this domain. Such a concept might unsettle some minds in the higher caste, "make them lose their faith in happiness as the Sovereign Good," and believe "that the purpose of life" is "some intensification and refining of consciousness, some enlargement of knowledge." While the Controller reflects that this may be true, he decides that it is not to be allowed because of the social risks involved. "'What fun it would be,' he thought, 'if one didn't have to think about happiness!'" Alas, he is not given such a choice.[36]

In his foreword, added to his book some years after its original publication, Huxley criticizes himself for presenting two queer alternatives in his imaginary future world: "An insane life in Utopia, or the life of a primitive in an Indian village." He had thought "that human beings are given free will in order to choose between insanity on the one hand and lunacy on the other." In the later foreword he changed his opinion and expressed the thought that sanity, though a rare phenomenon, can be achieved.[37]

This self-criticism seems to be unwarranted. Fiction is not a philosophical essay, even when it deals with ideas. The novel may present contrasting situations — or civilizations, in this case — in order to stimulate the reader's mind, but without resolving the posed problem. Otherwise, it would be accused of being didactic — a mortal sin for novelists.

As a matter of fact, Huxley hints at an alternative to the two brands of insanity. It is implied in the arguments of the Savage, when he speaks of his craving for poetry, freedom and goodness, even if he mixes his speech with talk about danger and sin. "I'm claiming the right to be unhappy."[38] The musings of the Controller, noted above, that it would be fun not to have to think about happiness, create some points of contact between the two characters and the civilizations they represent. Indeed, there is a class of people who combine some of the qualities of the two cultures — the dissatisfied individuals of the brave new world, who are not exterminated as in Zamiatin's *We*, but sent to an island where they meet "the most interesting set of men and women to be found anywhere in the world.... All the people who aren't satisfied with orthodoxy, who've got independent ideas of their own."[39]

Indeed, Huxley in his foreword points out that this community of exiles and refugees from the brave new world offers a third, sane alternative, which is the kind of world he would recommend. Its "prevailing philosophy of life would be a kind of Higher Utilitarianism, in which the Greatest Happiness principle would be secondary to the final end principle."[40] In other words, if we understand Huxley correctly, the community would combine beneficial scientific achievements with the continuous quest of people for aims and dreams transcending their basic needs. No static paradise, but a continuous search for meaning.

It is tempting to evaluate Huxley's projection of the future in relation to our present state of civilization. Even though we are not yet in the middle of the third millennium according to the customary counting, the dating of Huxley's *Brave New World* need not be taken too strictly. Indeed, Huxley himself tried to evaluate his prognostication mere fifteen years after the publication of the book.

To start with the unfulfilled prophecies, these are apparent on the political scene. The one world, or the entire world under one government, with the apparent disappearance of national awareness, as the names of the characters seem to indicate — Bernard Marx, Lenina Crowne, Mustapha Mond — has not been established. Even though the logic of the nuclear menace, or the logic of the anthrax bombs, would lead to the conclusion that the survival of humankind and its rescue from catastrophic calamities justifies and demands a global control of power, reality has not followed reason. What could be deemed a scientific political solution has been resisted by the irrational atavistic forces of group allegiance and xenophobia. This particular failure of humanity to follow the dictates of reason would probably be deplored by Huxley.

Another political prediction, namely the ascendancy of totalitarian regimes everywhere, also failed to be realized — this time to our and Huxley's relief. Interestingly, even fifteen years after the publication of the novel, Huxley expected that the rapid technological changes of our times would lead to the concentration and increase of government control, designed to deal with the social confusion resulting from techno-economic changes. Such totalitarianism, however, did not have to resemble the old oppressive one. "A really efficient totalitarian state would be one in which the all-powerful executive of political bosses and their army of managers control a population of slaves who do not have to be coerced, because they love their servitude" — which is one of the salient themes of the novel itself.[41] As we have discovered by the end of the twentieth century, the techno-economic development led to competitive decentralization in the socio-economic organization even in the totalitarian states, let alone in the democratic societies. As to the population of workers and otherwise, they cannot be described as enslaved — openly or discreetly — by political bosses, or even by industrial managers.

As to social stratification and its solidification into a caste system, another imperative of the novel's logic, present reality corroborates Huxley's predictions only to some extent. The gap between manual and semi-skilled workers and the highly professional experts and managers is as deep as ever. Then there are strata of workers in between these two extremes. Moreover, with technological advancement, the need for unskilled workers diminishes, so that there are less and less economic demands for "epsilons" and "deltas." At the same time, there is considerable social class mobility, which makes the rigid caste system of *Brave New World* not a plausible scenario. Again, social reality refuses to adhere — at least to adhere strictly — to the logic of theoretical speculation.

There are, however, features of Huxley's utopia which make us feel uncomfortable, because we discern in our society developments pointing in their direction. While human beings are not yet produced in bottles, the surrogate mothers, the experimental cloning (be it of animals so far), and other attempts at biological engineering, make the specter of artificial and controlled procreation not quite unreal. The inroads on the traditional family as a basic social unit, with the ascendancy of the single-parent household as an acceptable arrangement (and not merely an occasional phenomenon due to deplorable or tragical circumstances), and with the high rate of divorce, are compatible with the dire predictions of Huxley. The easy and early sex life in contemporary society, and the superficiality of emotional attachment, also comport with the "happy life" of Huxley's creation. We may not yet be there, but we cannot be confident that society is not heading in that direction.

Psychological conditioning and propagation of opinions and attitudes by repetition, if not yet hypnopedia, are very much with us. We witness it increasingly and incessantly in advertising—on radio, on television and in print. These media have resorted to both techniques, with considerable degree of success. Significantly, these techniques have expanded into the realm of politics, especially at election times. Rational argument is replaced by repetitious assertions, often presented in alluring form or pleasant association, on the assumption that so many repetitions create the belief in the truthfulness of the assertions. The perfected technique of applied psychology becomes a means for commercial and political interests. It amounts not to the control of the masses by the allegedly wise rulers of the brave new world, but to the seduction of the people by diverse interests, commercial and political. Despite the difference, the undermining of truth and the insult to human intelligence is similar.

The utopian bliss sarcastically outlined by Huxley, is it a threat to our civilization? Are we to resign our dreams, ambitions, yearnings, to a static existence of monotonous work and lowbrow distraction? Are we to be happy with feelies and *soma*, food and sensual pleasure? Will the entertainment beamed at us through numerous television channels, appealing to less than noble instincts, and disregarding any artistic consideration, be our daily portion of circus, added to the abundant amount of bread? If this be the case, then we are sunk deep in the brave new world, provided "happiness" at the expense of higher aspirations of humanity.

To be sure, this formula for happiness is not the result of the benevolent conspiracy of political and social leaders. It is not instilled from above. It springs from below, from the wishes of hoi polloi which, combined with the ingenuity of modern technology, can be easily and efficiently gratified.

Of course, there are some people, and they can be found also in Huxley's utopia, who are not happy with this kind of life. They may feel isolated, but in the present world they are not banished to an island. They may even speak up, though they are rarely heard—because of the noise of radio and television and what these media mostly represent. These few, while looking with approval at the benefits of science, see the menace of degeneration of a humanity happy with the currently apportioned bliss. They are weary of a life of uniform, predictable, placid happiness, life without imagination, reflection, striving, advancing.

It is true that people, afflicted with myriad misfortunes, have been striving to find a peaceful niche where their modest needs can be gratified and secured. Yet it is also true that some people are not satisfied with a return to the Garden of Eden, whether modest or embellished, but want to keep striving, to continue inquiring, to go on creating, to look beyond the horizon, even if they do not know what is to be found there. They may be rational and reasonable, they may have deep respect for science and knowledge, but they do not wish to have their lives, their mental aspirations, reduced to or controlled by a scientific and rational formula. Huxley is clearly on their side, as is superbly conveyed in his novel.

11

The Suicide of Civilization

Apocalyptic visions of the destruction of humanity and civilization are not a new idea. The biblical story of the flood provides a perfect model for the almost total destruction of humanity and life. The destruction of Sodom and Gomorrah by brimstone and fire, though limited in geographical extent, is no less dramatic in its horrific presentation of the disaster. Apocalyptic visions recur in the prophets, and reappear in Jewish post-biblical literature and then in Christianity. The cry that "the day of judgment is nigh" reverberates in some Christian sects to this day.

Thus, if with the ascent of the nuclear age and its inherent dangers a literature emerged and proliferated, preoccupied with catastrophes and disasters on a colossal and unprecedented scale, one could see it as merely an extension, or renaissance, of an old and long tradition of human preoccupation with disaster. Yet, there is a difference between the conventional literature of this kind and the modern version. For the latter is not based on some vague forebodings, nor does it originate in religious beliefs. It does not invoke divine intervention, or a mystical experience. It is based on the proven capacity of modern humans to annihilate their own civilization and even the human species. The means are available and technically easy to activate — all too easy. The day of judgment, if we want to call it that, can be enacted at a very short notice.

The realization of such immediacy has transposed the prophetic visions into an actual menace. Moreover, the menace is perceived not only by believers, but also by quite secular people. The threat of the new flood, a fiery flood, is believed as much by agnostics as by the devout. It is interdenominational, and it also encompasses those who are outside any organized church. This, of course, enhances the relevance and the importance of the new cataclysmic literature — whether systematic inquiry or fictional story.

Interestingly, the new literature — notably in its fictional manifestation — occasionally forges links with the ancient apocalyptic stories.[1] Whether by using old metaphors, or making deliberate analogies, describers of the new, real menace evoke the old imagined beliefs and sanctified stories. This need not surprise us, for as long as civilization continues, people perceive their great problems not only in their actual appearance, but also in the context and framework of their cultural traditions and mental images. Indeed, the connection is useful, for it presents the new concerns in a manner more easily absorbable and comprehensible — an important factor when one of the basic difficulties in this case is how to comprehend the incomprehensible. Thus, the traditions and beliefs of nonscientific origin help us to absorb the new realities of an advanced and sophisticated science and technology — and perhaps to avert the menace inherent in them.

Gloomy as the modern scenarios of nuclear catastrophe are — and how could they be otherwise? — they need not be fatalistic. Even when appearing to be so, they may well invite another interpretation. Indeed, they may intentionally depict a total disaster in order to convince the reader to act and prevent it. The frightening picture may be an educational device aiming at the salvation of humanity from a self-inflicted destruction. Just as the prophecy of Jonah about the impending divine destruction made the people of Nineveh repent and thus escape the punishment, so the horrific stories of our own age may make humanity take the steps necessary to reduce, or even abolish, the threat of its own making.

The intent, to be sure, is not explicitly made in these stories, for the fear that they may be deemed didactic. Nonetheless, the moral is there — palpable, though not proclaimed. It suggests a way of escape, even as the sword of Damocles is suspended over our advanced civilization. To put it in a more direct way, the stories attempt to frighten humanity into doing something to prevent its own demise. The conclusion must be reached by the readers themselves, just as the decision to repent was made not by Jonah, but by the people of Nineveh.

The literature concerned with the menace of nuclear disaster has proliferated since the power of the atomic bomb became manifest. Indeed, forebodings about some kind of cataclysmic weapons preceded their actual invention. Out of the plethora of such works, two will be examined here — both published in the fifties, but each quite different from the other. The first is entitled, rather mystifyingly, *A Canticle for Leibowitz*; the second, bearing a more earthly title, is *Level 7*. Both have been classified as science fiction, though it is not this aspect which conveys their main characteristics. For it is not fantastic inventions that dominate the two stories, but — with the exception of the ending of the first book, introducing interstellar travel — the technology involved is essentially available and virtually deployed today, and this situation was clearly predictable at the time of the composition of these books. This does not mean that there is not a considerable amount of fantasy in these works, only that this fantasy is devoted to an extrapolation or a projection of available science and technology, indeed pursuing the warfare technology to its logical, if not inevitable, conclusion.

One basic difference between the two novels is that while the *Canticle* looks at the nuclear threat in the wide setting of history, past and future, *Level 7* explores the menace in the limited time-frame of its occurrence, that is to say, the weeks preceding the disaster and following it. Consequently, the latter book is almost exclusively focused on the disaster, its antecedents and its ramifications, while the former roams into the boundless sphere of Western civilization, including religion, science, politics. Of course, all these either affect or are affected by the new power of cataclysmic weapons.

Homo Erratus

A Canticle for Leibowitz, by Walter M. Miller, Jr., was first published in 1959, though the three parts of the book, in somewhat different form, had appeared respectively in 1955, 1956 and 1957 in *Fantasy and Science Fiction Magazine.* The book has seen many reprintings in the following years and decades. The title sets it apart by associating the story with a church service on the one hand and with a person bearing a Jewish surname on the other hand. The combination of the two is intriguing, and it becomes clear in the sequence of the story. The three parts are entitled *Fiat Homo, Fiat Lux,* and *Fiat Voluntas Tua.* The biblical phrasing and the use of Latin, which is generously dispersed throughout the book, again point to the deliberate connection to the Bible and the Christian church, or, strictly speaking, the Roman Catholic Church.

The time framework of the novel spans centuries, or even millennia. It starts around A.D. 2600 and ends around A.D. 4300, but there are significant references to the end of the twentieth century, when the first nuclear world catastrophe occurred. History is divided into epochs of six hundred years, though there is no attempt to present a continuous historical sequence, but rather to pick out three representative fragments in the historical development of civilization, with recollections of the original catastrophe — a preamble which started it all. It is a future history as seen from the vantage point of a detached philosophical observer, who selects what is crucial for the understanding of the whole. The primary, though not exclusive, geographical setting is an abbey in a desert, somewhere in the North American continent, which persists through millennia.

Though the novel is a story of destruction and calamity, of catastrophe and suffering, of cruelty and folly, which by and large override the elements of sanity and goodwill, still, the tragic vicissitudes of human history and civilization are presented in contrast with some stubbornly persistent elements representing continuity and permanence. One such element is the Leibowitz Abbey, apparently symbolizing the Roman Catholic Church, or perhaps Christianity at large, faithful to its doctrine and faith, irrespective of the changes of history over centuries and millennia. Another is a wandering Jew, a mythical figure in tangible shape, who also survives, apparently symbolizing the persistence of Judaism despite persecution and suffering. The monks, representing the church, are committed, dedicated, selfless, and adhere to their ways, despite the reality which confounds their belief. The Jew, a beneficiary of long experience and perennial wisdom, appears skeptical, almost cynical. Yet, he too adheres to his religious belief, and despite the disillusionment, expects the coming of the Messiah and the delivery of mankind which will follow his appearance. It is against these backgrounds of human belief that the cruel vicissitudes of history in general, and of nuclear disasters in particular, are depicted.

Then there is — or was — Leibowitz, who in a way provides a connection between the Jew and the church, as well as a link between science and religion. A technician, engineer, or nuclear scientist, who lived in the late twentieth century, he gave up his scientific commitment following the nuclear catastrophe and became a monk, only to be martyred because of the popular rejection of science and the persecution of scientists. Thus the Albertian Order of Leibowitz was established, with its monks expecting the beatified martyr to be canonized some day and thus attain sainthood. This introduction of Leibowitz into the story, and even its title, offers an intriguing, even comical element, for — pace the original Jewishness of Peter, Paul and, of course, Jesus — turning a Jewish scientist into a Catholic monk strikes one as somewhat bizarre. The adoration of the monks in subsequent generations only augments the irony of the transformation of Leibowitz. Yet the strange linkage has its serious aspect, for it conveys the perplexity of the somewhat enigmatic and often strained relations between science and religion, between knowledge and belief, as well as between Judaism and Christianity. The choice of Leibowitz as a symbol of coexistence — or even ecumenical understanding — of the two may well be meant to be taken seriously.

The opening chapter of the book sets the somber tone and grievous mood for the whole story. It presents Brother Francis of Utah, a novice in the Leibowitz Abbey, spending his Lenten fast isolated in some hovel in the desert. The place is hot and desolate, abounding in scattered stones of ancient destroyed structures, and in buzzards hovering above, eager for carrion to feed on. The thriving buzzards are repeatedly referred to in the book, as beneficiaries of human self-destruction.

The half-starved and dehydrated novice has to build a night refuge for himself to protect himself from wolves and buzzards — a task which reflects the primitive conditions of humanity six hundred years after the Flame Deluge, as the nuclear catastrophe is referred to. He is helped in his endeavor by the wandering Jew, after initial mutual suspicion and confrontation, who points to a stone which would fit to complete the structure. What is more important, by moving the stone, the novice finds a fallout survival shelter. "Fallout," a term in pre–Deluge English, remains an enigmatic word, and is taken by Brother Francis to mean some kind of a devil, against whom he takes the established religious precautions, such as crossing himself.

Among the remnants of skeletons, lockers and a desk found in the shelter, the novice comes across some notes and a diagram described as "circuit design" by Leibowitz. The meaning of the words and of the mysterious signs is a mystery to Brother Francis and to his superiors, including the abbot, but the sanctity of the relic linked to Beatus Leibowitz is not in doubt, and Francis spends the following fifteen years illuminating the diagram. When eventually Leibowitz is canonized, Brother Francis, by now a monk, is sent to New Rome — somewhere in America — to present the holy relic and the illuminated copy to the pope. He is robbed of the illuminated copy, to which the thief takes fancy, and on the way back is killed and partially eaten by cannibals. The wandering Jew buries the remains, saving them from buzzards.

The general description of this first six-hundred-year period, broadly speaking, brings to mind the early Middle Ages. There is no central authority to assure peace and keep law and order. There is banditry and the life of the individual is precarious. The economic conditions are primitive, and the ancient civilization is known mainly by its ruins. In this social chaos and cultural desert, it is the church which remains the keeper of civilization, if not its actual agent. The monks are the literate people, and the abbey devoutly preserves the memorabilia of antiquity, even if it does not always understand the meaning of the writings in its possession.

Still, the new Middle Ages are worse than the old ones. For they evolved after a terrible disaster, whose memory informs the consciousness of humanity even hundreds of years after it occurred. They are reminded of the Flame Deluge not only by the physical remnants of destroyed buildings, but also by a variety of physical monstrosities which have persisted over generations due to genetic mutations caused by radiation. These continue to persist throughout the millennia traced in the story.

The historical background to this situation is remembered and recounted from the vantage point of the monks, and couched in biblical terms, striking by their simplicity and power: "It was said that God, in order to test mankind which had become swelled with pride as in the times of Noah, had commanded the wise men of that age ... to devise great engines of war such as had never before been upon the Earth, weapons of such might that they contained the very fires of Hell, and that God had suffered these magi to place the weapons in the hands of princes." They were advised to avoid striking each other for fear of retaliation. Yet, not heeding the warning, they thought each to himself, "If I but strike quickly enough ... I shall destroy those others ... and ... the earth shall be mine." There followed the Flame Deluge, and within weeks — or maybe days — it was all ended. Cities and nations vanished from the earth. Fertile land turned into desert, and many of the survivors were sickened by the poisoned air.[2]

This upheaval led to great wrath of the surviving people against the princes and the inventors of weapons. They set on destroying them, "and all their works, their names, and even their memories." They wanted to start a new order: "Let us make a great simplification, and then the world shall begin again." The simplification was a cruel slaughter of rulers, scientists, technicians, teachers.[3] The dark ages ensued.

As the first epoch was coming to its conclusion, there were signs of change and progress, as city-states rose. A new era was beginning, described in Part Two, entitled *Fiat Lux*. This era could be characterized, even if the author does not say it explicitly, as parallel to the Renaissance. For though there is no mention of great works of art, there are intrigues and warfare among princes and cities, and there is an awakened interest in old books and in new science. The leading political and military personality is the crafty and scheming Hannegan, whose ambition is to unite the continent under one dynasty. Thon Taddeo, a gifted and promising scientist, is his kinsman.

The latter, a prominent member of the Collegium in Texarcana, a major city, go to the Leibowitz Abbey to study the ancient incomprehensible Memorabilia and to make sense of them. Independently, one of the monks in the Abbey invents a dynamo which produces electric light. Thon Taddeo unravels the mysteries of mathematics and science and approves of the ingenuity of the monk-engineer. The practical and the theoretical meet. The incomprehensible wisdom of the twentieth century is gradually revived.

Thon Taddeo is courteously received by the abbot, even if they differ in their philosophical outlook. It looks as if the new age holds out the promise of a new, enlightened and better world. Hope seems to illuminate the future. This is expressed in the sanguine speech of Thon Taddeo to the monks of the Abbey. "Tomorrow, a new prince shall rule. Men of understanding, men of science shall stand behind his throne, and the universe will come to know his might. His name is Truth. His empire shall encompass the Earth. And the mastery of Man over the Earth shall be renewed."[4]

Yet the author dashes such forecasts of a noble and blissful age. He does it through the reaction of the wandering Jew. The Jew approaches the scholar and looks hopefully into his eyes, but then his face clouds. "A great keening sigh came from the dry old lungs as hope vanished. The eternally knowing smile of the Old Jew ... returned to his face. He turned to the community... 'It's not *Him*,' he told them sourly...."[5] Taddeo is not the Messiah, and his message does not offer salvation. And, indeed, the war and the atrocities go on, even if they are still conducted in a comparatively primitive way. This will not be the case in the future.

As we cross into the Year of Our Lord 3781, we make a transition into a new era, an age of a renewed civilization. There are again spaceships and technology thrives. There is even a race to the stars. Alas, also the old maladies return. The Atlantic Confederacy and the Asian Coalition confront each other. A nuclear disaster with thousands of casualties at Itu Wan is attributed to a weapons test of the Asians (say the westerners) and to an accidental rocket strike of the West (say the Asians). Retaliation on both sides follows, and the world faces a ten-day cease-fire in anxious anticipation.

On the face of it, there is good reason not to despair. For, as the abbot of our abbey argues, "we all know what *could* happen, if there's war. The genetic festering is still with us from the last time Man tried to eradicate himself." At the time of Saint Leibowitz humanity did not foresee the consequences of such war, "the madness and the murder and the blotting out of reason." Having had the actual experience, "they cannot do it again. Only a race of madmen could do it again."⁶ Yet the church in New Rome is cautiously pessimistic. It orders the abbot to prepare a group of monks to be ready to embark in a starship to a designated planet in another solar system, in order to continue the mission of the church. A few human colonies in distant planets, living in precarious conditions, have been in existence for some time.

Then one day the bombs start falling. The abbey and all of its inhabitants are destroyed, along with humanity at large. As "the visage of Lucifer mushroomed into hideousness above the cloudbank," the monks climbed into the ship. The last one, looking at the glow, murmured, "*sic transit mundus.*"⁷

What is the meaning of this ending? Did the writer intend to point to the final calamity of humankind, after it repeated its original nuclear sin? Did he suggest some hope of redemption by saving a handful of dedicated monks and sending them to another planet? And what about the future of those distant planets? Are not humans doomed to repeat there the mistakes they committed on earth? Or is the starship with its monks simply an assertion of indomitable faith in the face of human folly and its consequent disaster? There is no answer offered in the book, and readers are free to indulge in their own interpretations. Of course, the warning against the suicide of civilization and humankind remains intact, whatever the reading of the peculiar, slightly ambiguous, ending.

While the issue of science and knowledge is touched upon at various junctions of this story, as has been exemplified to some extent in our account, Miller occasionally deals with it in a direct and focused way. It could be said that, by and large, his attitude to science and technology is not negative, as one might have suspected. For though science is a prerequisite for the cataclysmic weapons which destroy the world, it is also a condition of material well-being and civilized life. The author does not in any way romanticize the Dark Ages. Nor does he sympathize with the ferocious attack on science and scientists by the propagators of the policy of simplification. The Age of Enlightenment, or Renaissance, is looked at with approval, as far as the cultural development is concerned.

Indeed, some of the approval and praise lavished on the abbey is due to its preservation of ancient knowledge, even when it is incomprehensible to the monks. The copying of mystifying documents and the artistic illumination of the circuit design of Leibowitz may appear as comical, but the selfless devotion of the monks in treating the memorabilia as sacred objects and assuring their preservation for posterity is a model of dedication to knowledge.

As the pope puts it to the humble Brother Francis, commenting on the work of the monks in the abbey: "Without your work, the world's amnesia might well be total."[8] The author himself refers to Brother Francis, shortly before his death, as "the small keeper of the flame of knowledge."[9]

Yet this generally positive attitude to knowledge and science should not be confused with unqualified admiration. For though science can be of great benefit to humankind and though knowledge may be of intrinsic value, there looms danger in these expressions of human genius, which must be addressed and curtailed if humanity is to survive. The historical account of the Flame Deluge, mentioned above, clearly points to the danger of the link between science and power. It is the scientifically designed cataclysmic weapons, the product of great ingenuity and profound knowledge, which in the hands of the prince, of the wielders of political power, turn into a disaster. The intent of the scientists, or of God who allowed them to succeed, may have been good — to prevent war altogether by making it catastrophic and suicidal. Yet the rational argument for the deployment of such weapons did not prove effective. The princes listened to their greed for power, or to the voice of Satan, saying: "Fear not to use the sword, for the wise men have deceived you in saying that the world would be destroyed thereby... Strike, and know that you shall be king over all."[10]

If, however, the liaison between science and power, between scientists and princes, is so dangerous, what ought scientists to do? Should they withdraw into some obscure place, into a monastic abbey of some kind, and hide the fruit of their inquiries? Hide it and "save it all up for the day when Man is good and pure and holy and wise?" Thon Taddeo, who discusses this issue with the abbot, cannot accept such voluntary withdrawal. For him, as probably for most dedicated scientists, curbing the urge to inquiry, hiding knowledge and keeping it arcane, is well nigh impossible. In his words: "If you try to save wisdom until the world is wise, Father, the world will never have it."[11] There seems no way for science but to advance and proclaim its findings, even at the risk of being misused by power.

Such a conclusion does not satisfy the reader, and apparently not the writer either. Miller's conclusion seems to be conveyed through the reflections of the abbot: "But neither infinite power nor infinite wisdom could bestow godhood upon men. For that there would have to be infinite love as well."[12] Thus, it would seem that humanity's destiny is controlled by three principles — power, knowledge and love. Only the proper coordination among these can assure its future. Science, though on the whole beneficial, can become a horrible menace, if abused by power. Power guided by knowledge and wisdom would be salutary. Yet, for power to follow knowledge, and not to be guided by hubris, and for knowledge to be constrained, and not become intoxicated with its own discoveries, they have to be informed by love of humanity. In other words, it is the ethical principle which should guide political life and scientific inquiry.

De Profundis

Level 7, by Mordecai Roshwald, was first published in 1959 in England. Like *A Canticle for Leibowitz,* it was written at the time of the Cold War, at a juncture when both superpowers, the United States and the Soviet Union, were expanding and refining their nuclear weapons and the means for delivering them. *Level 7* is clearly and directly a reaction to this frightening situation.

As already noted, unlike the millennial time framework of Miller's story, Roshwald's tale is confined to a few months — starting on March 21 and ending on October 12, to be precise. This conciseness lends the story a dramatic tension: it becomes akin to a ticking explosive device, which in a moment produces devastation and horror. The story precedes the nuclear collision, briefly gives an account of it, and follows up on the results. All this is done from the perspective of one man, Push Button Officer X-127, who commits his experiences and reflections to a diary. This perspective is necessarily partial and limited, and colored — in fact, almost deprived of color — by the personality of a man who is a participating spectator of an unprecedented calamity.

Level 7 carried a clear political intent, as it was dedicated to Dwight (Eisenhower) and Nikita (Khrushchev) in its first editions, the names changed to their respective successors, Ronald (Reagan) and Leonid (Brezhnev) and George (Bush) and Mikhail (Gorbachev), in subsequent editions. While there is no detectable expectation in the dedication of the book itself of infusing the potentates with love for each other, there may be an implicit, if vague, hope of stimulating their common sense. That, too, would help to prevent a catastrophe.

The book, though not turning away from international politics and the confrontation of power, deliberately avoids taking a partisan position — siding with the West or the East. Its target is the menace of the weapons in the context of international confrontation, and not the ideological dispute, significant as it may be. This approach is consistent with the characteristically lucid position of Bertrand Russell, that the prevention of nuclear war should not be confused with the arguments about the merits or demerits of communism or democracy. The concern should be with "the welfare of the human species as a whole," which coincides with the self-interest of each party.[13]

To preserve the neutrality of the book, the author avoids giving names to his characters. They are identified by letters and numbers, such as X-127, or Ph-107. Had the author intended to depict the American scene, he would have called them John and George. (This, incidentally, also serves another purpose of presenting the characters as essentially dehumanized human beings—not unlike those in Zamiatin's *We*.) Thus, the push-button officer and his colleagues can be equally Americans and Russians, as indeed the weapons systems and deployment of the two opponents have, broadly speaking, been the mirror images of each other.[14] Both the logic and the senselessness of the ultimate nuclear scenario apply equally to both sides.

The protagonist, X-127, is a career officer, training at the Push-Button Training Camp. One day, at the conclusion of his training, he is promoted to the rank of major, promised a two-week leave after finishing an impending assignment of a day or two, and ordered to mysterious underground installations which are the location of his prospective military duty. He is whisked off immediately and inconspicuously, feeling pleased with himself at his promotion and prospective leave.

As he reaches the destination through a well-camouflaged tunnel and a fast elevator, he passes through a turnstile into the underground installations, 4,400 feet below the crust of the earth. The installations are suitably provided for all the personnel, which include not only push-button officers, but also administrators, medical workers, psychologists and so on. Level 7, which is the designation of the place, is the location of the offensive branch of the military machine of the entire country. In other words, here the nuclear-armed rockets would be electronically dispatched, if the command was given, to their predetermined targets, and the push-button officer would do the dispatching.

While all this is hardly a surprise for X-127, who knew what he was training for, and who observes with professional interest the "real" facilities—what comes next is a shock. For the loudspeaker—the principal way of communication here—announces that Level 7 has been sealed off from the world above, and that all its personnel will remain in the facilities indefinitely, or at least till the day of victory over the enemy, victory by the PBX Command. As X-127 figures out, this must mean an indefinite imprisonment, for even a victory in a major nuclear conflict would leave the surface contaminated with radioactivity for a long time.

The loudspeaker voice sugarcoats the bitter pill by pointing to the great moral responsibility involved in this arrangement: to defend the country and to protect the defenders from danger, and thereby secure their retaliatory capability. Therefore they were assigned to the deepest shelter, sealed off against eventual radioactive pollution, and the shelter made self-sufficient and well provided for all the human needs of its occupants. All the crew have to do is to adjust to the new environment.

The conditions in the underground are spartan, but efficient. Space is allocated in a sparing but adequate manner, with some advantages accorded to the push-button officers. The normal duty of X-127 and his colleagues is being stationed at the push-button panel during a six-hour shift. With twelve buttons, arranged in three rows, they can dispatch the rockets to their targets — each button controlling a certain class of bombs and a specific region in the enemy territory. A screen displaying this territory and targets facilitates the viewing of the eventual attack on and destruction of these targets.

To prevent a catastrophic mishap, two officers, simultaneously on duty but some distance apart, have to follow the order to strike in a coordinated manner. To prevent collusion of the two, an actual strike cannot be activated without the participation of a supervisor, unknown to the officers and seated in another room.

The initial sense of despair and isolation of X-127 on the news of confinement to Level 7 diminishes somewhat, as he becomes acquainted with his roommate, X-l07. A man of more fatalistic disposition, the latter accepts the inevitable philosophically. Indeed, he agrees with the logic which makes a secluded and sealed-off push-button facility a necessary condition for the defense of the country at the present junction of military technology. Meeting other people in the lounge promotes some social contact.

The number of people on Level 7 is 500 and they have provisions for 500 years. These include a supply of compact dehydrated food, made edible by the injection of water, supplied from underground sources, nuclear-powered energy for a thousand years, waste disposal arrangements, perfect temperature control, and so on — all very ingeniously and efficiently designed. Cultural needs are satisfied by two twelve-day-long tapes, playing either classical or popular music.

11—The Suicide of Civilization

The perfect mechanical arrangements — one could say, the infrastructure of the new civilization — are supplemented with some human activity and intellectual creativity. Of course, they are circumscribed by and responsive to the conditions of Level 7. One such activity is live talks conducted by Ph-107, a kind of court philosopher. He uses his dialectical skills to prove that Level 7 has attained the highest level of democracy and freedom. Cut off from the rest of humankind, there is no fear of spies, and so people can discuss everything freely. R-747 (R standing for "Reserve Officer") is eventually to become T-747, an elementary school teacher. In the meantime she writes stories for the future children, in which some basic perceptions are inverted, such as depicting heaven as hell because of radiation pouring from above, and the underground as paradise. Level 7 starts forming its own ideology and myth. X-127 contributes a story, too.

The planning for future generations is based on the assumption that the inhabitants of Level 7 will marry. Indeed, this was taken into consideration when the crew were divided into an equal number of men and women, all of the age group of twenty to thirty. The institution of marriage is announced on the loudspeaker and is soon taken advantage of by some of the residents. The wedding ceremonies are reduced to a declaration of each partner of the intent to marry, and the confirmation of agreement by an anonymous officer through the loudspeaker. Each partner retains his or her own accommodation, though they are allotted strictly defined periods for conjugal privacy.

X-127, who is courted by a psychologist, P-867, marries her without much enthusiasm. Indeed, he prefers another woman. He decides, however, that being in love on Level 7 would create a problem, for one's privacy would be very curtailed. With a lukewarm relationship, such a limitation would not matter. He also hopes to be helped emotionally by marrying a professional psychologist. In line with the ethos of Level 7, he makes the rationally right decision.

In fact, he may need psychological help. For though accepting his lot and seeing the necessity for Level 7 and its arrangements, he is not entirely free from longing for sunshine and green fields, and his life on the surface of the earth. Moreover, he suffers from strange dreams and nightmares, related to personal danger or nuclear disaster. If X-127's peace of mind is disturbed, one of his fellow push-button officers, X-117, exhibits clear symptoms of neurosis and hysteria. Apparently he was not properly selected. Still, he undergoes a treatment, in which P-867 participates, and eventually returns to his duties. X-127, less sensitive and without prior personal attachments, plods on.

Besides Level 7, there are six other levels, each designated for its own specific sector of society. Level 6 is the location of the PBY Command, the defensive branch of the military, designed to intercept enemy missiles. It is technically more complex and requires a larger personnel, but it is not as crucial for the country's military might as PBX Command, and therefore situated at a lesser depth underground. Moreover, the personnel there is not cut off from the surface, but changes guard every two weeks. Levels 5, 4 and 3 are further up, and are intended to house the civilian elite of the country — the most important hiding in the lowest level. Level 2 is reserved for peacemongers and other unruly elements, in a successful attempt to neutralize their obstructive impulses. Level 1 is designed for the rest of the population, though it will take considerable time before such universal facilities can be constructed.

While there are only one Level 7 and Level 6, there are multiple locations of the other levels. At the same time, the higher up the level, the more people it accommodates, while offering less protection. The levels, excluding the top two, can accommodate altogether over 600,000 people, which leaves the bulk of the population with no shelter at all. Thus, with all the technological ingenuity and despite the rational organization, the country remains highly vulnerable to a nuclear attack. Level 7 is a notable exception in this respect, followed by Level 6, and perhaps Levels 5 to 3.

The structure of the shelter system and the underlying military and political considerations are explained through the loudspeaker for the benefit of the community of Level 7, and thus, in their own sinister way, the new perceptions of social order are established. The new order is presented, tongue in cheek, as the best of all possible worlds — under the conditions of nuclear menace, to be sure. As to X-127, who faces emotional difficulties in accepting the new situation and who suffers from nightmares and delusions (chiefly because of his longing for the outer world), he is treated for a week with drugs and electric shocks, and recovers.

With the setting thus ready for a static and stable existence on Level 7 and in the world at large, one morning there is an alert in the PBX Operations Room, followed by successive commands to push various buttons. The operation starts at 9:12 and ends at 11:20. The simplicity of the performance is almost an anticlimax to the preceding story. The complex and sophisticated technological and strategic arrangements are put into action, as far as the PBX Command is concerned, with utmost simplicity. As the thousands of rockets hit their targets, the map on the screen starts displaying the devastated

11—The Suicide of Civilization

areas. The results prove highly effective. X-127 sums it up in a characteristically laconic way: "The whole war lasted two hours and fifty-eight minutes — the shortest war in history. And the most devastating one."[15] To be sure, the operation was accompanied by a brief local drama. While X-127 and his colleague X-117 were performing their duty and pushing the buttons as ordered, at one point X-117 refused to continue. He had to be dragged out of the room and replaced by X-107, who scrupulously followed the instructions. X-127, our protagonist, experienced no emotional difficulties in following the orders and doing his part in the operations.

Then, as a matter of historical interest, the sequence of events is related to the crew of Level 7. It all started with twelve thermonuclear missiles of the enemy allegedly escaping their electronic controls and heading toward their targets. The enemy informed "our" government of the mishap only three minutes before the actual explosion, asking us not to retaliate. Our government, upset that the warning came too late for the missiles to be intercepted, and suspecting ruse, retaliated forcefully. From this point on, the exchange escalated and continued till the entire arsenal was used up.

One interesting feature of the war, which was made clear, was that the exchanges were essentially automatic. In order to avoid a situation in which the leaders' decision-making might fail because of human frailty, a technical device had been installed which would automatically activate a retaliatory strike in case of an attack of a certain magnitude. It is this device that issued the orders to the officers to push the buttons. The enemy had a similar arrangement, and thus his retaliation to our retaliation was automatic as well.

Why, then, was there a need for the human PBX Command at all? The reason for this, speculates X-127, must have been to make it possible for the leadership of the country to initiate an attack, or to retaliate with even greater force than planned to an enemy attack. Actually, however, the war was a feat of automation, with only minimal human link of the push-button officers.

X-127 asks himself why he was subjected to an elaborate training, if the job he was expected to perform was merely to push buttons on order, a task a child could perform. The answer, he muses, is that the technical training must have been a crafty psychological design intended to camouflage the simplicity of the task and to instill a sense of the importance of the job in the officer. As to the job itself, once it has been accomplished, X-127 and his colleagues have nothing left to do, and the Operations Room, formerly out of bounds to others, turns into a kind of a museum open to all. The visitors can play with the buttons and look at the screen, which displays the blackened enemy territory — evidence of its total devastation.

Before long it becomes clear that total devastation has occurred on both sides. There is no radio communication from the surface at all, which is an ominous sign. Shelters on Level 1 are also silent. The other levels, however, seem to be mostly alive and Level 7 gets information from them. The contact with other levels, precluded before the war to avoid emotional longing for the outer world among the crew of Level 7, is not avoided now, as everybody realizes the advantages of staying in the deep underground shelter. At the same time, the radio contact with the outer world, or what is left of it, enlivens the atmosphere of Level 7. The quarrels, the accusations, the abusive comments, are an entertainment for X-127.

The broadcasts, transmitted by radio from all over the globe, report total devastation. The allies of both superpowers, as well as neutral countries, have been affected too, the last because of stray missiles. The actual destruction has been compounded by the fallout from the rigged bombs. Civilization and human life are victims of the nuclear conflict. There are accusations by the neutral countries against the belligerents and requests for information about the kind of metal used for rigging the bombs, which would provide a clue about the duration of radiation. Such information is refused by both sides, for fear of divulging the secret to the enemy.

X-127 records his basic indifference to the new world situation. "Out of billions of people only a few millions survived?" Why, he reflects, should it matter if there are less people on earth? "Libraries and museums destroyed?" Who cares about these? He himself attributes his indifference to the plight of humanity to his existence underground, where he has been cut off from the world, as well as to the psychological treatment he has received.

The case of X-117 is different. Since his collapse on duty he has fallen into a state of despair and remorse, which seems beyond the curing capacity of the psychologists. He accuses himself and others, including the psychologists, of the disaster inflicted on humankind. Finally he hangs himself. Curiously enough, X-127 feels sorry for him, despite his indifference to the demise of millions. Puzzled by this inconsistency, he attributes it to the smooth, clean, mechanical way of performing his military duty.

The news from the world continues and grows progressively more alarming. There are reports of widespread radiation sickness on Level 2 and similar news from neutral countries. People are dying like flies. Radio contact is interrupted. The polluted radioactive air penetrates everywhere, except for the deeper levels of shelters, which are equipped with a self-sufficient air supply, and do not depend of filtered outer air. Gradually the realization sinks in that the only humans to survive — apparently on both sides of the political divide — are those in the deep underground shelters. These deep installations were made self-sufficient for varying periods of time — from twenty-five years on Level 3 to 500 years on Level 7. Yet it is not known what is the expected duration of the radioactive environment on the surface. It could last hours, or years, or millions of years.

The monotonous but speedy disappearance of humanity is enlivened by a couple from Level 3, who decide to leave their shelter and drive on the surface and report what they see by radio. They know they are going to face a certain death, as against the prospect of twenty-five years of life in their shelter, but they do not mind. Their chilling description of total devastation, contrasting with their humanity and devotion to each other, move the listeners — including X-127. While he has been largely indifferent to the horrendous plight of humankind so far, and even his earlier emotional problems had revolved on his own longing for sunshine and nature, he now feels stirred by the suffering of his fellow human beings. He discerns within himself a warm feeling for the brave couple, and even for humanity in general. Is it compassion? Is it love?

X-127 turns introspective as he reveals a new self in himself. He attributes the change to the couple, who "have pushed the hidden button" in his soul. "The lost, forgotten, decayed button.... It makes me realize that I am not alone in the world," but "that there are other beings like myself."[16] Ironically, this discovery of a better self within himself comes too late, as far as humanity is concerned. Of course, this may well symbolize a warning for humanity at large not to wake up before it is too late.

The change of heart of X-127 gets on the nerves of his wife. She cannot endure, perhaps because she cannot scientifically explain, this transformation. So after a while she divorces him and marries X-107, a very well adjusted push-button officer.

In the meantime, three months after the war, the living world in one hemisphere has shrunk to levels 3 to 7, with a total of over 600,000 people. Presumably a similar number continues existence on the enemy side. Yet even this does not last. Progressively there is trouble in the deeper levels too — apparently through polluted water sources.

As people realize their end, there is a revolt against the political leaders on level 5, and the leaders are hanged. The executioner is a general who accuses the politicians of being responsible for the creation of the sophisticated weapons which have caused the total catastrophe. All this cannot stop the dying on Levels 3 to 5. Before long only Level 6 and Level 7 remain, with a mere 2,500 men and women.

A communication from the enemy announces that their country has been completely devastated, with only one thousand people left in a deep shelter, self-sufficient for centuries. They suggest making peace, as there is nothing in dispute anymore. However there is no authority to make peace, as the politicians were on Level 5, now extinct. Curiously enough, there is no contact with Level 6. Something is gone wrong there, though there is no way of knowing what. The apparent catastrophe there makes people on Level 7 concerned about their own future. In the meantime, on the authority of a referendum, Level 7 decides to make peace with the enemy.

The only benefit of peace is its entertainment value. Both sides exchange patriotic slogans, in a mock praise of their respective ideologies, which have become quite meaningless. While one radio message proclaims "Cave-men of the world, unite!" another responds "Freedom and democracy for all cave-men!" A terse conclusion proclaims: "Divided we live, united we die!"[17]

Yet even this belated manifestation of human coexistence comes to a sudden stop, as the other side grows silent. Apparently some mishap occurred there and they are doomed. The realization spreads terror in the hearts of the remnants of humanity on Level 7. And, indeed, the fear becomes soon justified. A problem with the nuclear energy supply, on which life on Level 7 entirely depends, results in a radiation leak, which spreads and causes illness and death.

As X-127 is dying, perhaps the last specimen of *Homo sapiens*, he acutely feels his loneliness. He ends his diary with disjointed words, like "friends people mother sun." They seem to express his regained humanity — alas, regained too late.

Level 7 is clearly a novel with a message, and the message is to warn humanity against the menace of a total thermonuclear war, a menace inherent in the preparation for such a war. A book of such intent and scope naturally touches on issues of technology and science, which are at the base of nuclear weapons and their means of delivery. It is no less compelling for such a work to deal with the "logic" of the new strategic thinking, which has no precedent in the annals of military theory, though it has been a major topic of theoretical analysis since the middle of the twentieth century. The human underpinnings of nuclear strategy, including the psychological qualities of the nuclear warriors, repeatedly addressed in *Level 7*, deserve some further elaboration in the context of the present study.

By and large, *Level 7* is a sarcastic exposition of the potential catastrophic failure of both nuclear-missile technology and the strategic thinking and planning based on the possession and control of such weapons. While the book delves into the intricate sophisticated planning for a peace founded on nuclear threat, it points to the vulnerability of the system, however meticulous its planning.

Underlying the overall strategy, leading to an extensive system of nuclear missiles on the one hand and the underground shelters on the other hand, is an implicit trust in scientific competence and clear logical reasoning. The bombs are trusted to bring devastation, the missiles to carry the bombs, the guidance systems to lead the armed missiles to their targets. Then there is the anti-missile system designed to destroy enemy rockets. Yet, due to the implicit assumption of the limited reliability of the latter, there is need for shelter protection. As it is technically impossible to provide it for the entire population, the shelters are limited and graded, with the best and deepest secured for the PBX Command — to assure the operation of the thermonuclear missile system. A fringe benefit is the secured survival of humankind in case of a nuclear deluge.

The belief in the system at large and in the perfect scientific planning for Level 7 is expressed by X-107, the cool, unperturbed, rational officer. "To him Level 7 is still the best of all possible worlds," comments X-127 somewhat skeptically. He quotes X-107 enthusiastically praising the technological achievement of creating a self-sufficient community four thousand feet underground: "To achieve all this is nothing less than a miracle of human ingenuity and scientific progress."[18]

X-107 argues with compelling logic for the necessity of Level 7, and the seclusion of the PBX Command in the deep underground. To have the Command on the surface — even in a remote desert — would leave it vulnerable to a surprise attack. This could knock out the country without allowing it "to fire back a single shot." Equally, the staff of Level 7 *had* to be imprisoned, argues X-107 in response to X-127's complaint. "If you were able to get out, you might come back with a destructive weapon, or a destructive idea, which could put PBX Command out of action. Contact with the outside world could mean contact with spies, with enemies, with pacifists" — a risk the government could not take.[19]

The mistrust in people, the concern about their unreliability, is compensated by the reliance on scientific, technological capability. Therefore the strategists largely delegate the decision to fire the missiles to an automated system — though reserving the authority of the human leadership to initiate an unprovoked nuclear attack, a rather unlikely contingency. Thus, it is a gadget, called the "atomphone," which fulfills a crucial role in a thermonuclear conflict. Sensitive to atomic explosions occurring within a certain range, "it would react to an explosion in our country." Utilizing "the principle of the seismograph, its function depended also on its sensitivity to acoustic waves, electromagnetic radiation and some other properties. Thus it would not react to a mere earthquake. Moreover, it could classify the strength of the explosion. Once the atomphone had registered an atomic explosion, it would automatically issue the order for retaliation of the appropriate strength."[20]

Yet, it is the supposedly irrefutable logic and the allegedly invulnerable science and technology which, in the story of *Level 7*, lead to a total and disastrous failure. The perfect system does not prevent a seemingly innocent mishap of rockets escaping their controls. Once this happens, the logic and the technology work perfectly — with disastrous consequences. Eventually, the perfect technology maintaining Level 7 also falls prey to a minor technical failure in the nuclear energy supply. Logic, science, and technology turn into a broken reed, and ironically do so with the alacrity characteristic of the scientific era.

Paradoxically, though science proves a broken reed in one sense, it is a powerful stick in another way. It may fail to defend, but it is all-powerful in attack. It fails to save, but it succeeds to destroy. It makes destruction and killing easy enough, even to be performed by squeamish individuals, as X-127 happens to be. As he puts it, while he could not be an executioner, "to push a button ... is a very different thing. It is smooth, clean, mechanical."[21]

Thus, the whole scientific and logical edifice is exposed as a failure, and its designers, whether strategists or engineers, appear to have been scientists and logicians gone mad. This, to be sure, need not be read as an indictment of logic and science as such. It is merely criticism of the hubris of people of doctrine and science, as they repudiate the counsel of common sense and ignore fundamental moral considerations. An exclusive rule of science, an absolute trust in the inventions of applied science, may prove dangerous, or even catastrophic.

There is another danger the book warns us about, namely the tendency to ignore the natural needs and feelings of people and to favor the artificial amenities of technology. This is symbolized by X-127 who — though not a very illustrious specimen of humanity — persistently craves sunshine and the surface of the earth.

The intent seems to be to point out that people, however civilized and advanced and modern, have some basic ties and urges which cannot and should not be substituted by technological artifice. Level 7 cannot be the best of all possible worlds, as long as humanity retains some of its elemental qualities.

Of course, the designers of Level 7, who may well represent a widespread modern trend, try their best to train, or condition, people to assimilate modern science and technology into their own mental and behavioral disposition. For only in this way can they be relied upon to fulfill their own function without compunction and hesitancy. X-127 wonders what the difference is between himself and an electronic brain. He is almost as indifferent to the plight of others as an electronic device — which is what his trainers intended. The residual difference lies in his feeling of self-pity. Thus, he describes Level 7 as a "community of self-pitying gadgets."[22] This deliberately planned dehumanization is linked to the psychological selection of the push-button officers and their treatment in case of need. The author of *Level 7* devotes a considerable amount of attention and criticism to the role of applied psychology in facilitating the dehumanization of people, which is necessary for making them a ready and complacent functionaries of the political authority and its technological apparatus.

The very choice of X-127 for his role is based on certain personality characteristics. As the loudspeaker explains in response to his loud musing, "You were chosen because of your personal qualities. You must have proved to be a man of a stable disposition, technically skillful, ambitious, intelligent and very healthy. Also you must have got a very high score in claustrophobia tests."[23] While this sounds perfectly sensible, and the practice of taking into consideration personality traits when filling some complex functions has been long established, this issue turns into a sinister element in the context of the story. For in the design to select and train future mass killers, the psychological selection assumes the role of a devilish plan.

It seems callous in respect to the future victims, and it appears ruthless toward the chosen executioners. For these are not regarded as worthwhile human beings, as ends in themselves and sovereign rulers of their own lives, but rather as means to a political and military objective of a questionable merit, to put it mildly, who are not consulted about their own stand, and who are condemned to eventual imprisonment underground without their consent — only because their function requires it and their tolerance of claustrophobia facilitates it. Thus psychology fulfills a significant role in the grand design of Level 7 and all it stands for, and becomes another element in the moral failure of science and reason.

The psychological approach to the malaise of X-127, and particularly to the qualms of X-117, offer an opportunity for a more outspoken criticism of the theory and practice of the science of the human mind or soul. The neurotic symptoms of X-117 are not related to his profound abhorrence to pushing the buttons which would kill millions of people, but, with the assistance of the psychoanalytic theory, are attributed to the repression of some urges in childhood. His argument that the hysterical paralysis "is a punishment from 'above' for his readiness to ... destroy the world" is rejected and substituted by linking it to parental strictures.[24] In other words, ethical judgment is considered as a mere psychological phenomenon, and a sickly manifestation at that. Psychology is a science, while morality becomes a human weakness. Psychology as an applied science tries to cure X-117 and others of his ilk from their mental infirmity.

This is emphatically rejected by X-117, who clearly is here a spokesman for the author of *Level 7*. He turns his indignation and fury at P-867, whom he addresses, "You psychologist, you soul-killer!" His argument is contained in a nutshell: "You managed to cure me of my conscience so that I'd be able to kill humanity."[25] Psychology, with its tricks and drugs, can be a powerful instrument, but it may be directed at human conscience and thus prove destructive of human soul, of the essence of humanity in the good sense of the word.

Thus, in the last resort, the world comes to an end because of the combination, the unholy alliance of technology and psychology, the manipulation of physical forces and of the human mind. The source of the trouble is that the ethical element, the distinction between right and wrong, is ignored. Morality is not accorded its rightful place in the scheme of human affairs, which are determined by science, or subject to an arbitrary will, using scientific knowledge. Without ethical control, without moral judgment, civilization is doomed, and even humankind itself may perish, as the scientific means expand human power even beyond its original intent and willful design. Unguided by fundamental values, humankind faces the danger of becoming the victim of its rational ingenuity.

Conclusion

In exploring the perception of science and technology in various examples of myth and fiction, we have found a diversity of notions and attitudes. In some cases science and technology are seen as powerful means for the expansion of human capacity and the increase of humankind's well-being. In others science and technology are presented as a menace to humankind and its civilization. In some, science and technology are tools and servants, while in others they usurp the role of superiors.

Is there a way to conclude which is the right image? Is there a clear verdict on the role of this human endeavor in shaping the human condition? Are we in danger of subjection to Čapek's robots, or will human inventions be controlled and mastered by Bacon's Solomon's House? Can humankind remain in control of its ingenuity as exemplified by the mythological figure of Prometheus, or will it succumb to its own fascination with its machines and gadgets and scientific manipulation to produce a brave new world? Or may it even fall victim to its own ingenious weapons?

There are no conclusive answers to these questions, and there cannot be. Science and technology are not created and do not exist in a vacuum, but form a relationship with humanity, and this relationship is anything but simple. They exist in a complex setting which consists, inter alia, of the genius and inventiveness of some human beings, the complacency and apathy of many others, broad vision of a few and myopia of many — besides human ambition, power-seeking, greed, social conflict, class tension and so on.

There is the human quest for truth for its own sake, which may animate many scientists, and there is curiosity which may be idle. There is science aiming at the comprehension of reality and the mastering of it for human benefit. And there are experiments which are futile, like some in the Grand Academy of Lagado in *Gulliver's Travels*, which, as some skeptics may assert, are followed in outer space these days. There are some unquestionable benefits of technology, and both intellectual and practical achievements of science.

But then there are costs, detriments, risks and dangers. Some of these, as in the case of the nuclear weapons, are clear and present. Some, like biological control and psychological conditioning, even when well-intended, may turn a utopia into a travesty.

In this Babel of possibilities, exemplified in our analytical presentation, there is no clear guidance, or obvious model of perfection. One can read the various points of view conveyed in myth and fiction, and benefit from their insights, but one has to reach one's own conclusion. However, to reach such a conclusion, one must realize the complexity of the issue, as suggested above, and, having done so, one must address a moral judgment to decide on the specific issues under consideration. The quest for truth, informing scientific inquiry, and the quest for comfort and well-being, motivating technological innovation, must be steered by the norm of right, by the notion of good, to maximize the chances that human genius and ingenuity will not turn against humankind, or even send it to perdition. We may be sailing on an exceptionally advanced and comfortable boat. Yet it is up to us to decide where we want to go and how to steer the boat in the right direction.

To be sure, most of the works explored here explicitly or implicitly point to the right direction as they see it. The Golem is controlled by a wise and concerned rabbi. Huxley advocates the preservation of the freedom of the individual mind. A *Canticle for Leibowitz* proclaims the need for love and compassion to secure the salvation of humankind.

Still, pointing to the right direction for humankind is one thing; applying the advice to a concrete situation is another. The social application of compassion and humanity may be more difficult than the technological application of science, which makes the overall improvement of humankind, its moral progress, so difficult and tricky, and strewn with frustration and failure. The path to success in such a comprehensive sense, the road to a moral Eldorado, remains much more winding and bumpy than the road of scientific discovery and technological invention.

Chapter Notes

Chapter 1

1. Cf. *Lexicon Biblicum* (in Hebrew), Tel-Aviv: Dvir, 1964, Vol. II, p. 455, "*Mabul*" (Flood).
2. The English translation of the Hebrew text, here and in some further instances, deviates somewhat from the King James Version (further referred to as K.J.V.), in order to render the original more faithfully.
3. See *Lexicon Biblicum*, Vol. II, p. 882, "*Tevah*" (Ark).
4. K.J.V. translates the Hebrew text more freely, making Noah the first farmer: "And Noah began to be a husbandman, and he planted a vineyard" (Genesis 9:20).
5. The translation is an attempt to find out the true meaning of the Hebrew wording, which is not quite clear. K.J.V. reads: "And he called his name Noah, saying, This same shall comfort us concerning our work and toil of our hands, because of the ground which the Lord hath cursed."
6. Translated from Bialik and Ravnitsky, *Sefer Ha-Aggadah: A Selection of Legends from the Talmud and Midrashim* (in Hebrew), Tel-Aviv: Dvir, 1960, p. 19, #108. The book is available in English translation, under the title *The Book of Legends*, New York: Schocken Books, 1992.
7. "Landmark" might be a better translation of *shem* in this context. "*Shem*" means "name" and is so translated in the K.J.V. However, the Hebrew word has also other connotations, including "a memorial sign." "Landmark" seems here more appropriate, for though the "sign" may well be intended to be respected by posterity and thus assure the continuity of social-human identity, the text seems primarily to be concerned about the present geographical concentration and humanity's unity.
8. *Adam* in Hebrew is both the name of the first man and man in general. When the phrase *bnei Adam* is used, as in the present case, it makes better sense to translate it as "the sons (or children) of Adam" than "the children of man," (as does K.J.V.).
9. The second part of the verse is translated differently from the literal translation of K.J.V., as the latter does not convey the sense of the text as clearly.
10. K.J.V. translates literally: "upon the face of all the earth"—both here and in verse 9. The intent of the Hebrew text is better conveyed by "upon the surface of the entire earth."
11. The statement makes no sense in translation. In the Hebrew text the word for "confound" is *balal*, which sounds close enough to *Bavel* (Babel), to make the linguistic connection between the story and the name of the city. To be sure, it can be argued that this is a contrived connection, for the meaning of Babel in the original Akkadian is *Bab-ilu*, "the gate of God." Such meaning is well in line with the story of God coming down to see the city. All this may suggest the Babylonian origin of the myth. This, however, is not our concern in the present context.
12. The translation and summary of Ibn Ezra's Hebrew commentary, here and further on, follows the Hebrew text of *Mikraot Gedolot*, Vienna, 1859. *Mikraot Gedolot* contains the text of the Pentateuch with several major traditional commentaries. The commentaries concerned are appended to the relevant biblical verse.
13. Quotations from Ramban and Rashi from *Mikraot Gedolot*, the relevant commentaries to the text.
14. Translated from *Sefer Ha-Aggadah*, p. 23, #136.

Chapter 2

1. See "Introduction" of Sir James George Frazer to his translation of Apollodorus, *The Library*, The Loeb Classical Library, 1921, especially p. ix, and p. xvi.

2. Apollodorus, *The Library*, "Introduction," p. xvii.
3. Ibid Ibid., III, xv, 8.
4. Ibid Ibid., III, i, 4.
5. Ibid Ibid., III, xv, 8 and *Epitome* I, 7–9.
6. *Epitome*, I, 12–15.
7. Ovid, *Metamorphoses*, Latin with English translation by Frank Justus Miller, Loeb Classical Library, Third Edition, 1977, VIII, 183–187. The English translation in our text does not necessarily follow Miller's version verbatim. The section covered in our presentation is found in VIII, 183–262.
8. Ibid Ibid., VIII, 188–189.
9. Ibid Ibid., VIII, 217–220.
10. Ibid Ibid., VIII, 233–234.
11. See Liddell and Scott's *Greek-English Lexicon*, abridged edition, Clarendon Ppress, Oxford University Press, 1871.
12. Apollodorus, *The Library*, III, xv, 8. Note 2 (Vol. II, pp. 120–121).
13. Ibid Ibid., II, iii. 2. See also Homer's *Iliad*, VI, 183–231. Pegasus, further mentioned, does not appear in the version of Homer.
14. Apollodorus, *The Library*, I, vii, 1. See also Hesiod, *Theogony*, 521–531.
15. This and the following quotations from *Prometheus Bound* follow Aeschylus, *Prometheus* and *other Plays*, translated by Philip Vellacott, The penguin Classics, Penguin Books 1961, P. 27, lines 233–237.
16. Ibid Ibid., p. 24, lines 109–112.
17. Ibid Ibid., pp. 33–35, lines 442–500.
18. Ibid Ibid., p. 24, lines 103–104.
19. Ibid Ibid., p.22, lines 45–48.
20. Ibid Ibid., p. 22,lines 49–50.
21. Ibid Ibid., p. 28, lines 240–241.

Chapter 3

1. The first four volumes of the Arabic stories, by Antoine Galland, were published in Paris in 1704, under the title *Les Milles et Une Nuits*.
2. One prominent work is a novel by a German writer, Gustav Meyrink, *Der Golem*, 1915. (English translation 1928.). Another is a drama in Yiddish by H. Leivick, *Der Golem*, 1921, which was staged in Hebrew by the Habimah Theatre. A study of the legend and its use in German literature can be found in Beate Rosenfeld, *Die Golemsage und ihre Verwertung in der deutschen Literatur*, Breslau: Verlag Dr. Hans Priebatsch, 1934.
3. The above presentation follows the authoritative study of the problem by Gershom Scholem, "Die Vorstellung vom Golem in ihren tellurischen und magischen Beziehungen," *Eranos-Jahrbuch 1953*, Band XXII, Zurich: Rhein-Verlag, 1954, pp. 235–289. The summary refers to pp. 244–246.
4. Ibid Ibid., pp. 283–284.
5. Rosenfeld, pp. 17–18.
6. Scholem, pp. 284–287.
7. Scholem, Ibid., pp. 288–289.
8. Scholem, Ibid., p. 260.
9. Cf. Rosenfeld, p. 28.
10. Rosenfeld, p. 28Ibid.
11. Scholem, pp. 261–262.
12. Scholem, Ibid., p. 255.
13. Scholem, Ibid., pp. 277–279.
14. See Rosenfeld, p. 25, footnotes.
15. Scholem, pp. 287–288.
16. Scholem, Ibid, pp. 274–275.
17. Christopher Marlowe, *Doctor Faustus*, 1604. Quoted here from the Signet Classics edition, New York: New American Library, 1969. Act I, Scene I, p. 26.
18. Ibid Ibid., Act I, Scene I, p. 28.
19. Ibid Ibid., Act I, Sscene III, p. 35.
20. Ibid Ibid., Act III, Oopening, p. 53.
21. Ibid Ibid., Act II, Scene I, p. 43.
22. Ibid Ibid., Prologue, p. 23.
23. Ibid Ibid., Act I, Scene III, p. 34.

Chapter 4

1. *New Atlantis* was written in 1624 and published posthumously in 1629. The subsequent quotations and page references are from Francis Bacon, *Selected Writings*, New York: The Modern Library, 1955.
2. Ibid Ibid., p. 557.
3. Ibid Ibid., pp. 47–48.
4. Ibid Ibid., p. 583.
5. Ibid Ibid., p. 574.
6. Ibid Ibid., pp. 374ff.
7. Ibid Ibid., p. 581.
8. Ibid Ibid., p. 576.
9. Ibid Ibid., p. 579.
10. Ibid Ibid., p. 577.
11. Ibid Ibid., pp. 582–583.
12. Ibid Ibid., pp. 562–563.
13. Ibid Ibid., pp. 583–584.
14. 1 Kings 3:12 (K.J.V.).
15. 1 Kings 3:16–28.
16. 1 Kings 4:29–34, especially 4:33; 1 Kings 5:9–14, especially 5:13 (in the original Hebrew Bible).
17. The subsequent quotations from *Gulliver's Travels* follow the edition off A.B. Gough,

Oxford: At the Clarendon Press, 1924. The division into parts and chapters is common with other editions of Swift's book.

18. Ibid Ibid., Part IV, Chapter VIII, pp. 303–304.
19. Ibid Ibid., Part IV, Chapter VIII, p. 302.
20. Ibid Ibid., Part IV, Chapter V, ii, VII, p. 295.
21. Ibid Ibid., Part IV, Chapter VII, p. 296.
22. Ibid Ibid., Part II, Chapter VI, p. 145.
23. Ibid Ibid., Part IV, Chapter XII, p. 336.
24. Ibid Ibid., Part IV, Chapter V, p. 280.
25. Ibid Ibid., Part IV, Chapter VI, p. 281.
26. Ibid Ibid., Part IV, Chapter VI, p. 282.
27. Ibid Ibid., Part IV, Chapter V, pp. 282–283.
28. Ibid Ibid., Part IV, Chapter VII, p. 295.
29. Ibid Ibid., Part IV, Chapter X, p. 316.
30. Ibid Ibid., Part IV, Chapter XI, p. 324.
31. Ibid Ibid., Part II, Chapter VII, p. 150.
32. Ibid Ibid., Part III, Chapter V, pp. 204–205.
33. Ibid Ibid., Part III, Chapter V, p. 208.

Chapter 5

1. The author is sometimes referred to as Mary Wollstonecraft Shelley, or as Mary Godwin Shelley, following her maternal or paternal ancestry. The following quotations from *Frankenstein* follow the Bantam Classic edition, Bantam Books, 1981.
2. Ibid Ibid., Letter 1, pp. 1–2.
3. Ibid Ibid., Letter 1, p. 3.
4. Ibid Ibid., Chapter 3, p. 32.
5. Ibid Ibid., Chapter 3, pp. 33–34.
6. Ibid Ibid., Chapter 4, pp. 35–36.
7. Ibid Ibid., Letter 6, p. 15.
8. Ibid Ibid., Chapter 6, p. 52.
9. Ibid Ibid., Chapter 20, p. 152.
10. Ibid Ibid., Chapter 7, p. 61.
11. Ibid Ibid., Chapter 23, p. 184.
12. Ibid Ibid., Chapter 20, pp. 150–151.
13. Ibid Ibid., Chapter 15, pp. 114–115.
14. Ibid Ibid., Chapter 15, p. 115.
15. Ibid Ibid., Chapter 13, p. 104.
16. The following references and quotations from *Dr. Jekyll and Mr. Hyde* follow the Tor Book edition, New York: Tom Doherty Associates, 1991.
17. Ibid Ibid., pp. 60–61.
18. Ibid Ibid., p. 62.
19. Ibid Ibid., pp. 63–64.
20. Ibid Ibid., p. 67.
21. Ibid Ibid., pp. 70–71.

22. The Hebrew *yetzer*— which may be translated as "imagination" in the Bible (as in the verse from Genesis quoted above) — becomes "inclination" or "impulse" in the rabbinical literature. In the latter sense it conveys a trait stronger than mere "tendency," which is better rendered by "impulse." Yet it is not an accidental manifestation, as "impulse" would be, but an expression of a deeply set psychological inclination. Thus it is a combination of (continuous) tendency and (strong) impulse.
23. See Plato, *Phaedrus*, 253–254. B. Jowett's translation.
24. *Dr. Jekyll and Mr. Hyde*, p. 58.
25. Genesis 19:30–38.
26. Psalm 104:15.
27. *A Midsummer Night's Dream*, Act II, Scene I, 169–172.
28. *Dr. Jekyll and Mr. Hyde*, p.66.

Chapter 6

1. The original French title is *Voyage au centre de la Terre*. The English translation used here is by Lowell Bair, published by Bantam Books, 1991. Subsequent quotations indicate the chapter and the page in this edition. Occasionally, to convey more precisely the French text, the translation is modified or made by the present writer, in which case the French excerpt is reproduced in the corresponding note. The French edition is by Paris: J. Hetzel et Co., undated but apparently 1864.
2. Jules Verne, *Voyage to the Center of the World*, Chapter 3, p. 13. Avicenna (980–1037) wrote in Arabic on medicine and other sciences. Bacon, assuming it is Roger Bacon (1214–1294), an English philosopher, wrote works on alchemy. Raymond Lully (or Ramon Lull) (1236–1315), a Catalan philosopher and mystic, in later generations gained the reputation of being a magician. Paracelsus (1493–1541) was a Swiss physician, alchemist and chemist.
3. See Ibid Ibid., Chapter 6, pp. 32–34. Siméon Denis Poisson (1781–1840) was a French mathematician and physicist. Sir Humphry Davy (1778–1829) was an English chemist and physicist.
4. Ibid Ibid., Chapter 6, p. 32.
5. Ibid Ibid., Chapter 3, p. 16. Modified translations of two quotations: (1) "Eh bien, appliquons mon procédé au document en question." (2) "La tête du savant ne pouvait comprendre les choses du coeur."
6. Ibid Ibid., Chapter 5, pp. 26–27. "Mon

oncle, a cette lecture, bondit comme s'il eût inopinément touché une bouteille de Leyde. Il était magnifique d'audace, de joie et de la conviction." (Leyden jar is an electrical condenser, invented in the mid eighteenth century, which can cause a violent shock if not handled properly.)

7. Ibid Ibid., Chapter 8, p. 44.

8. Ibid Ibid., Chapter 7, p. 39. "Quelle gloire attend M. Lidenbrock et rejaillira sur son compagnonl."

9. Ibid Ibid., Chapter 11, pp. 63–64.

10. Ibid Ibid., Chapter 32, pp. 172–173. "Mon corps se subtilise, se sublime à son tour et se mélange comme un atome impondérable à ces immenses vapeurs qui tracent dans l'infini leur orbite enflammée!"

11. The French title is *De la Terre à la Lune*. The quotations are from the English translation in *Jules Verne Omnibus*, Philadelphia and New York: J.B. Lippincott. Co. (The name of the translator and the date of publication are not indicated.)

12. The French title is *Vingt mille lieues sous les Mers*. The quotations are from the English translation of Anthony Bonner, Bantam Books, 1962, 1981.

13. *Twenty-thousand Leagues under the Sea*, Chapter II, pp. 20–22.

14. *From the Earth to the Moon*, Chapter IV, p. 563.

15. *Twenty-thousand Leagues under the Sea*, Chapter XXVIII, pp. 210–211.

16. From *the Earth to the Moon*, Chapter XXV, pp. 658–659.

17. Ibid Ibid., Chapter I, p. 547.

18. Ibid Ibid., Chapter III, p. 559.

19. Ibid Ibid., Chapter I, p. 549.

20. Ibid Ibid., Chapter XVIII, p. 622.

21. *Twenty-thousand Leagues under the Sea*, Chapter XI.

22 Ibid Ibid., Chapter XI, p. 75.

23. *From the Earth to the Moon*, Chapter I, p. 550.

24. Ibid Ibid., Chapter X, p. 589. The New Testament version of the Golden Rule, attributed to Jesus, is: "As ye would that men should do to you, do ye also to them likewise" (Luke 6:31; Matthew 7:12). The wording of Hillel (70 B.C. A.D. 10) was: "What is hateful to thee, do not to thy fellow being" (*Babylonian Talmud*, Tractate *Sabbath* 31a).

25. *Twenty-thousand Leagues under the Sea*, Chapter XXXVI, pp. 281ff.

26. Ibid Ibid., Chapter XLV, p. 359. It is noteworthy that while Nemo insinuates that it is a certain nation he is hostile to (p. 359), he elsewhere makes a sweeping comment about the ubiquity of savages, who obviously populate also the supposedly civilized regions of the world.

"'Where won't you find savages?'" he sarcastically asks Aronnax (Chapter XXII, pp. 154–155).

27. Quoted from Jules Verne, *The Begum's Fortune*, London: Bernard Hanison, 1958, Chapter III, p.40.

28. Ibid Ibid., Chapter VII, p. 88.

29. Ibid Ibid., Chapter VIII, p. 104.

30. Ibid Ibid., Chapter XVIII, p. 186.

31. Ibid Ibid., Chapter III, p. 37.

32. Ibid Ibid., Chapter I, p. 20.

33. Ibid Ibid., Chapter XII, p. 143.

34. Ibid Ibid., Chapter X.

35. Ibid Ibid., Chapter V, p. 68.

Chapter 7

1. H.G. Wells, *The Outline of History*, Revised edition, New York: Doubleday & & Company, 1949, Book I, Chapter 1, #3, p. 16.

2. Quoted from *Encyclopaedia Britannica*, 1960 edition, Vol. II, "Huxley, Thomas Henry," p. 949a.

3. H.G. Wells, *The Island of Dr. Moreau* (1896). Quoted from New York: Tor edition, 1996, Chapter 6, p. 27.

4. Ibid Ibid., Chapter 22, p. 141.

5. Ibid Ibid., Chapter 14, p. 74.

6. Ibid Ibid., Chapter 14, p. 75.

7. Ibid Ibid., Chapter 15, p. 84.

8. Ibid Ibid., Chapter 8, p. 38.

9. Ibid Ibid., Chapter 14, p. 77.

10. Ibid Ibid., Chapter 14, p. 78.

11. Ibid Ibid., Chapter 22, p. 141.

12. Ibid Ibid., Chapter 19, p. 114.

13. Ibid Ibid., Chapter 16, p. 101.

14. Ibid Ibid., Chapter 22, p. 142.

15. H.G. Wells, *A Modern Utopia*, 1905. Lincoln: University of Nebraska Ppress, 1967, Chapter 11, #3, p. 363.

16. Ibid Ibid., "A Note to the Reader," p. xxx.

17. Ibid Ibid., Chapter 1, #7, p. 30.

18. Ibid Ibid., Chapter 1, #1, p. 5.

19. Ibid Ibid., Chapter 1, #5, p. 22.

20. Ibid Ibid., Chapter 2, #3, p. 49.

21. Ibid Ibid., Chapter 3, #4, p. 88.

22. Ibid Ibid., Chapter 6, #2, p. 181.

23. Ibid Ibid., Chapter 9, #4, p. 278.

24. Ibid Ibid., Chapter 9, #8, p. 311.

25. Ibid Ibid., Chapter 9, #6, p. 299.

26. Ibid Ibid., Chapter 3, #6, p. 98.

27. Ibid Ibid., Chapter 3, #8, pp. 110–111.

28. Ibid Ibid., Chapter 2, #5, p. 60.

29. Ibid Ibid., Chapter 12, #1, pp. 318–319.

30. Ibid Ibid., Chapter 12, #1, p. 324.

31. Ibid Ibid., Chapter 12, #1, p. 320.

32. Ibid Ibid., Chapter 7, #7, p. 244.

Chapter 8

1. B.F. Skinner, *Walden Two*, 1948. Quoted here, and subsequently, from the Macmillan paperbacks edition, 1962, Chapter 27, p. 223.
2. Ibid Ibid., Chapter 15, p. 126.
3. Ibid Ibid., Chapter 4, pp. 30–31.
4. Ibid Ibid., Chapter 6, p. 45.
5. Ibid Ibid., Chapter 13.
6. Ibid Ibid., Chapter 4, pp. 29–30.
7. Ibid Ibid., Chapter 8, p. 56.
8. Ibid Ibid., Chapter 19, p. 157.
9. Ibid Ibid., Chapter 29, p. 254.
10. Ibid Ibid., Chapter 29, pp. 259–260
11. Ibid Ibid., Chapter 20, p. 175.
12. Ibid Ibid., Chapter 32, pp. 292–293.
13. Ibid Ibid., Chapter 14, pp. 105–107.
14. Ibid Ibid., Chapter 29, pp. 256–257.
15. Ibid Ibid., Chapter 20, pp. 174–175.
16. Ibid Ibid., Chapter 23, p. 196.
17. Ibid Ibid., Chapter 29, P. 257.
18. Ibid Ibid., Chapter 33, pp. 296–297.
19. Ibid Ibid., Chapter 29, p. 273.
20. George Orwell, *1984*, 1949. Quotation from Signet Classics, New American Library, 1961, Part Ttwo, IX, pp. 171–172.
21. Ibid Ibid., Part Two, IX, pp. 173–174.
22. Ibid Ibid., Part One, I, p. 5.
23. Ibid Ibid., Part One, IV, p. 36.
24. Ibid Ibid., Part Three, III, p. 217.
25. Ibid Ibid., Part One, I , p. 19.
26. Ibid Ibid., Part Three, II, p. 211.
27. Ibid Ibid., Part Two, IX, p. 159.
28. Ibid Ibid., Part One, III, pp. 32–33.
29. Ibid Ibid., Part One, I , p. 7, and p. 17.
30. Ibid Ibid., Part One, V, pp. 45–47.
31. Ibid Ibid., Appendix, p. 254.
32. Bertrand Russell, "The Psychoanalyst's Nightmare" in *Nightmares of Eminent Persons and Other Stories*, London: The Bodley Head, 1954, p. 21.
33. Ibid Ibid., p. 24.
34. Ibid Ibid., p. 27.
35. Ibid Ibid., p. 29.
36. Ibid Ibid., p. 29.
37. Ibid Ibid., p. 28.
38. "Dr. Southport Vulpes's Nightmare," *Nightmares of Eminent Persons*, p. 64.
39. See Bertrand Russell, *Common Sense and Nuclear Warfare*, New York: Simon and Schuster, 1959.
40. "Dr. Southport Vulpes's Nightmare," *Nightmares*, p. 63.

Chapter 9

1. Quoted from Karel Čapek, *R.U.R.* (*Rossum's Universal Robots*), translated by Paul Selver, New York: Doubleday, Page & Company, 1923, Act I, pp. 16–17.
2. Ibid Ibid., Act I, p. 42.
3. Ibid Ibid., Act III, p. 133.
4. Ibid Ibid., Act II, pp. 112–114.
5. Ibid Ibid., Act II, p. 109.
6. Ibid Ibid., Act II, pp. 86–88.
7. Ibid Ibid., Act I, p. 51. Cf. also Act III, pp. 130–131.
8. Ibid Ibid., Act III, p. 131.
9. E.M. Forster, *The Collected Tales*, New York: Alfred A. Knopf, 1964, "Introduction" (1946), pp. *vii–viii*. The following quotations from "The Machine Stops" are made from this volume.
10. Ibid Ibid., p. 144.
11. Ibid Ibid., p. 150.
12. Ibid Ibid., p. 151.
13. Ibid Ibid., p. 153.
14. Ibid Ibid., p. 197.
15. Ibid Ibid., p. 164.
16. Ibid Ibid, p. 164.
17. Ibid Ibid., p. 176.
18. Ibid Ibid., p. 184.
19. Aldous Huxley, *Ape and Essence*, New York: Harper and Brothers, 1948, p. 32.
20. Ibid Ibid., p. 45.
21. Ibid Ibid., p. 35.
22. Jonathan Swift, *Gulliver's Travels*, Part IV, Chapter V, pp. 282–283. See also above, Chapter 4, ii.
23. Huxley, *Ape and Essence*, pp. 51–52.
24. Ibid Ibid., p. 53.
25. Ibid Ibid., p. 54.
26. Ibid Ibid., p. 111.
27. Ibid Ibid., pp. 120–124.
28. Ibid Ibid., pp. 124–125.
29. Ibid Ibid., p. 190.

Chapter 10

1. Aldous Huxley, *Ape and Essence*, pp. 6–7.
2. Eugene Zamiatin, *We*, English translation by Gregory Zilboorg (1924). Quoted from New York: E.P. Dutton paperback edition. Each quotation indicates the Record number, and book page. Record Three, pp. 12–13.
3. Ibid Ibid., Record One, p. 4.
4. Ibid Ibid., Record Two, p. 5.
5. Ibid Ibid., Record Thirty, p. 164.

6. Ibid Ibid., Record Two, p. 6.
7. Ibid Ibid., Record Three, p. 15.
8. Ibid Ibid., Record Twelve, p. 63.
9. Ibid Ibid., Record Twelve, pp. 62–63.
10. Ibid Ibid., Record Fifteen, pp. 76–77.
11. Ibid Ibid., Record Seven, p. 31.
12. Ibid Ibid., Record Four, p. 17.
13. Ibid Ibid., Record Nineteen, p. 102.
14. Ibid Ibid., Record Twenty-One, p. 112.
15. Ibid Ibid., Record Eighteen, pp. 96–97.
16. Ibid Ibid., Record Thirty-One, pp. 166–167.
17. Ibid Ibid., Record Twenty-Five, p. 193.
18. Ibid Ibid., Record One, p. 3.
19. Jean-Jacques Rousseau, *The Social Contract* (1762), Book I, VII: Of the Sovereign.
20. See Gilbert Ryle, *The Concept of Mind* (1949), Penguin Books, 1963, Chapter III (5), pp. 74–75.
21. Aldous Huxley, *Brave New World*, 1932, with author's "Foreword," 1946. Quoted from Bantam Books edition, 1958, Chapter One, p. 10.
22. Ibid Ibid., Chapter Three, p. 26.
23. Ibid Ibid., Chapter Three, pp. 22–23.
24. Ibid Ibid., Chapter Three, pp. 35–36.
25. Ibid Ibid., Chapter Nine, p. 94. The quotation is from *The Tempest*, Act V, Scene I, verses 183–184.
26. *Brave New World*, Foreword, pp. ix–x.
27. Ibid Ibid., Chapter Ten, pp. 98–99.
28. This is one of the most shocking illustrations of the education process depicted in *Tthe Brave New World*. See Ibid Ibid., Chapter Two, pp. 12–15.
29. Ibid Ibid., Chapter Fifteen, p. 146
30. Ibid Ibid., Chapter Three, p. 31.
31. Ibid Ibid., Foreword, p. xii.
32. Ibid Ibid., Chapter Seventeen, p. 161.
33. Ibid Ibid., Chapter Seventeen, p. 159.
34. Ibid Ibid., Chapter Sixteen, pp. 152–153.
35. Ibid Ibid., Chapter Sixteen, p. 155.
36. Ibid Ibid., Chapter Twelve, pp. 119–120.
37. Ibid Ibid., Foreword, pp. vii–viii.
38. Ibid Ibid., Chapter Seventeen, p. 163.
39. Ibid Ibid., Chapter Sixteen, p. 154.
40. Ibid Ibid., Foreword, pp. viii–ix.
41. Ibid Ibid., Foreword, pp. xi–xii.

Chapter 11

1. Cf. David Dowling, *Fictions of Nuclear Disaster*, Iowa City: University of Iowa Press, 1987, Chapter 5. Dowling comments that "the language of Biblical apocalypse has been transferred effortlessly and wholesale to the description of late twentieth century angst and, in particular, the secular menace of nuclear destruction" (p. 115).
2. Walter M. Miller, Jr., *A Canticle for Leibowitz*, 1959, Bantam Books, 1976, Part I, Chapter 6, pp. 57–58.
3. Ibid Ibid., Part I, Chapter 6, p. 59.
4. Ibid Ibid., Part II, Chapter 20, p. 197.
5. Ibid Ibid., Part II, Chapter 20, pp. 199–200.
6. Ibid Ibid., Part III, Chapter 25, pp. 255–256.
7. Ibid Ibid., Part III, Chapter 30, p. 312.
8. Ibid Ibid., Part I, Chapter 11, p. 103.
9. Ibid Ibid., Part I, Chapter 11, p. 107.
10. Ibid Ibid., Part II, Chapter 18, p. 170.
11. Ibid Ibid., Part II, Chapter 21, pp. 207–208.
12. Ibid Ibid., Part II, Chapter 22, p. 220.
13. Bertrand Russell, *Common Sense and Nuclear Warfare*, 1959, "Introduction," pp. 11–13.
14. Many reviewers of the book and undoubtedly many readers missed the point and saw *Level 7* as an exposition of the American system of nuclear defense. This for two reasons. One was that the author lived in the United States, though the book was first published in the United Kingdom. Another reason was that the American publisher, though basing his edition on the British text, slightly revised the following original phrasing, "Our attitude probably resembled that of a bunch of aristocratic officer-cadets," by Americanizing it into "Our attitude probably resembled that of a bunch of Ivy-league college boys." This was done without the author's knowledge. See "Afterword" by H. Bruce Franklin to Mordecai Roshwald, *Level 7* (1959), Lawrence Hill Books, Chicago 1989, page 189 and note 8 on page 192. In this edition, the phrasing was restored to its original intent, though the wording was slightly modified, substituting "privileged" for "aristocratic." Quotations from *Level 7* refer to this edition and, except for "Introduction," indicate the date of entry in the diary, and the page in the book. This corrected text was reprinted (page numbers included) in the edition of *Level 7* published by Wisconsin University Press, edited by David Seed, 2004.
15. *Level 7*, June 10, p.121.
16. Ibid Ibid., July 2, p. 156.
17. Ibid Ibid., September 28 and 29, pp. 172–173.
18. Ibid Ibid., April 4, pp. 43–44.
19. Ibid Ibid., March 25, pp. 25–26.
20. Ibid Ibid., June 11, p. 126
21. Ibid Ibid., June 19, p. 141.
22. Ibid Ibid., April 11, p. 56.
23. Ibid Ibid., March 23, p. 22.
24. Ibid Ibid., April 14, pp. 58–59.
25. Ibid Ibid., June 18, p. 139.

Bibliography

Aeschylus. *Prometheus and Other Plays.* Translated by Philip Vellacott. Hammondsworth: Penguin Books, 1961.

Apollodorus. *The Library.* Greek text with English translation by Sir George Frazer. Loeb Classical Library, 1921.

Arabian Nights. Translated by Husain Haddawy. New York: W.W. Norton and Company, 1995.

Bacon, Francis. "New Atlantis." Francis Bacon's *Selected Writings.* New York: The Modern Library, 1955.

Bialik, H.N. and J.H. Ravnitzky. *Sefer Ha-Aggadah* (in Hebrew). [*A Selection of Legends from the Talmud and Midrashim.*] Tel-Aviv: Dvir, 1960. English translation: *The Book of Legends.* New York: Schocken Books, 1992.

Bible. Hebrew Bible. English translation: King James Version.

Čapek, Karel. *R.U.R. (Rossum's Universal Robots).* Translated by Paul Selver. New York: Doubleday, Page and Company, 1923.

Dowling, David. *Fictions of Nuclear Disaster.* Iowa City: University of Iowa Press, 1987.

Forster, E.M. "The Machine Stops." *Collected Tales.* New York: Alfred A. Knopf, 1946.

Franklin, H. Bruce, *War Stars: The Superweapon and the American Imagination.* New York: Oxford University Press, 1988.

Homer, *Iliad.* Translated by Lord Derby. London: J.M. Dent and New York: E.P. Dutton, 1910.

Huxley, Aldous. *Ape and Essence.* New York: Harper and Brothers, 1948.

_____. *Brave New World,* 1932. With author's foreword, 1946. New York: Bantam Books, 1958.

Lexicon Biblicum (in Hebrew). Tel Aviv: Dvir, 1964.

Liddel and Scott. *Greek-English Lexicon* (abridged edition). Oxford: Clarendon Press, Oxford University Press, 1871.

Marlowe, Christopher. *Doctor Faustus,* 1604. New York: New American Library, Signet Classics, 1969.

Meyrink, Gustav. *Der Golem,* 1915. English translation, 1928.

Mikraot Gedolot (in Hebrew). Text of the Pentateuch with major traditional commentaries. Vienna, 1859.

Miller, Walter M. *A Canticle for Leibowitz.* New York: Bantam Books, 1959.

Ovid, *Metamorphoses.* Latin with English translation by Frank Justus Miller. Loeb Classical Library, Third Edition, 1977.

Rosenfeld, Beate. *Die Golemsage und ihre Verwertung in der deutschen Literatur.* Breslau: Verlag Dr. Hans Priebatsch, 1934.

Roshwald, Mordecai. *Level 7,* 1959. Madison: University of Wisconsin Press, 2004.

Rousseau, Jean-Jacques. *Du Contrat Social,* 1762. English translation: *The Social Contract.*

Russell, Bertrand. *Common Sense and Nuclear Warfare.* New York: Simon and Schuster, 1959.

_____. *Nightmares of Eminent Persons and*

Other Stories. London: The Bodley Head, 1954.

Ryle, Gilbert. *The Concept of Mind*, 1949. Penguin Books, 1963.

Scholem, Gershom. "Die Vorstellung vom Golem in ihren tellurischen und magischen Beziehungen." *Eranos-Jahrbuch 1953*, Band XXII. Zürich: Rhein-Verlag, 1954.

Seed, David. *American Science Fiction and the Cold War*. Edinburgh: Edinburgh University Press, 1999.

Shelley, Mary Godwin. *Frankenstein*, 1818. New York: Bantam Books, 1981.

Skinner, B.F. *Walden Two*, 1948. New York: Macmillan paperback edition, 1962.

Stevenson, Robert Louis. *Dr. Jekyll and Mr. Hyde*, 1886. New York: Tom Doherty Associates, 1991.

Tripp, Edward. *The Meridian Handbook of Classical Mythology*. New York: New American Library, 1970.

Verne, Jules. *De la Terre à la Lune*, 1865. English translation: *From the Earth to the Moon. Jules Verne Omnibus.* Philadelphia and New York: J.B. Lippincott Company, no date.

_____. *Le Cinq Cents Millions de la Bégum, 1879.* English: *The Begum's Fortune*. London: Bernard Hanison, 1958.

_____. *Vingt mille lieues sous les Mers*, 1869. English: *Twenty Thousand Leagues under the Sea,* translated by Anthony Bonner. New York: Bantam Books, 1962.

_____. *Voyage au centre de la Terre,* 1864. English: *Voyage to the Center of the World.* New York: Bantam Books, 1991.

Warner Rex. *Men and Gods: Myths and Legends of the Ancient Greeks*, 1950. Oxford: Heinemann Educational Books, 1951.

Wells, H.G., *The Island of Dr. Moreau*, 1896. New York: Tor, 1996.

_____. *A Modern Utopia*, 1905. Lincoln: University of Nebraska Press, 1967.

_____. *The Outline of History*, Revised Edition. New York: Doubleday and Company, 1949.

Index

Aaron 15, 17
Abel 5, 9
Accadia 5, 6
Achilles 12, 27, 36
Adam 11, 38, 64, 142, 211*n*
Aeschylus 29, 30, 31, 33, 34, 212*n*, 217
Aladdin 36
Alchemy 35, 76, 213*n*
Ali Baba 36
America, American 73, 78, 80, 84, 85, 91, 125, 141, 154, 190, 191, 197, 212*n*, 215*n*, 216*n*, 217, 218
Ape and Essence 153, 159, 215*n*, 217
Apollo 20
Apollodorus 21, 22, 29, 211*n*, 212*n*, 217
Ariadne 22
Ark 6-9
Astronomy 57, 94, 100
Athens 22, 23, 175
Avicenna 76, 213*n*

Babel 10-14, 210, 211*n*
Bacon, Francis 45-52, 55-57, 63, 76, 106, 209, 212*n*, 217
The Begum's Fortune 88, 91, 214*n*, 218
Bellerophon 27-29
Bibliotheke see *The Library*
Biology 76, 82, 94, 96, 100, 107, 137, 179, 182
Boyle, Robert 51, 57
Brave New World 111, 153, 162, 174, 178, 179, 181, 183-185, 209, 216*n*, 217

Cain 5, 9
A Canticle for Leibowitz 188, 189, 196, 210, 216*n*, 217
Čapek, Karel 140, 142-146, 209, 215*n*, 217
Caucasus 30, 136, 150
Cellini, Benvenuto 27
China 6, 125
Christianity 32, 41, 43, 44, 46, 154, 176, 187, 190, 191
Communism 116, 138, 163, 172, 197

The Confessions of an English Opium Eater 71
Critias 50

Daedalus 2, 21-28
Darwin, Charles 57, 90, 93, 100, 107, 108
Darwin, Erasmus 57
Devil 38, 41, 43, 63, 68, 88-90, 131, 132, 155, 191, 207; *see also* Satan
Doctor Faustus 36, 40-43, 45, 47, 56, 212*n*, 217

Egypt, Egyptian 15-18
Eldorado 210
Epimetheus 30
Eugenics 57, 103
Evolution 79, 80, 93-97, 99-102, 104, 107, 108, 128, 146, 159

Fantascienza 61
Fascists 161, 162
Faust, Faustian 38, 41, 44, 58
Flood 2, 7, 9, 10, 14, 187, 211*n*
Flying 2, 24, 25, 28, 42, 48, 55, 150, 164
Forster, Edward Morgan 146, 149-152, 215*n*, 217
Franco-Prussian War 88
Frankenstein 59-65, 66, 97, 142, 146, 213*n*, 218
Freud, Sigmund 68, 69

Galton, Francis 57
Galvani, Luigi 61
Genesis 5, 6, 9-11, 13, 17, 68, 211*n*, 213*n*
Gilgamesh 6
Golem 36-40, 41, 46, 60, 97, 139, 140, 142, 310, 211*n*, 212*n*, 217, 218
Good and Evil 65, 88, 112, 138
Greece, Greeks 6, 112, 118, 150, 218
Gulliver's Travels 45, 51, 52, 55, 56, 157, 209, 212*n*, 215*n*

Harvey, William 51, 57
Hephaestus 33

Index

Heracles, Hercules 36
Hillel 87, 214*n*
Hollywood 153–155
Homo sapiens 26, 45, 53, 56, 94, 95, 156, 170, 204
House of Salomon *see* Salomon's House
Hubris 12, 14, 38, 43, 47, 63, 81, 137, 158, 163, 196, 206
Huxley, Aldous 93, 111, 153, 154, 156–162, 174, 176–186, 210, 214*n*, 215*n*, 216*n*, 217
Huxley, Thomas Henry 93, 95, 96

Ibn Ezra 13, 211*n*
Icarus 23–26, 43
Iceland 75, 79
India 6, 89, 177, 182
Industrial Revolution 73, 93, 139
Isaiah 87, 106
The Island of Dr. Moreau 95, 99, 100, 108, 112, 214*n*, 218
Israel, Israelite 5, 11, 15–18, 20, 32, 50, 115

Jabal 5
Jesus 120, 121, 190, 214*n*
Jews, Jewish 13, 36–38, 69, 187, 189, 190
Jonah 32, 188
Jubal 5
Judaism 38, 39, 190, 191

Kibbutz 115, 116

Labyrinth 22, 23, 25–27
Lagado, Grand Academy of 55, 56, 209
Laputa 55, 56
Lavoisier, Antoine 61
Leeuwenhoek, Antony van 51
Level 7 188, 189, 196–208, 216*n*, 217
The Library 21, 22, 86, 211*n*, 212*n*, 217
Loew, Rabbi 37, 38
Lully 76, 213*n*

Machine 2, 55, 58, 73, 84, 105, 138–142, 144, 146–152, 158, 160, 165, 171, 180, 181, 197, 209, 215*n*, 217
Magic, Magician 15–18, 35–38, 40–43, 45, 46, 60, 213*n*
Marlowe, Christopher 41, 42, 44–46, 56, 212*n*, 217
Marx, Marxian, Marxist 108, 145, 161, 173, 176, 177, 180, 183
Mephistopheles 41, 43
Mesopotamia 6, 10
Metamorphoses 22, 142, 212*n*, 217
Middle Ages 22, 142, 212*n*, 217
Midrash see Rabbinical literature
Minos 22, 23, 27
Minotaur 22, 23, 26

A Modern Utopia 100, 101, 105, 107, 109, 110, 146, 214*n*, 218
Morality 10, 27, 87, 88, 208
Moses 10, 27, 87, 88, 208

Nautilus 82–84, 86–88
Nemo, Captain 82–84, 86, 87
New Atlantis 45–47, 49–52, 63, 212*n*, 217
New Testament 87, 214*n*
Newton, Sir Isaac 51, 55, 57, 100
Noah 6–10, 13, 14, 192, 211*n*

Olympus 20, 24
Orwell, George 124, 125, 131, 132, 215*n*
Ovid, Ovidius 22–25, 212*n*, 217

Paracelsus 76, 213*n*
Pasiphae 22, 26, 27
Pegasus 28, 29, 212*n*
Phaedrus 68, 213*n*
Pharaoh 15–17
Plato, Platonic 50, 51, 68, 69, 101, 104–106, 110, 116, 124, 161, 167, 213*n*
Prague 37, 38
Proteus 28
Progress 2, 14, 16, 57, 61–63, 67, 72, 73, 78, 87, 89, 91, 92, 95, 97, 100, 102, 103, 107, 108, 117–119, 130, 135, 144–146, 149, 150, 156, 158–160, 181, 192, 202, 203, 205, 210
Prometheus 10, 29–34, 51, 209, 212*n*, 217
Psychology 68–70, 72, 93, 99, 112–115, 119–124, 129, 130, 133, 135, 139, 176, 179, 185, 207, 208

Rabbinical literature 9, 10, 68, 211*n*, 213*n*
Ramban 14, 211*n*
Rashi 14, 211*n*
Religion 18, 46, 78, 91, 105, 112, 121, 148, 155, 174, 176, 181, 189, 190
Robots 63, 135, 136–138, 140, 142–146, 209, 215*n*, 217
Rome 18, 175, 191, 194
Roshwald, Mordecai 196, 216*n*, 217
Round the Moon 81, 83
Rousseau, Jeans-Jacques 172, 216*n*, 217
Russell, Bertrand 132–137, 215*n*, 216*n*, 217
Russia, Russian 18, 136, 162, 163, 197

Salomon's House, House of Salomon 48, 49, 55, 56, 63, 106
Satan 72, 195; *see also* Devil
Shakespeare 68, 71, 133, 134, 178
Shelley, Mary 59, 60, 61, 63–66, 213*n*, 218
Shinar 10
Sicily 23, 75
Sinai 5
Skinner, B.F. 114–124, 215*n*, 218

Sociology 107–109
Sophocles 21
Soviet Union 113, 124, 125, 163, 172, 196
Sparta, Spartan 18, 110, 198
Spartacus 18
Spencer, Herbert 93
Stevenson, Robert Louis 65, 66, 68–72, 112, 218
The Strange Case of Dr. Jekyll and Mr. Hyde 65, 66, 97, 112, 213*n*, 218
Strength 33, 37, 38, 42, 60, 131, 180, 206
Submarine 74, 81–84, 86
Sumeria, Sumerian 6
Swift, Jonathan (also Swiftian) 45, 52–56, 85, 157, 213*n*, 215*n*

Tabernacle 5
Theseus 22, 25, 27, 36
Thoreau, Henry David 115
Thousand and One Nights 35
Timaeus 50
Tiryns 28

Tubal-cain 5
Twenty Thousand Leagues under the Sea 80, 81, 214*n*, 218

Verne, Jules 58, 73–89, 91, 92, 139, 149, 213*n*, 214*n*, 218
Voyage to the Center of the World 74, 75, 213*n*, 218

Walden 115
Walden Two 114, 116, 117, 119, 122, 124, 215*n*, 218
We 162, 163, 173, 183, 197, 215*n*
Wells, H.G. 93–103, 105–111, 112, 146, 149, 214*n*, 218

Yahoo 53–56

Zamiatin, Eugene 162, 163, 167, 169, 172–174, 183, 197, 215*n*
Zeus 20, 29, 30, 33

www.ingramcontent.com/pod-product-compliance
Lightning Source LLC
Chambersburg PA
CBHW032053300426
44116CB00007B/720